Web Site Cookbook™

b11170840

Other resources from O'Reilly

Related titles

PHP Hacks™
PHP Cookbook™
Perl for Web Site
   Management

Web Design in a Nutshell
Webmaster in a Nutshell
Web Site Measurement
   Hacks™

oreilly.com

oreilly.com is more than a complete catalog of O'Reilly books. You'll also find links to news, events, articles, weblogs, sample chapters, and code examples.

oreillynet.com is the essential portal for developers interested in open and emerging technologies, including new platforms, programming languages, and operating systems.

Conferences

O'Reilly brings diverse innovators together to nurture the ideas that spark revolutionary industries. We specialize in documenting the latest tools and systems, translating the innovator's knowledge into useful skills for those in the trenches. Visit *conferences.oreilly.com* for our upcoming events.

Safari Bookshelf (*safari.oreilly.com*) is the premier online reference library for programmers and IT professionals. Conduct searches across more than 1,000 books. Subscribers can zero in on answers to time-critical questions in a matter of seconds. Read the books on your Bookshelf from cover to cover or simply flip to the page you need. Try it today for free.

Web Site Cookbook™

Doug Addison

O'REILLY®

Beijing · Cambridge · Farnham · Köln · Paris · Sebastopol · Taipei · Tokyo

Web Site Cookbook
by Doug Addison

Published by O'Reilly Media, Inc., 1005 Gravenstein Highway North, Sebastopol, CA 95472.

O'Reilly books may be purchased for educational, business, or sales promotional use. Online editions are also available for most titles (*safari.oreilly.com*). For more information, contact our corporate/institutional sales department: (800) 998-9938 or *corporate@oreilly.com*.

Editor: Brett McLaughlin
Developmental Editor: Mike Hendrickson
Production Editor: Laurel R.T. Ruma
Copyeditor: Laurel R.T. Ruma
Proofreader: Ann Atalla

Indexer: Johnna VanHoose Dinse
Cover Designer: Karen Montgomery
Interior Designer: David Futato
Illustrators: Robert Romano, Jessamyn Read, and Lesley Borash

Printing History:

February 2006:   First Edition.

 This book uses RepKover™, a durable and flexible lay-flat binding.

ISBN: 0-596-10109-0
[M]

*To my wife, Amy Chamberlain, and my
daughters, Eleanor and Jane.*

—Doug Addison

Table of Contents

Preface

Web Site Cookbook is about building web sites that people will visit, use, bookmark, and revisit. It is the book I wish I had when I started building my first web site almost 10 years ago—a one-stop source for answers to the questions that come up when building a web site. In it, you'll find solutions to everything from choosing, registering, and protecting a site's domain name to keep spammers from harvesting the addresses you display on its pages.

Rather than being the authoritative volume on how to be a webmaster, web designer, web developer, or expert in any of the Internet's myriad technologies, acronyms, or buzzwords, the *Web Site Cookbook* instead shows you how all of those disciplines (and others) can be combined for a common purpose: serving and engaging—even delighting—an audience of visitors to your site. Without them, of course, your efforts will be for naught.

Producing and maintaining a web site requires both halves of your brain, as well as a closet full of hats for assuming the various roles you will take on to ensure the web site's success. In the course of bringing a site to life, you might find yourself playing strategic planner, interface designer, programmer, database administrator, quality assurance manager, and promotional guru—often in the same week. That's why this book strives to present a wide range of design-, coding-, and marketing-oriented solutions to real-life problems that come up regularly when creating and growing a web site.

Do not feel compelled to read this book from start to finish. Unless you're just getting started building web sites, you may find that your own knowledge will serve you just as well as the recipes on that subject. (But remember, even a gourmet chef needs a refresher now and then.) This book is intended to be a ready reference for the site builder who needs a quick solution to an immediate problem that falls outside of his area of expertise. For example, the designer who needs a crash course in document types or setting up a cron job, the programmer who needs advice on choosing a color scheme or clip art for a site, or the marketer who wants to set up a weblog or email newsletter.

Regardless of your abilities or the role you play in building a site, you share a common trait with millions of other people building and publishing web sites: you have a message in need of an audience and want to find that audience on the Internet. The *Web Site Cookbook* can lead the way in showing you how to publish a site that is not only a useful and attractive representation of the business, organization, or person behind it, but is also easy to build, maintain, and update.

Assumptions

This book assumes that you have a hands-on role in the creation and ongoing life of a web site. It will not help you decide *if* you should build a web site, *what* kind of web site to build, or *whom to hire* if you can't build it yourself. If you oversee or manage one or more web designers, web programmers or other web experts, you may find useful background information in the book's solutions. Their true value, however, will be apparent to those who can implement the solutions on a working web site.

Many of the more technical recipes—including those that cover server setup, dynamic web pages, and database techniques—overwhelmingly favor the open-source, or LAMP, approach. By LAMP, I mean Linux (or, more generally, Unix) for the server platform, the Apache web server, MySQL as database server, and the PHP scripting language. By far, most solutions are platform-agnostic and alternatives for the Windows Internet Information Server (IIS) platform worth mentioning are noted in the "See Also" sections of selected recipes.

You should have a working knowledge of HMTL code. Although WYSIWYG-oriented site builders will find much in this book that will help them improve their work, the code samples presented in many of the solutions are geared toward those who are comfortable reading and writing web page source code. On the other hand, several recipes describe server command-line instructions, JavaScript functions, and moderately complex PHP routines in a step-by-step method intended to help newcomers become more familiar with these common web techniques and technologies.

Other Sources

The web is teeming with web sites about web sites. There seems to be an inexhaustible supply of advice and opinion about what to do with the space between the <html> and </html> on your web pages. In the process of writing this book, I availed myself of much of it—condensing, synthesizing, updating, and improving on what I found for the solutions presented here.

See for yourself. If you need more information on any of the topics presented here, I recommend the following sources:

- The discussion forum of my favorite web hosting company, Dreamhost (*http:// discussion.dreamhost.com/*).

- The mailing list archive of the online web development community Evolt (*http:// lists.evolt.org*).

- The online forums at WebmasterWorld.com (*http://www.webmasterworld.com/*).

Conventions Used in This Book

The following typographical conventions are used in this book:

Plain text
> Indicates menu titles, menu options, menu buttons, and keyboard accelerators (such as Alt and Ctrl).

Italic
> Indicates new terms, URLs, email addresses, filenames, file extensions, pathnames, directories, and Unix utilities.

Constant width
> Indicates commands, options, switches, variables, attributes, keys, functions, types, classes, namespaces, methods, modules, properties, parameters, values, objects, events, event handlers, XML tags, HTML tags, macros, the contents of files, or the output from commands.

Constant width bold
> Shows commands or other text that should be typed literally by the user.

Constant width italic
> Shows text that should be replaced with user-supplied values.

 This icon signifies a tip, suggestion, or general note.

 This icon indicates a warning or caution.

How to Contact Us

Please address comments and questions concerning this book to the publisher:

O'Reilly Media, Inc.
1005 Gravenstein Highway North
Sebastopol, CA 95472
(800) 998-9938 (in the United States or Canada)
(707) 829-0515 (international or local)
(707) 829-0104 (fax)

There is a web page for this book where we list errata, examples, and any additional information. You can access this page at:

http://www.oreilly.com/catalog/websiteckbk

To comment or ask technical questions about this book, send email to:

bookquestions@oreilly.com

For more information about our books, conferences, Resource Centers, and the O'Reilly Network, see our web site at:

http://www.oreilly.com

Safari® Enabled

 When you see a Safari® Enabled icon on the cover of your favorite technology book, that means the book is available online through the O'Reilly Network Safari Bookshelf.

Safari offers a solution that's better than e-books. It's a virtual library that lets you easily search thousands of top tech books, cut and paste code samples, download chapters, and find quick answers when you need the most accurate, current information. Try it for free at *http://safari.oreilly.com*.

Acknowledgments

First, thanks to my editor, Brett McLaughlin, for guiding and encouraging me through the sometimes arduous process of writing this book—without ever stressing me out.

I'd also like to thank my loyal web design clients, including Damond Benningfield, Sandra Preston, Ross Ramsey, Kenan Pollack, Martin Acevedo, and others, who over the last 10 years have allowed me to try out and develop many of the techniques described in this book. My expertise—and their web sites—are the better for their trust and indulgence.

Gratitude also goes out to my tenacious tech reviewers—Paul Mitchell, Carl Sieber, Sam Eder, and Terrie Miller—who in the process of putting this book's recipes through their paces made many constructive comments that helped improve the end result.

CHAPTER 1

Web Server Setup

1.0   Introduction

The process of designing a web site does not start in Photoshop, Dreamweaver, or your favorite text editor. Before the first line of code is written and the first image is optimized, a web site must have a home on the Internet and a virtual provenance of sorts that legitimizes its existence along with the millions of sites that have come before. Web sites must have a domain name, as well as disk space on a web server, to join the ever-growing club of online resources. In this chapter, we'll untangle the choices that confront web site builders during the process of getting a new web site off the ground.

1.1   Registering a Domain Name

Problem

You need to register a new domain name for your web site.

Solution

Choose the right domain name and registrar for your web site after weighing factors such as budget and goals for organizational identity.

Discussion

Choosing a new domain name for a web site can often seem like shopping on the last day of an end-of-season sale at a popular clothing store. The best choices were long ago snapped up by the early shoppers. Like a picked-over pile of extra-small beige golf shirts, the remaining choices may not be a perfect fit for your planned web site.

Check the registrar of your choice to see if the domain name you want is already registered. Assuming for a minute that you will not be able to acquire your first choice (or second, or even third), here are some guidelines to consider when registering a brand new domain name:

- Consider using your company or organization's short branding message or marketing slogan as your domain name. For example, if Wal-Mart's deep pockets and legions of lawyers were not able to wrest ownership of *walmart.com* from a hypothetical cyber squatter, they might consider *alwayslowprices.com* an acceptable alternative.

- Try to come up with an action-oriented phrase or common aphorism that dovetails with the mission of your web site, and build your web site around that domain. For example, a site that promotes good health through good diet might register *anappleaday.com*.

- Try adding your city, state, or other local identifier to your already-taken first or second choice to find an acceptable alternative that you can claim for your own, such as *austinwebdesign.com* or *youngstownyoga.com*.

- Avoid using hyphens and long acronyms in your domain name. You might be tempted to register an alternative domain name by tweaking your already-taken first choice with hyphens between key words, or by reducing your business name to an alphabet-soup acronym of unrelated letters. Don't do it. A fair share of your potential site visitors will trip over these grammatical stumbling blocks, leaving your web site lost in cyberspace. For example, *wsj.com* works; *the-wall-street-journal.com* does not.

- Consider registering a domain name from the ever-growing list of new top-level domains (TLDs)(see Table 1-1).

Table 1-1. Top-level domains: past, present, and future

Name	Description
Original TLDs	
.com	May be registered by anyone; operated by VeriSign Global Registry. Available since 1995.
.net	May be registered by anyone; operated by VeriSign Global Registry. Available since 1995.
.org	May be registered by anyone; operated by Public Interest Registry. Available since 1995.
.edu	Reserved for U.S. educational institutions, such as universities or high schools. Operated by EDUCAUSE. Available since 1995.
.gov	Reserved for U.S. government use since 1995.
.mil	Reserved for U.S. military use since 1995.
Other sponsored top-level domains (sTLDs)	
.aero	Sponsored by the Societe Internationale de Telecommunications Aeronautiques SC (SITA) and restricted to organizations within the air transport industry. Available since 2001.
.biz	Operated by NeuLevel, a joint venture between NeuStar, a Virginia-based telecommunications company, and Melbourne IT, an Australian domain name registration service. Must be used by businesses for commercial purposes. Available since 2001.

Table 1-1. Top-level domains: past, present, and future (continued)

Name	Description
.coop	Sponsored by Dot Cooperation LLC and the National Cooperative Business Association, based in Washington, D.C. It is restricted to cooperative organizations. Available since 2001.
.info	Operated by Afilias Limited, a consortium of 19 major domain name registrars including VeriSign, Register.com, and Tucows. Anyone may register a .info domain name. Available since 2001.
.int	Registrants must be an intergovernmental organization. Operated by the Internet Assigned Numbers Authority (IANA). Available since 1998.
.museum	Sponsored and administered by the Museum Domain Management Association, a nonprofit organization founded by the International Counsel of Museums and the J. Paul Getty Trust. Restricted to accredited museums worldwide. Available since 2001.
.name	Offered to individuals for personal web sites and email addresses; operated by Global Name Registry. Available since 2001.
.pro	Marketed to professionals, such as accountants, doctors, lawyers, and engineers. Operated exclusively by RegistryPro. Available since 2002.
Proposed, pending, and recently added TLDs	
.asia	Proposed by DotAsia Organisation Ltd. in early 2004.
.cat	Approved by ICANN in September 2005, but it is not for feline aficionados. From the applicant's web site: "Why do we want .cat? Because the Catalan language and culture are a community that wants to be identified with its own domain on the internet." Who's next? Klingons?
.jobs	Sponsored by the Society for Human Resource Management (SHRM); approved by ICANN in late 2004.
.mail	Proposed by the Spamhaus Project and others as an antidote to spam.
.mobi	Sponsored by Mobi JV, a consortium of Microsoft, Nokia, and Vodafone and other heavyweight multinational corporations. Geared toward web sites to be viewed on mobile devices, such as PDAs and cell phones. Approved by ICANN in July 2005.
.post	Sponsored by the Switzerland-based Universal Postal Union; approved by ICANN in late 2004.
.tel	ICANN approved Telnic's application to run a TLO for managing corporate and individual contact information in July 2005.
.travel	Sponsored by the Travel Partnership Corporation; approved by ICANN in late 2004.
.xxx	In August 2005, the Bush administration expressed its opposition to the creation of a new TLD specifically for the porn industry.
Notable country code TLDs (ccTLDs)	
.md	Originally for use by the eastern European Republic of Moldova; now marketed to physicians.
.tv	Administered by the .tv Corporation, a subsidiary of VeriSign. This TLD hit the free market in 2000 thanks to the South Pacific island nation of Tuvalu.
.us	Commonly used for city, county, and state web sites in the United States, now sold for commercial use to web sites with domains in every other TLD.
.eu	Proposed to ICANN by EURid for use by businesses and individuals in the European Union.

With your domain name chosen, it's time to claim it as your own by registering it. To make sense of the often complex and overlapping roles of domain name registrars and web site hosting providers, consider this great analogy (related on numerous sites on the Web) that recasts the process as one that should be familiar to car owners everywhere.

Imagine for a minute that your web site is an automobile—say, a red Lexus RX 330—and its domain name is a personalized license plate. To get a license plate for your Lexus, you register it with your local department of motor vehicles; to get a domain name for your web site, you must register it with an accredited domain name registrar. The Internet Corporation for Assigned Names and Numbers (ICANN) keeps a list of accredited registrars on its web site (*http://www.icann.org/registrars/ accredited-list.html*). If the registrar you want to use is not on the list, they are likely a reseller of an approved registrar's services. Many web hosting companies (more on them later) offer domain name registration in this way.

Most Lexus owners, it's safe to assume, keep their cars in a garage, be it semi-detached in a suburban subdivision or underground in spot C219. After you have registered your domain name, you have to find a place to keep it. Web hosting companies typically provide *domain name service* (DNS) and disk space on a web server where web site designers "park" their web sites.

But where the rubber meets the road, so to speak, is where you as the web designer draw the line between registration and web hosting. Many—if not most—registrars can host your site, and a growing number of hosting companies can register your domain name when you sign up for one of their hosting plans. But few Lexus owners would grant the clerks at the DMV the dual role of parking attendant for one of their most valuable assets (their car). For your domain name and web site, you would be wise to abide by the same separation-of-powers principle, choosing one company to handle your domain registration and a different one to do the hosting.

Why? Here are some gotchas to beware of and avoid when choosing a registrar and host for your domain name and web site:

- Hosting companies that offer to register your domain name have been known to list themselves as the owner of your domain name. Although this practice is less common than it once was, and by no means widespread, clearing up this administrative wrinkle in your DNS record can be a real headache if or when the time comes to relocate your web site to a new hosting provider. Bottom line: if you choose to register and host with the same company, read the fine print in your service agreement.

- Registrars that offer no-cost, or low-cost, registration in exchange for you also choosing them as your hosting provider may be doing so in hopes of collecting high fees when your domain comes up for renewal. Expect to pay $10 to $35 for a one-year registration. Bottom line: assume that you're getting what you pay for and make sure you know who's responsible for what.

See Also

ICANN-accredited registrars are listed at *http://www.icann.org/registrars/accredited-list.html*, and whois.net is another good domain lookup service, at *http://www.whois.net/*.

Netcraft (*http://netcraft.com*) tracks Internet technologies and compiles statistics, including hosting provider network performance and uptime. TopHosts.com (*www.tophosts.com*)and HostSearch (*http://hostsearch.com*) let you search for hosting plans based on price, platform, and features.

1.2   Managing and Protecting a Domain Name

Problem

You need to protect the investment you made in a domain name for your web site.

Solution

Learn how the domain registration system works and keep your domain from being neglected or stolen by:

- Knowing the expiration date
- Keeping contact information up to date
- Enabling domain security features
- Choosing a strong domain management password
- Registering your domain name as a trademark
- Reading every email your registrar sends to you carefully
- Consolidating multiple domains
- Registering domain name variants
- Using a domain-name monitoring service
- Planning ahead if you move your domain to another host
- Setting up a third-party, backup DNS service

Discussion

When comparing a web site to a car, as in Recipe 1.1, you should take into account one key distinction: cars depreciate in value the more you use them. But once you build a functioning web site at your domain—with growing traffic and name recognition—that domain becomes many times more valuable to you than the nominal fee you paid to register it. For that reason, you should treat your domain name as a valuable asset to your business or organization.

The process of choosing a registrar, name service, and hosting provider can be complicated considering all the overlapping options that a web site builder must sort out before making a decision. But the process of losing a domain name can be deceptively simple—with the emphasis on deceptive—and can happen right under the nose of the careless domain name owner.

Ownership of a domain name can be lost to the fraudulent actions of an aggressive domain name speculator, or simply for want of attention to detail. In most cases, a registered domain that is allowed to expire will be snapped up by a speculator within hours of it becoming available.

Learn from the mistakes of others, including me. A few years ago I was managing a Spanish-language web site for a client with a domain name listed with a registrar based in Spain. I thought I had all my bases covered early in 2002, well in advance of the expiration date listed in the whois database: 12-01-2002. But by mid-January, the domain was no longer in my control. The expiration date I had assumed to be December 1, 2002, was actually formatted in the European date style of day first, then month, and year. After my registration expired on January 12, the domain was purchased by a speculator who wanted $5,000 to sell it back to my client, a price the client could not afford.

Here are some important techniques for domain management that can prevent the inadvertent loss of your domain name:

Keep track of the expiration date.
> Put the date on your calendar and keep a print-out of your whois record—listing the administrative, billing, technical contacts, and expiration date—in your files. Use the buddy system: make sure at least one other person with an interest in protecting the domain knows the expiration date and whois record information. Choose a registration term that won't exceed the institutional memory of the domain name owners. Although many registrars offer domain-name periods of up to 10 years, I prefer to keep mine two or three years. That way, I get a chance every so often to review the value of the domain and even choose a new registrar if I want—and I was never very good at that "Where will you be in five years?" interview question either.

Make sure the contact information is up to date.
> The whois listing should have your correct contact data and list the proper owner: either the administrative contact, billing contact, or both. Make sure that you give your registrar, as well as your hosting company, an email address that's *not @yourdomainname.com* in case there are problems with your domain name or account that make your email inoperable.

Enable any and all security features that your registrar offers.
> A new ICANN domain transfer policy went into effect in the second half of 2004 that cut the time between a transfer request and its taking place to as little as five days. Basically, it allows anyone to request a domain transfer and the registrar to authorize the transfer if the current owner does not object. When this policy went into effect, one pithy online forum poster quipped that it spelled the end of

week-long, internet-free vacations for web builders everywhere. You can prevent this form of hijacking by enabling a *registration lock* on your domain. Only unlocked domains can fall victim to the new quick transfer procedure, and only the owner of the domain can unlock it. Other security features vary among registrars, so familiarize yourself with those that are available on your domain and use them to protect it.

Choose a complex, hard-to-guess domain management password.

Don't email this password to anyone. Most good registrars offer web-based tools for managing your domain, so you'll need to create a secure password for accessing your account. Choose one that contains at least eight characters, including both upper- and lowercase letters and one numeral. Don't base it on a real word, or any other bit of personal information that could be guessed by other means, such as your birthday, address, or phone number. If you need to give the password to a colleague or web designer, *do not* send it by email. Email can be intercepted and read by someone you can't trust en route to its intended recipient. When sharing sensitive passwords, deliver them in person, over the phone, or by fax, provided the receiving fax machine is in a trusted location. If you forget your password and your registrar emails it to you, log in and change the password immediately. Many registrars use a better method of resetting a forgotten password and requiring the domain owner to verify the change by logging in to their account. In either case, don't forget to make a note of your new password.

Register your domain name as a trademark, if possible.

If your web site address identifies a distinctive product or service that your business provides, then you might consider applying for trademark protection through the U.S. Patent and Trademark Office, and other national trademark offices as necessary. Trademark protection can be a potential weapon on your side, should a dispute over your domain name arise. Bear in mind, however, that the most insidious domain hijackers may re-register your domain in a country that does not have the same high regard for U.S. trademarks as you do. In that case, prepare for a long, costly—and usually fruitless—effort to reclaim your stolen domain. For more resources on handling domain disputes, refer to the organizations listed under "See Also" at the end of this section.

Read every email your registrar sends you carefully and skeptically.

ICANN now requires registrars to contact domain name owners annually to verify contact information. Unscrupulous domain name speculators also will try to contact you with an email that appears to come from your registrar, in an attempt to trick you into providing information to them that they can use to hijack your domain. If you're unsure about any communication you get regarding your domain, call your registrar or report the fraudulent email to them immediately.

Consolidate multiple domains with one registrar and a common expiration date.

It's tempting to shop around for the best deal when registering a new domain name, but before you know it you've got nearly as many domain management accounts with various registrars as you have domains under your control. The potential to lose one or more of your domains is an order of magnitude greater in this situation. Find the registrar with the best balance of features, prices and management tools that meet your needs, and stick with that registrar. Move domains at other registrars over to your preferred registrar when they're up for renewal. The little bit of extra money you will spend will be worth it for peace of mind.

Register as many variants of your domain as your budget will allow.

Often, the appearance of a hijacked domain can be more likely and more damaging than the hijacking itself. Take the case of a hypothetical nonprofit that registers only the dot-org (.org) variation of its name. A group with opposing views—or just a penchant for mischief—can set up a web site using the dot-com (.com) domain, leaving visitors who don't know any better confused about which site truly speaks for the organization.

Use a domain name monitoring service such as SnapNames or NameProtect.

SnapNames and NameProtect allow you to get alerts about potentially unwanted changes to domains you own and registration opportunities for domains you don't own, but want to own.

Plan ahead if you move your domain to another host.

One of the services your web-hosting company will provide for you is DNS on its domain name servers. The DNS system functions as the address book of the world wide web, matching up the internet protocol (IP) numbers by which network traffic gets routed with alphabetical domain names that are easier for humans to remember. Just as previous residents at your home address may periodically get letters in your mailbox, the DNS system of web site addresses does not get updated instantaneously when you move your site and domain to a new web hosting service. That's because when you move your site, the domain name remains the same but the IP number associated with it changes, and propagation of the new IP number associated with your domain name to the thousands of DNS servers around the world takes anywhere from 24 to 72 hours.

When moving your site, follow these steps in order or risk your site disappearing from the web temporarily while information about your move spreads throughout the DNS system:

a. Set up your new hosting account.

b. Copy all your web site files to the new account when you have confirmation that the account is set up (usually within 24 hours).

c. Place a hidden tag of comment text that distinguishes it from the file on the old web server on your home page file saved on the new web server, like this:

```
<!-- new host -->
```

d. Preview how the site will look by connecting to it with your web browser using the IP number of the new web server or a preview URL provided by the hosting company (e.g., *http://yourdomain.newhost.com*).

e. Notify your domain registrar that you want to change the DNS server information for your domain to those maintained by your new hosting company when you're satisfied that the site on the new host's servers looks and behaves like the site on the current host's servers. (They should give the IP numbers and/or host names of their DNS servers when you sign up.)

Usually you can update your DNS information via your registrar's web-based control panel for your account. At this point, the waiting period for the DNS change begins, so any changes you make to your site during this period must be made to files on both the old and new hosting account. I prefer to pull the trigger on DNS changes on a Friday, let the propagation occur over the weekend, and then check the site on Monday. Viewing source and finding the hidden tag confirms that the propagation is almost, if not entirely, done. By the middle of the week, you can cancel your old hosting account.

Consider setting up a third-party, backup DNS service.
This allows you to respond to web site outages quickly. If your hosting provider's DNS server goes down, then your web site will be down, too. For a nominal fee, you can set up a backup DNS listing through a company such as Ultra DNS to avoid this situation.

See Also

SnapNames (*http://www.snapnames.com/*) and NameProtect (*http://www.nameprotect.com/*) provide alert services for careful domain owners and administrators. The World Intellectual Property Organization Arbitration and Mediation Center, online at *http://arbiter.wipo.int/center/index.html*, works to resolve international intellectual property disputes. Ultra DNS, at *http://www.ultradns.com*, provides backup DNS listings to avoid web site downtime if your primary DNS services becomes unavailable.

1.3   Choosing a Server Platform and Hosting Plan

Problem

You need to narrow down the myriad web hosting choices to the best one for your web site.

Solution

First, consider which web server software and platform your site will be built on; open source Apache and Microsoft's Internet Information Servers (IIS) are by far the most common, although a handful of other web server applications offer special options for companies with particular web site needs. Then think about what features you may need—such as an e-commerce platform, SQL database, secure shell access, or phone-based tech support—to determine whether you should pay for a third-party hosting service or become your own webmaster and host the site yourself.

Discussion

Ten dollars a month will buy you a lot of web hosting, and $100 a month will buy you more than you ever knew you needed. Free hosting is worth just a little less than what you pay for it. And hosting your own site, especially if you've got real work to do, may ruin what little love for computers you may have. Before you let your cousin Mickey host your site from the server farm in his basement or jump at the first web hosting deal you find, spend time doing some long-range planning about how your web site may grow and change.

About 85 percent of the sites on the web these days are running either Apache, an open source and free descendant of the httpd code that served the first web pages, or IIS, a commercial application from Microsoft that is built into server versions of Windows. The rest of the web is covered by lesser-known server software such as Lotus Domino from IBM, Netscape Enterprise Server, Zeus, and StarNine's WebStar (among others).

Rather than present a biased pro and con of the two leading choices, here are some neutral observations and facts about Apache and IIS:

- Large corporations overwhelmingly favor IIS for their web sites.
- Apache has about 70 percent of the total web server marker, according to Netcraft.
- Some hosting providers offer only Apache or IIS, although some offer both. The cost of similar plans on either platform are comparable.
- IIS has a configuration utility with a graphical user interface (GUI).
- Apache is best configured through text files and shell-prompt commands, although there is a GUI for Apache called Comanche.
- Both Apache and IIS will run Perl and Python scripts, as well as JavaServer Pages applications.
- Both can access SQL databases, but IIS has the advantage of better integration opportunities with Microsoft's Windows-only desktop database application, Access, as well as Word and Excel.

- The server-side scripting languages PHP and Microsoft's Active Server Pages (ASP) can run on either platform, too. PHP is somewhat more common with Apache. Apache also requires an additional component to process ASP pages, while ASP is built into IIS.

- Apache runs on all common Unix-flavor servers, as well as Windows. IIS only runs on Windows.

- Both are fast, well-supported, and stable.

- Few of your web site visitors will know or care which you use, and none will notice any difference in how your site behaves.

The choice usually comes down to a matter a personal preference. This book is geared toward web sites running Apache, so, after you select your (Apache-based) hosting account, you'll have just one of many decisions about your hosting setup behind you. Shopping wisely for a place to host your web site will pay off in the long run. Although it's not impossible to transfer a site from one host to another, the process has been known to ruin more than its share of web designer's weekends.

With even the most basic, entry-level hosting plans offering more than enough disk storage and data transfer quota for a small- to medium-size web site, what are the features and factors that matter?

Secure-sockets layer (SSL) server options
  E-commerce transactions or other transmissions containing confidential information between your site visitors and your web server will require a certificate signed by a third-party certificate authority to verify your web site's authenticity (Recipe 8.5 covers setting up certificates). In addition to the fee you'll pay to the certificate authority, enabling the SSL functionality on your account to encrypt the data as it passes over the Internet usually involves a setup fee and ongoing monthly charges. Take those fees into account when choosing a hosting provider, even if you don't need an SSL server on day one.

Charges for extra disk quota or bandwidth
  A mild-mannered web site with predictably modest traffic patterns can easily fall victim to overuse fees when business booms or an unexpected link to the site causes web site activity to spike. Some hosting providers may shut down sites that exceed the account's allotments or email the owner when there's a problem. Others may grade your accounts usage numbers "on the curve," throwing out the high and low numbers and charging you for the average of the remaining days of the month. Be sure you know your hosting company's fees and policies on exceptional web site activity and how long it would take to upgrade your account and move your site to a better plan if your site's new-found popularity becomes the norm.

Phone-based technical support
  How quickly can you get someone on the phone if there's a problem? Hello?

Ease of adding other domains and web sites

At some point, you may want to host a second domain name and web site on your existing hosting account. Your hosting company may see this as new revenue stream from you to them. If you need to host more than one site, look for a provider with the most reasonable fees for this service.

Anonymous FTP access

A no-login-required "drop box" on your web server can be a faster, more convenient, and more reliable way to receive large files from your site visitors than receiving them as email attachments.

Secure-shell access

Many of the solutions to Recipes presented in this chapter require shell or command-line access to your server through a Telnet connection. A better, more secure method of connecting to your server to get a shell-prompt for running commands is through a secure shell connection. Some providers may require that you request this feature in writing before enabling it. Look for a provider that offers this feature and take the steps necessary to enable it.

Backups

The local files/remote files site management setup of popular WYSIWYG web site editing applications (such as Dreamweaver) automatically keep a backup of web site files on the hard drives of one, or more, of the people responsible for the site. But this type of backup doesn't include all the crucial files. Make sure your hosting account includes a regular backup scheme—preferably with an archive of older backups—that covers everything on the site: databases, CGI scripts, logs, and the like.

See Also

Recipe 8.5 on setting up self-signed certificates to work with SSL.

1.4   Enabling Server-Side Includes

Problem

You need to display the contents of one or more shared files in the body of your web pages.

Solution

Configure your web server to parse include tags for all files, or rename your files using the server-side include (SSI) friendly suffix for files that will be parsed.

A typical web server installation will have the module for parsing SSI tags enabled by default. If you have the ability to open and modify your Apache configuration file, check to make sure the following two lines are not commented out.

The location of Apache's configuration file—*httpd.conf*—is set at installation. The default location is */etc/httpd/conf/httpd.conf*. A commented, or inactive, line in the configuration file is preceded by a pound sign (#).

The two lines you're looking for should be near the top of the file:

```
LoadModule includes_module    libexec/httpd/mod_include.so
```

and:

```
AddModule mod_include.c
```

Any change you make to the file will require a web server restart to take effect (see Recipe 1.9). A file's suffix determines if it is eligible for parsing. Typically, files ending with *.shtml* are parsed for includes, but files ending with the more familiar *.html* will not. Since most web page editors create files ending in *.html*—and most visitors to your site will assume that pages on your site end with *.html*—it's a good idea to stick with that naming convention and enable SSIs on *.html* files, too.

Now, go back to the Apache configuration file, where you should find two lines together like this:

```
AddType text/html .html
AddHandler server-parsed .shtml
```

On that second line you want to add ".html" so it reads like this:

```
AddHandler server-parsed .shtml .html
```

If you don't have access to the master configuration file, you can still change the way Apache parses the files for your site with an *.htaccess* file. Just create the file in your web site root directory and paste in the first and third lines of code above, like this:

```
AddType text/html .html
AddHandler server-parsed .shtml .html
```

A web server restart is *not* required when you use this method.

Discussion

Server-side includes are one of the most powerful, yet easy to use, tools in a web designer's bag of tricks. Before the days of reliable web page templates built in a WYSIWYG web page editor or a content management system, SSIs were just about the only way to ensure web site consistency across a multipage site. Server-side includes allow a web designer to save shared content in a single file and display it on multiple pages.

If you're building even a modest-size web site, make sure that SSI functionality is available for every page on your web site.

Server-side includes have other magical powers, like displaying the date of a web page's last modification and executing and displaying the results of a CGI script in an otherwise static web page. We'll come back to these techniques in Chapter 4.

Bear in mind that parsing every *.html* file on your site for includes puts an extra load on your web server. You should not notice a decrease in your web site's performance if you follow a couple of guidelines about using SSIs. First, keep the number of SSI files included on your pages to a minimum. If you have two or three includes strung together in your page code, combine them into one file if possible. Don't build your pages out of includes.

Also, don't nest include files inside other include files. Since Apache parses files for includes based on the file suffix, give your include files—even though they might contain HTML code—a distinct suffix such as *.inc* or *.ssi* so Apache won't look through the include file for more includes to parse.

1.5   Setting the Default Filename for a Directory or Entire Site

Problem

You need to tell your web server the name of the default page for a given directory or all directories on your web site.

Solution

Add or modify the DirectoryIndex entry in your *httpd.conf* file, or a specific directory's *.htaccess* file. List the files that should be treated as default pages in the order you wish them to be served:

```
DirectoryIndex index.php index.html index.htm index.php3 welcome.html
```

Discussion

When a visitor to your web site requests a URL without a specific filename—say, *http://yourwebsite.com/news/*—the web server needs to decide which page to send back to the browser. The file can have any name, and be a static file or one that is dynamically generated. Regardless of how the file is created, if it's missing when requested, then your visitors will see an ugly list of every other file in the directory or, worse, a 403 Forbidden error telling them they don't have permission to access the directory.

For more about denying auto-indexing of a directory, see Recipe 5.5.

As you saw in Recipe 1.4 on server-side includes, the setting that determines the name of a directory's default page resides in the main Apache configuration file, and may be overridden by an *.htaccess* file. Apache configuration changes listed in an *.htaccess* file apply to all of the files in the same directory and to all of the files in subdirectories below it that don't have their own *.htaccess* file.

The line to look for in the configuration file—or to add to an *.htaccess* file—looks something like this:

```
DirectoryIndex index.php index.html index.htm index.php3 welcome.html
```

The setting can contain more than one default file option, listed in descending order of priority. In this example, the server will look for *index.php* first, then *index.html*, and so on down the line.

See Also

Recipe 1.4 on using configuration files to enable SSIs.

1.6 Making Sure Your Web Site Loads With and Without the "www" Prefix

Problem

You need to make sure that your web site can be accessed both with and without the "www" prefix.

Solution

If your web site won't load without the "www" prefix—or it won't load *with* "www"—then you may need to make a change to your DNS record. Some hosting providers allow customers with higher end accounts to change their own DNS records, but use caution if your account includes this feature and you're not sure what you're doing. If you're in doubt, contact your hosting company for clarification or guidance.

If you have access to the command-line network tools nslookup or dig, either on your own PC or through a Telnet shell provided by your hosting account, you can investigate the details of the various listings in your DNS record without changing them. Some web-based tools (see the "See Also" section in this Recipe) can access the same DNS record information if you do not have access to dig or nslookup.

In the example below, a dig request on *www.daddison.com* shows it to be a CNAME, or canonical name, listing for *daddison.com*. A CNAME listing is an alias to the main, or A RECORD, listing in the domain name's DNS record. Requests for either web site address—with or without the "www"—are answered with my web site:

```
Lookup has started ...


; <<>> DiG 9.2.2 <<>> www.daddison.com any
;; global options:  printcmd
;; Got answer:
;; ->>HEADER<<- opcode: QUERY, status: NOERROR, id: 40212
;; flags: qr rd ra; QUERY: 1, ANSWER: 1, AUTHORITY: 2, ADDITIONAL: 1

;; QUESTION SECTION:
;www.daddison.com.          IN      ANY

;; ANSWER SECTION:
www.daddison.com.   3600    IN      CNAME     daddison.com.

;; AUTHORITY SECTION:
daddison.com.       3600    IN      NS      ns22.pair.com.
daddison.com.       3600    IN      NS      ns0000.ns0.com.

;; ADDITIONAL SECTION:
ns0000.ns0.com.         7110    IN     A     216.92.61.2

;; Query time: 98 msec
;; SERVER: 151.164.20.201#53(151.164.20.201)
;; WHEN: Wed Apr 20 15:50:18 2005
;; MSG SIZE  rcvd: 113
```

Discussion

In the classic 1963 farce "It's a Mad, Mad, Mad, Mad World," an all-star cast from Hollywood's Golden Age raced against each other to find a treasure hidden under a big "W." In the late 1990s, during the Internet's first (we hope) Golden Age, legions of dot-com entrepreneurs also sought riches, in this case, under "www." With the wisdom of hindsight—and perhaps with a renewed appreciation for the farcical and tongue-tying nature of hyper-alliterative repetition—many web sites now present themselves on the World Wide Web *sans* "www."

But old habits die hard. Although it's now rare to find a reputable web-hosting provider that does not configure its servers to respond to browser requests for a web site both with and without the "www" prefix, the visitors to your site—especially novice web users—may assume that typing in the "www" is a requirement for getting to your web site.

From the perspective of the hosting company, the prefix is simply a shorthand for the type of Internet resource and server at their data center that handles the request. In a typical scenario, the DNS record for your domain has been configured to redirect requests starting with (or without) "www" to a host server that handles web requests. The DNS record may also have entries for "ftp," "mail," or other services enabled on your domain that are handled by other host servers.

There are also some good reasons to direct all of your visitors to your web site without the "www" prefix. Not only is it a time-wasting mouthful when spoken aloud in a broadcast or voicemail auto-attendant message, but some web site functionality— such as session cookies and SSL certificates—may be valid for web site addresses without the "www," but not with it.

If your web server has the rewrite module enabled, you can create rules that tell Apache to seamlessly change the URL requested by the browser to something else. For example, requests for *http://www.domain.com* become *http://domain.com*. To do this, create or modify the *.htaccess* file in your web root directory with a rewrite rule to remove the "www." from browser requests to your web site. First, find or create an *.htaccess* file. Then copy into it the code shown below, replacing *domain.com* with your domain name:

```
RewriteEngine On
RewriteCond %{HTTP_HOST} ^www\.domain\.com$ [NC]
RewriteRule ^(.*)$ http://domain.com/$1 [R=301,L]
```

See Also

No-WWW is an online campaign to purge the "www" from web site addresses. Visit the site at *http://no-www.org*. Sam Spade Tools offers a variety of web-based domain tools at *http://www.samspade.org/t/*.

1.7 Creating and Accessing Directories Outside the Web Site Root Directory

Problem

You need to place some files out of the reach of HTTP requests.

Solution

Put your web pages in a directory one level below your login's home directory and create and use directories at the same level as the "web root" to hide private files.

Discussion

I'm always a little annoyed when I FTP or Telnet into a new client's web server for the first time and find that the home directory for the hosting account and the root directory for the web site are one and the same. Such setups are typical of basic hosting accounts and likely keep tech support calls to a minimum by eliminating the need for novice and do-it-yourself web designers to remember file paths on the web server when uploading their web pages. Just FTP into your web server and the site files are right there in front of you.

In these bare-bones web site setups, any file that gets uploaded to the hosting account home directory, or that is created by an automated process on the web site, can potentially be viewed and downloaded over the web. Sensitive or restricted data can include files containing your weblog, email list, or credit card merchant account passwords, database login information or backups, downloadable files that are only made available to authorized site visitors, auto-generated order logs containing confidential information about your online customers, or future versions of important pages on your site to be published at a later date.

Restricted file permissions and password-protected directories are among the other popular methods of keeping private files out of reach of browser requests. But keeping files in a directory that's not even part of your web site (password protected or not) makes worrying about unauthorized web access unnecessary.

First, you'll need to relocate your web site's root directory with a few Apache rewrite rules placed in an *.htaccess* file, a technique first encountered in Recipe 1.6. You can start using this technique with either a new or existing web site. The changes will be immediate and transparent to your visitors.

Create a directory at the top level of your hosting account home directory—in other words, at the same level as your current home page HTML file. Call the directory something obvious, such as *www*, *web*, or *htdocs*. I'm going to use *htdocs* for the example below. Now create or modify the *.htaccess* file in your home directory. Copy into it the following rules for redirecting requests to your domain name to files in the *htdocs* directory:

```
RewriteEngine on

RewriteCond $1 !^htdocs/
RewriteRule (.*) / htdocs /$1 [L]

RewriteCond %{THE_REQUEST} ^[A-Z]+\ / htdocs /
RewriteRule .* - [F]
```

The first line ensures that the Apache rewrite engine is on. Lines two and three invisibly redirect browser requests to files in the *htdocs* directory, but keep the rule from looping indefinitely. Because the rules in the *.htaccess* file apply to the directory the file is in as well as all the directories below it—including our new *htdocs* directory—line 3 prevents Apache from appending an infinite number of *htdocs* to the browser request. Lines 4 and 5 prevent direct requests for files in the *htdocs* directory.

Copy all your web site files and directories into the *htdocs* directory, delete the original web site files and directories at the top level of your user account, and you're done. Now you can create other new directories at the same level as *htdocs*, such as *includes*, *backups*, and *downloads*. None of these new directories will be web accessible.

You can still use standard server-side include tags, introduced in Recipe 1.4, to reference files in the new "super" includes directory, like this:

```
<!--#include virtual="/includes/ssi_file.inc" -->
```

You can also add includes to your web pages that are saved in an *includes* directory, within your new *htdocs* directory, like this:

```
<!--#include virtual="/htdocs/includes/ssi_file.inc" -->
```

If your web site uses the popular server-side scripting language PHP, you can configure your scripts to read or write files to directories outside the *htdocs* directory. Apache's includes functionality begins looking for files at the DocumentRoot specified in its configuration file, which, despite our rewrite rule, is the home directory in our example. PHP, on the other hand, can roam the entire file system of the server, which can make tracking down the exact path to the file you want to include a bit of a mind bender.

Fortunately, you can usually specify a base include path for PHP in your *.htaccess* file. Open the *.htaccess* file that you put the rewrite rules into earlier and add the full server path to your home directory.

 If you don't know the full server path to your home directory, use the pwd utility at a command line to your web server to find out.

The line in your *.htaccess* file should look like this:

```
php_value include_path .:/path/to/your/hosting/account/home/directory/
```

An include statement in one of your PHP scripts that refers to a file above your new *htdocs* directory would look like this:

```
<? include ("includes/ssi_file.inc "); ?>
```

1.8   Automating Routine Tasks

Problem

You need to publish or change files overnight while you're sleeping.

Solution

Use your web server's built-in task scheduling utility, cron, to do the work for you.

Discussion

Web designers like their sleep just like anyone else—maybe more. The last thing any of us want to do is stay up late or get up early to post new information on a web site according to the boss or marketing department's schedule.

Fortunately, Unix-based web servers come with a built-in task-scheduling utility called cron that can do everything from executing simple file operations—like copying an updated web page from a private directory to a public one—to running complete scripts with instructions for more complex site maintenance routines. Let's look at the basics of cron and how you can use it to do simple site updates when you're otherwise busy having a life.

Say, for example, that your company's public relations department is working on an important news release for a new product announcement. The release is embargoed (held back from public view) until Wednesday morning, but they give you the final text of the release on Monday to build a page for the web site. The PR department wants the release to be posted on the site at 6:00 a.m. Eastern Standard Time, but your office is in Denver—two hours behind the East Coast—and you plan to be watching the back of your eyelids at that time. It's cron to the rescue!

First, create the updated web page (*newsrelease.html*) and upload it to your web server. If you're feeling lucky, and don't think that URL-fishing site visitors or Google will find the page before the embargo date, put the new page in a new public directory on your web site. If you're worried about your job security, you're paranoid, or both, put the file in a directory that is password protected, hidden, or outside the root web site directory on the server. Either way, cron will be able to find and move the file when the time comes.

Now, tell your web server to use cron to move the file to the URL that the PR department will announce on Wednesday morning. Your web server stores the list of tasks, or *cron jobs*, that it will run for your account in a file call a crontab. From the command-line prompt to your server, type **crontab -1** to list the tasks. Assuming there are no tasks yet, the server will respond with something like "no crontab tab for user doug." Type **crontab -e** to create a new crontab file using a command-line text editor.

crontab entries start with the time and day on which they should run, followed by the command. They are listed in this order:

1. Minute (0–59)
2. Hour (0–23)
3. Day of the month (1–31)
4. Month of the year (1–12)
5. Day of the week (Typically 0–6, with Sunday being 0 and Saturday 6, but some systems may use 1–7, starting with Monday. Double-check your system to be sure.)

Using the Unix move utility, mv, the crontab line for your scheduled site update should look like this, assuming the server is in the same time zone as you are:

```
0 4 * * 3 /bin/mv /private/newsrelease.html /public/newsrelease.html
```

Alternately, if the embargo date is the 15th of the month, you can use this line in your crontab:

```
0 4 15 * * /bin/mv /private/newsrelease.html /public/newsrelease.html
```

Asterisks are wildcards that cron will use to run the task on any day of the month, month of the year, and so forth. A crontab entry that begins with five consecutive asterisks will run on every minute of every day of the year.

 A crontab entry with five consecutive asterisks may also generate an email from your web server's system administrator if the scheduled task encroaches on server performance.

Tweaking your crontab

To schedule a recurring task, say every 15 minutes, use this syntax:

```
*/15 * * * * /bin/mv /private/newsrelease.html /public/newsrelease.html
```

If your web server is located in a different time zone than you are, you can tell cron to use your local time for running automated tasks. Add a time zone configuration line to the top of your crontab like this:

```
TZ=US/Central
```

Note that you can't easily change the overall time zone setting for your web server—especially in a shared hosting setup—because Apache takes its time setting from the server's system clock. If getting the correct time zone for things like time and date stamps on files and order receipts is important, consider hosting your account on a server that resides in your time zone. Or upgrade your hosting account to a virtual or dedicated server, which may give you more control over the server's clock, even if the server itself is in a different time zone.

Every time cron runs an automated task from your crontab, it will send an email to your login account's default inbox detailing the results of the command. Feedback from cron provides valuable debugging information, but emails from frequently recurring tasks can choke your inbox and eat up the disk quota on your hosting account. To turn off the notifications, add this line to top of your crontab:

```
MAILTO=""
```

 You can also create and modify your crontab in a text editor such as NotePad or BBEdit and then upload the file to your server.

Be sure to make the file you upload executable by the owner (you) by using the chmod utility to change the permissions on the file with this command:

```
chmod u+x /path/to/my_crontab_file
```

Then use this command to load the entries in your file into the server's notion of your crontab:

```
crontab  /path/to/my_crontab_file
```

Then double-check that the crontab was loaded correctly from your file by typing:

```
crontab -l
```

This should output your crontab file exactly as you entered it:

```
*/15 * * * * /bin/mv
    /path/to/your/privateorhidden/directory/newsrelease.html
    /path/to/your/public/directory/newsrelease.html
```

1.9   Restarting Your Web Server

Problem

You need to restart the HTTP daemon that processes requests for web pages on your server.

Solution

At the command-line prompt for your server, issue the apachectl graceful command, or the appropriate restart command for your web server.

Discussion

Restarting your web server has come up in several of the topics covered in this chapter. When you modify the configuration file for Apache, you have to restart it for any changes to take effect.

Basic webhosting accounts usually share Apache server processes with other web sites, so if that's the case with your web site, your provider may not want or allow you to restart Apache. Web designers with higher priced virtual server accounts, or accounts running on a dedicated server, have Apache all to themselves and usually can issue the commands for stopping and starting it as needed.

Later versions for Apache install with a control script called apachectl. With it, you can start, stop, and restart the HTTP daemon on your dedicated server or "virtual server" account.

Finding the script

You should be able to use apachectl at the command-line prompt to your web server by typing its name followed by a space and stop, start, or graceful. If that does not work, you will have to specify the full path to the script. To locate the script on your server, use one of these commands:

```
find / -name apachectl
```

or:

```
which apachectl
```

Stopping and starting Apache

The results of the commands `apachectl stop` and `apachectl start` are self-evident.

 The `stop` command immediately turns off the server, cutting off connections that may still be in the process of downloading pages from your web site.

Gracefully restarting Apache

A better way to restart Apache after a change to the configuration file is with the `graceful` argument to `apachectl`. In this case, Apache leaves current connections to browsers open and starts applying the changed settings to new connections.

See Also

The Apache Software Foundation web site has more information about stopping and starting the Apache web server on the manual page for `apachectl` at *http://httpd.apache.org/docs/programs/apachectl.html* and a guide to restarting Apache at *http://httpd.apache.org/docs/stopping.html*.

1.10   Monitoring Web Server Activity

Problem

You want to see programs your web server is running and user requests for web pages.

Solution

Use command-line tools to get a real-time snapshot of web server activity:

`tail`

Returns the last part of a file, such as most recent connection entries from the web server logfile

`grep`

Searches for a pattern in a file, such as specific filenames or error codes from the web server logfile

`ps`

Reports on the status of web server processes

Discussion

Almost any decent web hosting account will record connections to your web site in logfiles that you can view and process. A good hosting provider may even help you automate the task of purging the connection records—or *log rolling*—so the files do not consume your account's disk quota, and give you access to web site statistics software, such as Analog or Urchin, that will generate easy-to-read reports about activity on your web site.

If you're serious about your web site, then you should take advantage of the tools available to you and review web site traffic reports often to understand how visitors get to your site, what's popular, and what's working (or not working). How to look at and use web site traffic reports is covered in Recipe 9.9.

The access and error logs that provide the raw material for traffic reports are constantly updated. Traffic reports themselves, on the other hand, are usually generated less frequently—daily, or even weekly, in some cases. A situation may arise when you can't wait for the next traffic report to be created. You need to get an up-to-the-minute picture of the who, what, and how many of your web site's current activity. Here are some command-line tools you can use to take your web site's pulse.

Using tail to track web site requests in real time

First, you'll need to find your Apache access and error logfiles. They are usually saved in a separate *logs* directory and have names like *access_log*, *access.log*, or *apache.access_log*. The error log should be in the same directory with the access log, so once you've found the logs, Telnet into your web server and switch to the logfiles directory.

Now you can watch connections to your web site as they're handled by Apache with the Unix utility tail. Assuming your access log is named *access_log*, type this command at your Telnet prompt:

```
tail -f access_log
```

Your shell window should be filled with several lines, like this:

```
128.118.152.116 - - [14/May/2005:12:49:26 -0500] "GET
/swgr/index.php HTTP/1.1" 200 29070
"http://daddison.com/index.html" "Mozilla/4.0
(compatible; MSIE 6.0; Windows NT 5.1; SV1; .NET CLR 1.1.4322)"
68.142.250.83 - - [14/May/2005:12:49:30 -0500] "GET
/case_studies/cs01.html HTTP/1.0" 200 19604 "-" "Mozilla/4.0
(compatible; MSIE 5.01; Windows NT; .NET CLR 1.1.4322)"
165.83.120.231 - - [14/May/2005:12:49:33 -0500] "GET
/clients/index.html HTTP/1.1" 301 255 "-" "Mozilla/4.0 (compatible;
MSIE 6.0; Windows NT 5.1; SV1)"
```

Each line indicates the IP number, file requested, and status of each unique connection, or *hit*, to your web site. The -f flag on the command tells tail to show the last 10 lines in the access log, and to echo new lines to the shell window as they are appended to the file. See for yourself: open a browser window and, with your shell window still visible, hit a page on your web site. Your request should be duly noted by tail.

Using grep to find specific requests in the web server log

Going back to the problem in Recipe 1.8 about automatically updating pages on your site, let's say that your boss wants to know how many hits to the company's latest news release have been recorded today. And she can't wait until tomorrow, when a nice and neat traffic report will be waiting on the site with the answer. With grep, you can narrow your focus on the access log to just see recent requests for a specific file.

At the Telnet prompt to your web server, you can instruct the grep utility to search the access log for the filename of the news release in the content of the current access log by typing this command:

```
grep "GET /news/newsrelease.html" access_log
```

With the search string GET /news/newsrelease.html you're looking for all the requests for *newsrelease.html* in the */news* directory in the current server log. The results might look like this:

```
24.91.149.141 - - [14/May/2005:13:55:45 -0500] "GET
/news/newsrelease.html HTTP/1.1" 200 18912 "-" "Mozilla/4.0
(compatible; MSIE 6.0; Windows NT 5.1; .NET CLR 1.1.4322)"
213.219.80.16 - - [14/May/2005:13:56:36 -0500] "GET
/news/newsrelease.html HTTP/1.1" 200 18912 "-" "Mozilla/4.0
(compatible; MSIE 6.0; Windows 98; Win 9x 4.90)"
70.176.205.66 - - [14/May/2005:13:58:09 -0500] "GET
/news/newsrelease.html HTTP/1.1" 200 18912 "-" "Mozilla/4.0
(compatible; MSIE 6.0; Windows NT 5.1; SV1)"
```

You can also send the results of the search to file by modifying the command like this:

```
grep "newsrelease.html" access_log > newsrelease_report.txt
```

And if you want to get really fancy, you can put that second grep command in your crontab file, have it run every 15 minutes, and let the boss check the hits herself.

You also can use grep to sift the access log for errors and unsuccessful requests that visitors to your web site are encountering. Each line in the log also includes an error code indicating the result of the request. Some common error codes are shown in Table 1-2. For a complete list, see the World Wide Web Consortium (W3C) list referred to in the "See Also" section of this Recipe.

Table 1-2. Common error codes

Code	Meaning
200	OK, the request has succeeded
401	Unauthorized, the request requires authorization
403	Forbidden, the request was refused
404	Not found
500	Internal server error

Using ps to monitor web server processes

Finally, there may come a time when you want to see what processes are running under your user ID on your web server. Use the Unix process report utility—ps—with this command, replacing userid with your own ID (right after the -U flag):

```
ps -Uuserid
```

The results should look something like this, with httpd indicating Apache processes that are currently running on your web server:

```
PID   TTY     TIME CMD
11565 ?       0:00 httpd
 1715 pts/5   0:00 tail
11569 pts/6   0:00 tcsh
11560 ?       0:00 httpd
11567 ?       0:00 sshd
11512 ?       0:00 sh
11542 ?       0:01 httpd
29475 ?       0:01 sshd
29477 pts/5   0:00 tcsh
 6373 ?       0:00 sshd
11559 ?       0:00 httpd
11578 pts/6   0:00 ps
11557 ?       0:00 httpd
11553 ?       0:00 httpd
11554 ?       0:00 httpd
```

See Also

For a complete list of HTTP status code definitions, see the W3C page at *http://www. w3.org/Protocols/rfc2616/rfc2616-sec10.html.*

1.11 Building an Easy-to-Maintain Web Site with Free Tools

Problem

You need to set up a small web site and are willing to sacrifice some customization options in favor of saving money and getting it online quickly.

Solution

Employ a combination of free or inexpensive resources available on the Web to build a low-cost site that's easy to maintain. The ingredients for this Recipe are:

- A domain parked at a registrar that allows you to forward requests for the domain to another URL
- A small amount of free hosting space provided by your internet service provider, school, employer, or other reliable web server operator

- One or more blogs hosted by Blogger (or another free blogging service)
- A free Flickr account for storing and sharing images you want to display on your site
- A free del.icio.us account for managing links on the site, including its navigation
- A Google-based site search form

Discussion

Although the rest of this book is devoted to in-depth solutions for building a substantial, highly customized web site, there are times when you need to get something online fast, cheaply, and under control. Fortunately, a slew of free or inexpensive web services have become available recently (some referred to under the banner of *Web 2.0*) that make doing so fairly easy.

As I explained in Recipe 1.1, web sites start with a domain name. Expect to pay $5 to $10 for a one-year registration, although you may find a cheaper deal for a domain in one of the newer top-level domains (such as *.info* or *.biz*) if you shop around. For this Recipe, I registered the domain *dougaddison.info* at GoDaddy.com (*http://www. godaddy.com*). When choosing a registrar for the site, make sure you can "park" the domain on their DNS servers for free (or a nominal fee) and forward requests for the domain to another URL. In addition to free parking and forwarding, GoDaddy also lets registrants "mask" the forwarded domain, which means that the browser location window will always display the domain name (*dougaddison.info*), even though the pages themselves will be served from another URL.

Next, you'll need to find a small amount of hosting space for the site. I found mine through my internet service provider—SBC—who, through a partnership with Yahoo!, gives its customers a free GeoCities account with 15MB of disk space. The GeoCities control panel also has a web-based file manager for uploading and editing web pages stored on the account (see Figure 1-1). In my GoDaddy control panel, I set *dougaddison.info* to forward to *geocities.yahoo.com/daddison@swbell.net*. Because I also instructed GoDaddy to mask the domain, visitors to the site will never see the GeoCities address.

 For a design, I turned to another free online resource—the Layout-o-Matic at *inknoise.com*. Chapter 3 features additional resources on layout and color, including additional free resources for downloading pre-coded design templates and color schemes.

A free Blogger account solves the content management problem. With its user-friendly web-based writing and editing interface, Blogger's blogging tools circumvent the need for your less computer-savvy site contributors to set up an FTP client and understand the process of uploading files to the web server. Blogger also offers a variety of design templates for displaying your blog at an address on their server

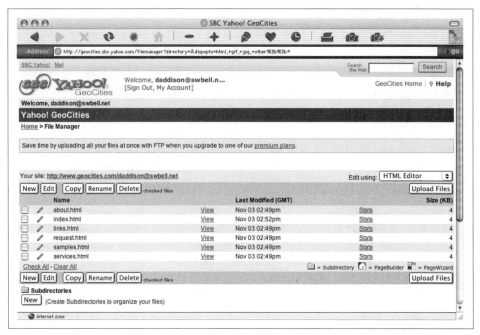

Figure 1-1. Free web space from GeoCities comes with a web-based file manager for uploading and editing web pages

(i.e., *dougaddison.blogspot.com*). But for this site, you will *self-syndicate an RSS feed* from your blog and display it on a page that you upload just once to your free hosting space. See Recipe 6.7 for a discussion of three methods for doing this.

Self-syndication will be the key to adding navigation and images to the site, and free accounts with del.icio.us and Flickr will provide the tools for doing so. As darlings of the Web 2.0 movement, Flickr and del.icio.us are leading the way in opening the web to new ways of managing images and links on the web. The tagging features of both services—dubbed *folksonomy* for their grass-roots inversion of traditional top-down categorization, or *taxonomy*, of online resources—enable novel and inspiring ways of communal publishing and sharing with the web.

At the most basic level, del.icio.us is an online bookmark storage service. With it, you can ditch the bookmark list that your browser saves on your PC's hard drive and have access to your favorite sites from any browser on any computer that you use. You also can define your own system for categorizing your bookmarks with one or more tags that you assign to each bookmark you add to your del.icio.us account. Flickr works in a similar way, but with images. A free Flickr account provides 20 MB of image-upload storage each month, as well as tools for tagging individual images, generating code for displaying them on another web site, uploading images automatically from your cell phone's camera, and posting the images with a short description to a blog hosted by another service (including Blogger).

Best of all for your fast, cheap, and under control site, both del.icio.us and Flickr generate RSS feeds for each tag that you define. So in my del.icio.us account I defined two tags for the links I want to display on the site: "sitenav" for the internal links and "sitelinks" for other web sites that I want to link to from dougaddison.info. Then, I plugged in the self-syndication code for the two tag feeds into the pages where I want those links to appear: "sitenav" in the sidebar of every page and "sitelinks" on my Links page (see Figure 1-2).

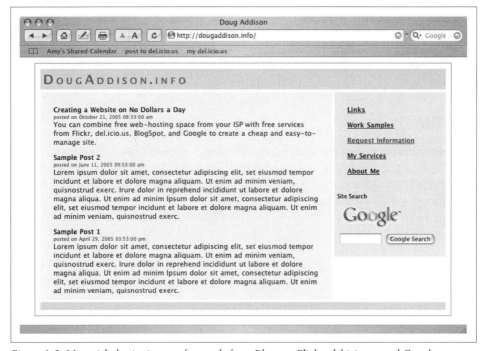

Figure 1-2. My quick, basic site uses free tools from Blogger, Flickr, del.icio.us, and Google

Likewise with Flickr, I created a tag called "worksamples," uploaded some screenshots of web sites I've worked on recently along with a short description, then copied the self-syndication code generated by a tool described in Recipe 6.7 onto my Work Samples page. Alternatively, you can post Flickr images to your Blogger blog directly from Flickr (which will cause images and your other text-only posts to be displayed together) or create a second images-only blog on your Blogger account, post your Flickr images to it, and then display those posts separately on a different page.

Finally, you can easily add a site-wide search tool with a free tool from Google or copy the code below and replace YOUR DOMAIN NAME with your domain:

```
<!-- SiteSearch Google -->
<FORM method=GET action="http://www.google.com/search">
<input type="hidden" name="ie" value="UTF-8">
```

```
<input type="hidden" name="oe" value="UTF-8">
<TABLE bgcolor="#FFFFFF"><tr><td>
<A HREF="http://www.google.com/">
<IMG SRC="http://www.google.com/logos/Logo_40wht.gif"
border="0" ALT="Google"></A>
</td>
<td>
<INPUT TYPE="text" name="q" size="31" maxlength="255" "value="">
<INPUT type="submit" name="btnG" VALUE="Google Search">
<font size="-1">
<input type="hidden" name="domains" value="YOUR DOMAIN NAME"><br><input
type="radio" name="sitesearch" value=""> WWW <input type="radio" name="sitesearch"
value="YOUR DOMAIN NAME" checked> YOUR DOMAIN NAME <br>
</font>
</td></tr></TABLE>
</FORM>
<!-- SiteSearch Google -->
```

See Also

For more information on the techniques described in this Recipe, see Recipes 1.1 and 6.7. To sign up and begin using the free tools, visit del.icio.us (*http://del.icio.us*), Blogger (*http://blogger.com*), Flickr (*http://flickr.com*), and Google Free WebSearch (*http://www.google.com/searchcode.html*).

CHAPTER 2

Site Planning and Setup

2.0 Introduction

By the time your web site launches you might finally be ready to let your visitors (collectively) start thinking about the site more than you have been. That's why a good web site starts with good planning. While it's tempting to start designing and coding right away, the more complex your project, the more you'll benefit from written documentation that helps you set a course for the work ahead of you. Planning can take various forms: the functional specification demands answers to questions such as who will use the site and what they will do. A flowchart helps smooth out an online transaction or process. Setting up and following specific coding standards for seemingly minor site details—page titles, file and directory names, and variables—provides a consistent experience on your web site. All together, these practices ensure that the web site you launch will be useful and enjoyable for the people who visit.

Before we begin, a warning to readers: this chapter is heavy on explanations and light on code. Although you might prefer to skip to a more code-oriented chapter, I urge you to study the Recipes in this chapter to understand why this early stage is critical. Good web site builders (many of whom learned the hard way) know that it's a waste of everyone's time and money to spend days writing great code, only to find out that it does all the wrong things.

2.1 Writing a Functional Specification for Your Site

Problem

You need to determine the purpose and goals for your site.

Solution

Write a functional specification that describes a road map for creating an online experience and get all the stakeholders interested in your web site's success to read the spec, approve it, and follow it.

A functional specification document can vary from a two-page outline for a small, quick turnaround web design project to a lengthy, multipart treatise for a complex web application. Regardless of the size and scope of your project, a functional specification for a web site should:

- Identify the audience
- State the goals of the web site
- Establish a method for measuring success
- Define interaction points
- Describe the site both textually and visually
- List key decisions to be made
- Identify and assess similar sites
- Outline a schedule
- Provide a guide for testing

Discussion

Most of your web site projects will benefit from some kind of blueprint to guide your work and manage the expectations of those for whom you're working. A functional specification document can do just that. By unifying the needs of users, the capabilities of available technology, the vision for a new site's look-and-feel, and the business needs of those who are paying the bills, a functional spec makes a web site project go much more smoothly than a project that proceeds without one. For web site builders at the crossroads of these oft-competing interests, a functional spec offers a useful tool for avoiding "feature-creep" along the way and deflecting criticism and complaints when the project it defines is complete.

> "Feature-creep" (a.k.a. *featuritus*) is the term jaded web site builders use to describe projects whose list of requirements grows and changes as the deadline looms.

In Recipe 4.8, I explain why it can be useful to maintain your web site the same way software companies do their products—as code to be compiled and delivered in its most streamlined state to users. Writing functional specifications is a key first step in any successful software development process, as well as most modestly complex web applications. Likewise, any web site—no matter how small—can benefit from using a functional spec as its starting point. That's because the prose, visuals, and schematics of a functional spec are almost always easier to argue over and change than the actual HTML code and graphics of a half-finished web site.

Reality Check

Before you begin writing a functional spec document for your project, do a reality check. Ask yourself "Is this process absolutely necessary?" Often, you will find that unless you're building a web site by yourself, for yourself, and plan to keep all the goals and requirements in your head, a functional spec is the best way to get a complicated project off the ground. But don't write it just because you can, and when you do, keep it shorter than you think it needs to be. You can feel more confident in the agreement a functional spec elicits when you know everyone has read it.

Beware that functional spec documents have inherent flaws: as political documents, they can be used incorrectly to appease stakeholders rather than make them aware of tough decisions ahead. As prognosticators, functional specs can fail to anticipate changes in the inherently uncertain world of web design—the inevitable phase that a friend in the business refers to as the point "when the wheels come off." Don't blindly follow your functional spec off a cliff. In the end, realize that your functional spec is a snapshot of what you know about a project before it starts and a compromise—the first of many you'll make to get the project finished.

Writing functional specs begins with information gathering. The three main questions you need answers for are:

- What will this web site do?
- Who will the web site do it (the answer to the first question) for?
- When does the web site need to be done?

If you're working one-on-one with a client, you might be able to get what you need in a short introductory meeting combined with a questionnaire. For larger projects involving more stakeholders, the first step of information gathering is often simply figuring out who has the information you need. Getting answers to these three big questions also usually requires shaping them out of answers to more specific questions posed in your client questionnaire, or in interviews with the key project players, such as:

- What is the intended launch date for the site?
- Do you have any user feedback about the current site (if there is one)?
- How will you measure the new site's success?
- Who is a typical user that visits (or will visit) the site?
- What is the site's key idea or "take-away" concept for visitors?
- What is the primary "action" the visitor should take during (or after) a site visit?
- Why do your target visitors choose to do business with your company?

- How does your company (or organization) differentiate itself from its competitors?
- What web sites do you find compelling?
- How do most people find out about your current web site?
- Who will be responsible for updating and providing content?

Start by listing all the goals that can be accomplished with the site (or a new component of an existing site), then prioritize the list from most to least important. Elevate the top two or three as primary goals (or core functionalities) of the site—the objectives the site must achieve. On the next tier, list secondary goals. Make sure you identify these as the "nice-to-have, if-there's-time" objectives. Also, list the non-goals—the wish list requests that this web site project will not accomplish. As time, budget, and technology limitations come into better focus in the creation of the functional spec, expect some goal-shifting among the three lists.

When defining your audience, remember that your visitors don't care about technology constraints or marketing plans, they just care about the subject of the site and getting what they want from it. Start by writing a real-life depiction of the web site's target audience and why they will use the site. Often a web site's audience is not comprised of just one stereotypical user, but a variety of distinct, but related, visitor profiles, or *personas*.

For example, consider the hypothetical user personas included in the specification for a web site that will promote new medical office space:

Target user
> Physicians who will move their medical practices to the new building.

Other users
> Therapists and pharmacists who might want to lease or sublet space or establish ground-floor retail establishments in the new facility, or prospective patients who live in the neighborhood.

Also, try to discover as much about the browsing requirements and technological capabilities of your audience as possible and include a benchmark statement in the general audience profile that anticipates those needs. For example: "Doctors in our target audience have access to newer PCs with high-speed Internet connections, but have little time for web browsing. The site will be designed for quick, productive visits using Version 5.0 browsers (or better)."

Finally, make sure the functional spec acknowledges realistic estimates for the time involved in meeting the goals, as well as external factors that affect the project completion date. The time to find out about the major tradeshow or direct mail campaign that the site needs to support is right now. Outline a schedule that works backward from a hard deadline and includes milestone dates and time at the end for testing (see Figure 2-1).

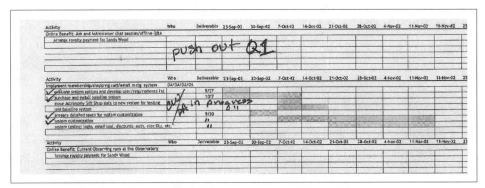

Figure 2-1. A timeline helps highlight task priorities and schedule conflicts

Lay out the interaction points between visitors and the site by providing as much detail as possible about screens, links, and buttons. Because people process information in different ways, provide both visual and textual descriptions of the site (see examples in Figures 2-2, 2-3, and 2-4). For small, simple sites, this can simply be a list of navigational elements, a site map showing how pages will be organized and linked to one another, and mockups of the page templates. More complex sites and web applications—such as membership or e-commerce sites—can benefit from flowcharts, wireframe layouts (see Figure 2-5), and dummy HTML prototypes that map out a user's interaction with the site (as discussed in Recipe 2.9).

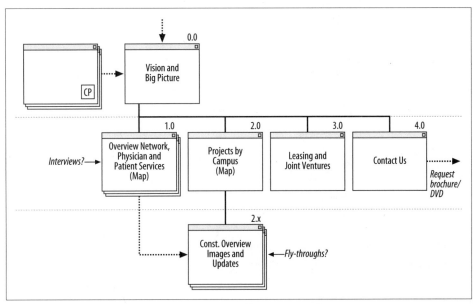

Figure 2-2. A schematic site map lays out a potential navigation scheme

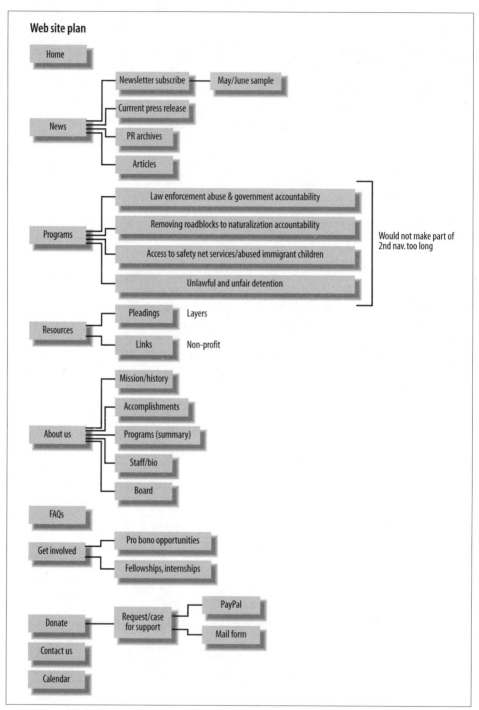

Figure 2-3. An icon-based site map outlines a site's levels and pages

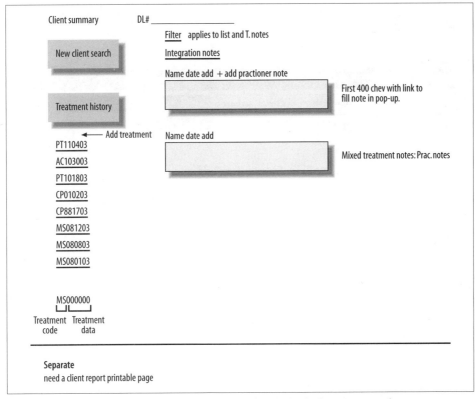

Figure 2-4. Details about a form-intensive layout should be hashed out on paper first

Along with these schematics and hands-on depictions of a web site project, a thorough, functional spec will also include individual descriptions for the components of the site. For example, a description of a user survey page might specify: "Respondents will be asked their gender (radio button choices for "male" and "female"), their age (pull-down menu with choices "13–19," "20–29," "30–39," "40–49," "50–59," "60–69," "70–79," "80+"), and how they heard about the site (checklist of choices providing by marketing department)."

Identifying decisions to be made over the life of a project is another main goal of the functional spec. Compiling a planning document before work begins on the site helps nail down answers to easily forgotten or overlooked project questions: who will provide the content, who will write the content that doesn't exist yet, who will maintain the site, who will get online order notifications by email, what will the text of the mailing list sign-up confirmation and error messages be.

Share your functional spec with the interested parties to help them understand their responsibilities, suggest changes, and fill in holes as necessary; and when you've got everyone's agreement and approval, begin the project.

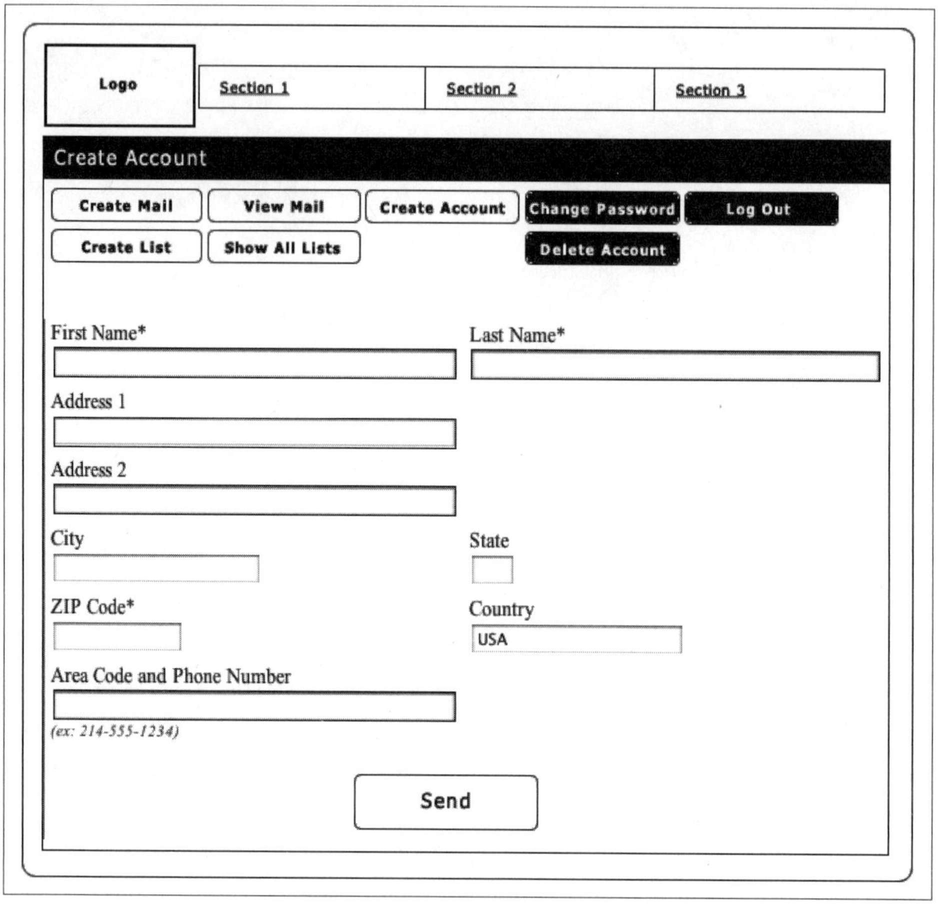

Figure 2-5. Wireframe designs isolate layout, navigation, and functionality from color and visual design

See Also

Recipe 2.9 talks about how to map your requirements to a flowchart. Recipe 9.10 explains the importance of getting feedback from potential visitors before your site launches. For a contrarian view on the need for a functional specification for your web site project (and the lively discussion that follows), see 37Signals's "Getting Real, Step 1: No Functional Spec" at *http://www.37signals.com/svn/archives/001050. php*.

2.2   Assessing Available Materials for a Site

Problem

You need to compile a list of documents, images, and other source files that you will need in order to build a site.

Solution

Create a content inventory or checklist to determine what text, images, and other assets are available and need to be part of the site. Your list should answer these questions:

- Who has the original materials?
- What formats are the materials in?
- Who will acquire, create, and approve the new material?
- What has to be resized, edited, or optimized for online use?
- How often will content be updated, and by whom?

Discussion

Compiling a content inventory, like writing a functional specification (detailed in Recipe 2.1), is a key step in successfully making your web site concept a reality. But these two tasks can create a "chicken-and-egg" dilemma for a web designer. By that, I mean it's hard to devise a navigational structure for the functional specification without a clear idea of the available content—and you might not know what content you'll need without knowing how the site will be organized.

You might want to integrate the two tasks so one informs the other. That way, a content inventory can help refine the decisions and responsibilities identified by the functional specification. That said, you'll want to be careful not to let the complete opus of available material dictate how to structure a site. Don't feel compelled to shoehorn every company newsletter article and holiday party photo into the site. It's almost always easier to add content than take it away (see Recipe 9.1).

Like the functional spec, a content inventory is a tool for managing expectations and developing a schedule for completing a web site project. Table 2-1 shows a list of a few of the typical *assets* that will be needed for a web site.

Table 2-1. A content inventory, such as this sample here, outlines the who, what, where, when, and how for source files that will be used to build a site

Asset	Who has	Who creates	What format	Edit/resize/optimize	Updates
Logo	Joe (graphic artist)	N/A	EPS file; Joe will provide on CD	Convert to GIF (web designer)	N/A
Data sheets	Traci in marketing	Traci	Word docs (~75)	Convert to PDF (web designer)	New ones added quarterly
Company history	Matt (founder's nephew)	Matt	Five long articles in one FrameMaker file	Shorten each to ~300 to 500 words each (Matt) and convert to HTML (web designer)	As needed (Matt)

Table 2-1. A content inventory, such as this sample here, outlines the who, what, where, when, and how for source files that will be used to build a site (continued)

Asset	Who has	Who creates	What format	Edit/resize/ optimize	Updates
Stock photos	N/A	Web designer (from online sources)	JPEGs	Web designer	CEO will approve choices

Like a site map or flowchart, a content inventory offers a way to visualize an important aspect of your web site. In this case, each asset's row in the list presents an at-a-glance view of the asset's lifespan on the site, from its originator to the need for ongoing updates. You might also want to add columns to further describe how site assets will affect the project schedule (such as who will approve the asset before it goes on the site), when assets from outside sources will be available, and whether the site can launch without a particular asset.

A content inventory also can be a useful tool for taking stock of an existing site. By combining information about each asset's name, location, and relationship to other assets, along with the names and dates of those who own and update the asset, this type of inventory can provide useful guidance when redesigning, re-engineering, or just uncluttering a site that's been around a while.

See Also

For more information on using a content inventory for ongoing site maintenance, read Janice Crotty Fraser's article "Taking a Content Inventory" online at *http:// webtechniques.com/archives/2001/10/fraser/* and Jeffrey Veen's "Doing a Content Inventory" at *http://www.adaptivepath.com/publications/essays/archives/000040.php*. Recipe 2.1 details putting together a functional specification, and Recipe 2.9 will help take these assets and place them into the overall flow of a site.

2.3   Organizing Your Files in Directories

Problem

You need a plan for putting site assets in their proper place, so you and others who work on the site can easily find and update the right file at a later date.

Solution

Group your files by content, method of creation, and access level, and then create directories on your web server where they can be uploaded and modified as needed.

From a command-shell prompt, you can create a directory with the Unix `mkdir` command. A full-featured FTP client or WYSIWYG site management applications should offer a menu command for creating directories on a remote server as well.

Discussion

Don't build a site where every file commingles with every other file in an unorganized mess at the top file level of your web server. Well-planned web site organization requires a lot of advance planning, but pays dividends as your site grows and changes. Try to mirror your web site's navigation—the links and buttons that visitors follow through your site—but keep in mind some of the limits of the server file system as you do.

Unlike the folders you create on your desktop PC, web site directory names should not contain spaces. The server will convert spaces to the unaesthetic (but not unusable) encoding %20. Likewise, avoid special characters: The server might mistake ampersands (&) and questions marks (?) for delimiters in a CGI script argument; the number (or pound) sign (#) is used in HTML markup to create a link to another section of the same web page. Hyphens and underscore characters are safe, but—as you saw in Recipe 1.1—they add an unnecessary stumbling block to people trying to memorize a URL or recite it over the phone. Best to leave them out, if possible. Finally, use all lowercase; on Unix servers, the directory and filenames that make up a URL are case sensitive.

Every site should have separate directories for the supporting files that are not linked to directly on your site, such as GIFs, JPEGs, and PNGs (in */images*), server-side includes (in */includes* or */ssis*), Flash or QuickTime files (in */movies*), stylesheets (in */styles* or */css*), and client-side scripts (in */scripts*, */javascripts*, or */js*).

Generic directory names for supporting files are better than names that describe the technology of the files they contain. */styles* is usually better than */css*, and */scripts* is usually better than */javascripts*. And, it makes upgrading to different technologies a lot easier. (Who wants to refer to */javascript/validate.php*?)

On a large site, you may want to divide these directories into subdirectories that reflect the site structure. For examples, images for the products section could go in */images/products*, images for events in */images/events*, and so forth.

Separating files by content and creator makes keeping track of everything much easier. Keeping the web page for a product demo in the */demos* directory and the movie of the demo in */movies/demo* prevents you from deleting or overwriting the wrong file. It's all too easy to overwrite *widget.mpg* when you meant to replace *widget.html* if all of your files are in the same directory.

Maintaining separate directories for site files has other practical benefits. Although Unix can easily store and retrieve several thousand files in one directory, I start to get dizzy when sorting through a list of more than a couple of hundred files. Grouping files in directories also allows you to segregate files with different security settings or permissions. Web hosting companies commonly restrict CGI scripts that run on the web server—in other words, *executable* files—to the */cgi-bin* directory. You may have other files to protect, such as customer order logs in a directory for which only you have read access, or downloadable files in a directory that require a password from visitors to gain access.

See Also

To define the page that visitors see when the URL they request does not include a filename, see Recipe 1.5. Recipe 3.7 explains how to use your directory structure to create "you are here" link trails on your pages. Recipe 9.1 discusses ways to make sure visitors don't get lost after you reorganize your site's files and directories.

2.4   Establishing a Naming Convention for Your Files

Problem

You need to name web page files so they convey meaningful information to your visitors—as well as you and others who work on the site.

Solution

Web server file naming should follow the same guidelines discussed in Recipe 2.3: you should avoid spaces and special characters, use other punctuation sparingly, and keep them all lowercase. Unlike a web site directory—whose primary, if not only, purpose is to organize and contain site files—the files themselves are on the site for a variety of reasons. A one-size-fits-all naming scheme won't work. The right way to name a downloadable PDF file differs from the right way to name a GIF file of the site logo because the two files have different purposes.

Despite their differences, all the files on your site should have names that:

- Have a valid file extension, such as *.html*, *.gif*, or *.pdf*
- Convey something about the source, contents, or nature of the file
- Follow a logical and consistent scheme across similar files

Discussion

The various files on your site come together on pages, the Web's most basic building block. As files themselves, your HTML pages have filenaming requirements depending on where they exist in the site structure. I'll cover some of those issues first, and then address some additional guidelines to consider when naming supporting files such as images and downloads.

Index pages

As its name suggests, the index page offers an overview of the contents of the directory and provides links to the other pages in it. If a directory of files requires a main page, call it *index.html*. Although it's possible to modify or override the server's configuration to use an alternate filename for the main page in a directory or entire site (see Recipe 1.5), you should employ this technique sparingly. Don't set up custom directory home pages that reiterate the directory name—for example */about/about.html* or */products/products.html*. Deviating too often from the *index.html* standard will end up confusing you and your visitors.

Subpages

Each directory of pages on your site might have its own naming scheme, depending on the nature of the files it contains. For example, you might use date-oriented notation to name files in your directory of archived newsletters according to their issue date (*200504.html*, *200505.html*, and *200506.html*), while pages in your case studies section might be named according to the client they highlight (*gm.html*, *ford.html*, and *honda.html*). Likewise, template files that generate pages from content in a database can be structured with coded logic (or URL rewriting as described in Recipe 2.8) to convey human-readable information about their contents: *issue.php?date=200506* or *casestudy.php?client=honda*. The goal is to use a consistent scheme for all related pages. Also, use subdirectories to avoid redundancy in filenames. Consider a directory of web pages containing information about a company's staff, locations, and history:

```
/about/stafflist.html
/about/staffbios.html
/about/northlocation.html
/about/downtownlocation.html
/about/aboutfounder.html
/about/historyearly.html
/about/historyrecent.html
/about/future.html
```

As Big Bird would say, some of these things are not like the others. By subdividing the */about* directory, each page can have a more succinct filename that conveys its subject:

```
/about/staff/list.html
/about/staff/bios.html
/about/locations/north.html
/about/locations/downtown.html
/about/history/founder.html
/about/history/early.html
/about/history/recent.html
/about/history/future.html
```

In this case, the main page for the */about* directory (which should, of course, be named *index.html*) can adequately serve as the index page for all the subdirectories.

Images and movies

File extensions (the three or four characters after the "dot" in a filename) say a lot about a file. The web server uses them to determine a file's *MIME type*, which when combined with a user's browser settings, determine whether the file is downloaded, opened automatically in a helper application, or viewed in place on a page.

Useful filenames for site assets that get viewed inline—such as images and movies—are more important to the web designer than the web surfer. Adding references to a file's source, quality, and/or dimensions can make finding the right file when laying out a page a lot easier. For example, you might take the *logo.eps* file you get from a graphic designer and optimize it as *logo_120x65.gif*. The width and height notation will help you keep track of the various versions of the logo you will create. Likewise, you can add shorthand details to movie files that indicate their playback quality, such as *widget_hq.mpg* for the high-quality, broadband version of a product demo movie, and *widget_lq.mpg* for the low-quality dial-up connection version.

Downloadables

Offering files that a visitor can take away from your site temporarily joins the file-naming scheme on your site with the one on their PC's hard drive. Everyone has experienced—either personally or vicariously—the bewilderment of a novice web surfer trying to locate a file downloaded from a web site. Assuming they can find the file, the name you've given it should be more for their benefit than yours. Rather than using generic names like *orderform.pdf* or *application.pdf*—which end up in an amorphous clump with other like-named files in the downloads folder—give your downloads distinctive names that indicate the site they came from. For example, the ABC Nutriceuticals company might offer a downloadable order form named *ABC_orderform.pdf*.

See Also

Web pages are also known by the label that appears in the browser title bar. For more information, see Recipe 2.5. To define the page that visitors see when the URL they request does not include a filename, see Recipe 1.5.

2.5   Establishing a Naming Convention for Page Titles

Problem

You need to give meaningful and reliable titles to your web pages so they are easily distinguished from one another in search results and browser history lists.

Solution

Set up a scheme for formatting the content that goes between the `<title>` tags in your web page code and follow it throughout your site. The title goes in the head section of the HTML code, like this:

```
<head>
...meta tags...
 <title>page title information</title>
...CSS styles and other head content...
</head>
```

Other guidelines to follow include:

- Maintain a consistent format.
- Use specific language.
- Make page titles unique.
- Keep page titles brief.

Discussion

The page title is one of the most important *and* overlooked web page elements. Often without knowing so, web surfers use page titles to get to your web site and move around on it once there. In general, page titles are the linked text that appears in a list of search results (see Figure 2-6). They're also used to keep a running archive of recently visited pages, available through a browser's History or Go menu.

Web designers often neglect writing a useful (or any) page title for a variety of reasons. First, they may be focused on the content and design of a page's main section, and, after completing that, they forget to go back and add a page title. Likewise, their web page editor may have a default page title such as "Untitled" or "Designed with Adobe GoLive," but this title is just as useless as having no title at all, if it doesn't get changed to something more meaningful. Second, many content management and shopping cart systems do not provide a way to give unique page titles to dynamically generated pages, so every page gets created with the generic "Article" or "Catalog Item" page title.

Page titles are really a string of information about a page. At the very least, they should start with a summary of the page contents, then identify the site section or category the page lives in, and then the name of the site. On your home page, list the site name and/or URL, and the site's tagline. For example:

Smith Enterprises—Serving Springfield Gardeners Since 1949

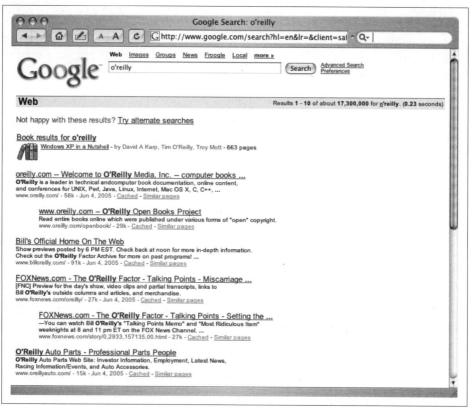

Figure 2-6. Search engines use the contents of a web page's title tag to build a list of search result links; Google's own meaningful page title (top bar of browser window) reiterates the search term

Search engine optimization consultants often advocate filling page titles with offers and tantalizing keywords (instead of meaningful wayfinding text) to juice a site's click-through rate. Striking the right balance between the needs of a site's users and the marketing department is left to the reader.

Each piece of information in the page title should be separated by punctuation, such as a hyphen, colon, pipe, asterisk, or (for novelty's sake) a combination of two or more of these separators. Choose one style, and then use it consistently for all the page titles on your site.

Start with something unique about the page, such as a short headline or product name. When seen together in a list of search results or browser history list, the first two or three words are what users will scan and use to differentiate one page from another. Then add information to the title in decreasing order of specificity.

For example, in this hypothetical page title, the information gets more specific moving from right to left:

4hp Widget (blue)—Widgets—Online Store—Smith Enterprises

Don't get carried away, though. If your site has a deep directory structure or hierarchy, don't feel compelled to list every section and subsection that lies between the current page and the site's home page. First, few—if any—of your visitors need that much information. And some browsers will truncate page titles in the history list after 40 or 50 characters. Keep your page titles short and to the point to maximize their benefit for your site's audience.

See Also

The art of creating page titles and link text are closely related. For more information, see Recipe 6.2. To add extra oomph to the way your pages appear in browser bookmark and history lists, see Recipe 8.3.

2.6 Establishing a Naming Convention for Your Variables

Problem

You need to follow a dependable pattern for naming variables in your web site scripts.

Solution

Develop coding guidelines that make sense to you, your team, and your web site, and then stick to them.

In general, a good variable naming scheme:

- Uses unique, concise terms
- Limits abbreviations
- Avoids reserved words in its programming language
- Serves as a form of self-documentation

Discussion

Variables are used to store alphanumeric values that will be manipulated by a script or program. Variables can have a constant value defined permanently in the code, or be changed from one value to another through logic or input from a user.

For example, a PHP script might take a Fahrenheit temperature value entered on a web site form (call it $temp), perform a calculation on the variable to convert it to Celsius, and then echo the same variable (with a new value) back to the user.

The variable name $temp has several disadvantages (that's why I chose it). As a generic abbreviation for temperature, $temp easily could be misconstrued as representing a temporary value (or the user's temperament) by another programmer reviewing the code.

 If you find that you have to use abbreviations or shorthand for your variables, compile a glossary and add it to a central comment block in your script.

While the name $temp meets the simple needs for a hypothetical temperature converter, it becomes woefully inadequate as soon as you try to add other functionality to the converter. Say, for example, that you improve the script to accept two temperature values from a user—the current indoor temperature and the current outdoor temperature. Which one of the two should be $temp? Neither. A better strategy is to use more meaningful names for the two variables, such as $indoor and $outdoor.

Now, let's suppose that you want to let users specify how to convert the temperatures: from Fahrenheit to Celsius or from Celsius to Fahrenheit. For this, the script will need another variable—whose value is chosen by the user through either a radio button or select menu—that dictates which conversion to perform on $indoor and $outdoor. Let's call it $convert.

So far, so good. Two temperature values and a trigger value ($convert) go in, and two new temperature values come out. But wait: now let's add the ability to convert atmospheric pressure readings—from inches of mercury to millibars or vice versa— at the same time for both indoor and outdoor readings (Our hypothetical user has a great weather gauge!).

Now the script needs six variables: two for temperature, two for pressure, and two for the types of conversion to perform. And now you should start to see why having a naming scheme can be valuable. Six good variable names for the converter would be:

```
$indoor_temp;
$outdoor_temp;
$convert_temp;
$indoor_pressure;
$outdoor_pressure;
$convert_pressure;
```

For PHP variables, I recommend using all lowercase letters with underscores separating words to improve readability. An alternate technique uses so-called *camel case*, or inner-cased, variable names, meaning that words in a name are capitalized (except the first) and run together without spaces—$indoor_temp would become $indoorTemp.

The latter method has pitfalls because variable names in PHP (as well as JavaScript and Perl) are case sensitive. The names $indoortemp and $indoorTemp would represent two *different* variables. Whichever technique you choose, be consistent and avoid naming two variables whose names differ only by case.

 Variable names for constants should be all uppercase, such as $EARTHS_GRAVITY.

The uniqueness of a variable also can be affected by the order of the words in its name, which in turn can affect how well variable names "self-document" a script or program. Easy-to-read and understand variable names are critical for projects with more than one programmer (or for just one programmer who does not look at the code very often—you know who you are). For the six variables needed for the sample converter script, I chose names with better distinctiveness at the beginning of the name. Three variables beginning with $temp_ and three beginning with $pressure_ would not provide the same benefit to another programmer scanning the code to distinguish between adjacent references to two variables.

See Also

For a list of reserved words that can't be used as variable names in PHP, see *http://us4.php.net/reserved.variables*. For JavaScript, see *http://javascript.about.com/library/blreserved.htm*

2.7 Downloading All Files from a Site

Problem

You need to create a backup, mirror, or offline copy of your web site.

Solution

Use the Unix utility wget to mirror the files on the server to another location either by HTTP with this command:

```
wget --mirror http://yourwebsite.com
```

or by FTP:

```
wget --mirror ftp://username:password@yourwebsite.com
```

Alternatively, you can use GUI-based utilities on your PC. Some choices are listed in the "See Also" section of this Recipe.

Discussion

With wget, you can perform heroic feats of webmastering, whether it's copying a single file from one site to another, or an entire site to another server.

 When spidering a site over HTTP, wget will only copy files it finds links to. Unused images and old web pages still lingering on the server will be skipped. Using FTP, wget will copy everything.

Some scenarios where wget can be indispensable include:

Keeping frequently updated pages or images in sync on two sites
Say you want to display a real-time webcam image on your site, but don't want to (or can't) use an absolute URL to the site where the camera saves the image in the image tag's src attribute. (Perhaps the other site's server is slower or less reliable than yours, or outside linking to the image has been disabled, as described in Recipe 5.5.) With wget, you can specify the URL of the file, a local directory on your server where it should be copied, and the number of times to retry a flaky HTTP connection. Combined with cron (see Recipe 1.8), wget can perform its connect-and-copy task as often as you (or your system administrator) want it to.

Setting up a mirror version of a site
Because wget also can connect via FTP, you can use it as part of your backup strategy. When wget retrieves a file with HTTP, you get the same rendered code that you would see if you viewed source on the page in a browser. Server-side code, such as PHP scripting and include file tags, won't show up. Using FTP, which requires adding a username and password to the wget command, yields the actual files with all the "pre-rendering" code intact. If an unexpected outage or traffic spike knocks your site offline, wget can help you quickly relocate it on another server.

Getting all the files needed for an offline copy of a site
Offline copies of a site can be useful in situations where connecting to the real thing is impractical or not feasible. For example, the sales staff wants to demonstrate your password-protected tech support site for a prospective customer. Putting a copy of the site on a CD or laptop hard drive can prevent connection or login problems that could sink the demo. In HTTP mode, wget can negotiate HTTP authentication logins (the type that appear in a browser-based pop-up dialog box). With its cookie-handling options, wget can load authentication information from a previously created session cookie to access a protected site, a technique reserved for power users who review the wget manual (referred to in the "See Also" section of this Recipe).

However, one shortcoming of wget is its ability to handle dynamically generated sites. With the --html-extension option enabled, wget will append a *.html* suffix to dynamically generated pages, but links to those pages that include the query string will not be updated.

For example, a site might have several FAQs stored in a database and displayed on the site through a PHP template that retrieves the content based on a record ID. A link to the page might look like this:

```
<a href="/faq.php?id=1">Question No. 1</a>
```

This link's destination file, retrieved by wget, will be named faq.php?id=1.html (or faq.php?id=1 without the extension option enabled). But the link itself won't be changed, which will detract from the offline browsing experience.

A PC site-downloading utility (two are listed in the "See Also" section of this Recipe, and there are surely others) can take the extra step of converting a dynamic site to a static site. For each dynamic link the utility finds while crawling a site, it creates a unique file (such as *faq60148.php* for the hypothetical FAQ) *and* updates all the links to point to the new static page.

See Also

You can use cron to schedule recurring uses of wget. For more information, see Recipe 1.8. For more on using wget, see *http://www.gnu.org/software/wget/wget.html.* Grab-a-Site for Windows (*http://www.bluesquirrel.com/products/grabasite/*) and Site-Sucker for Mac (*http://www.sitesucker.us/*) are two desktop applications that go where wget does not. Both provide the ability to download dynamic sites to static pages, among other features.

2.8   Making URLs Easy to Find and Remember

Problem

You need to turn complex content management system, blog, or shopping cart URLs into easy-to-remember URLs.

Solution

Use mod_rewrite rules in an *.htaccess* file to invisibly turn simple URLs into complex query strings that return dynamic pages to the visitor's browser. For example, an e-commerce site that sells men and women's clothes might offer a variety of men's shoes, such as boots, oxfords, sandals, and loafers.

A URL for the list of loafers might look like this:

> *http://mensandwomensclothes.com/store/list.php?type=mens&cat=shoes&subcat=loafers*

Using rewrite rules, you can tidy up the URL to something like this:

> *http://mensandwomensclothes.com/store/mens/shoes/loafers/*

A rewrite rule in the *.htaccess* file that you create or modify in the */store* directory takes care of converting the clean URL to the more complex query string that the store template (*list.php*) needs to generate the list of loafers from the store database. Here's the code for the rewrite rule:

```
RewriteEngine On
Options +FollowSymLinks
RewriteRule ^(.*)/(.*)/(.*)/$ /store/list.php?type=$1&cat=$2&subcat=$3
```

Assuming the mod_rewrite module has been compiled into your installation of Apache (typically, it has), the first line (RewriteEngine On) prepares the module for the rewrite rule or rules to follow. The second line (Options +FollowSymLinks) can be left out if it's already in the main Apache configuration file (typically, *httpd.conf*).

The third line contains the rule. Three consecutive wildcard search patterns followed by a slash—(.*)/—match the structure of the simple URL. The patterns would match other clean URLS, too, such as ...*womens/skirts/mini/* or ...*mens/hats/stetsons/*. Note that the URL has to end with a slash (marked by the $ at the end of the search pattern) for a successful match.

Discussion

Investing the time to create rewrite rules that turn simple URLs into complex, behind-the-scenes queries pays off in several ways for you and your site's visitors. First off, because the resultant URLs are generally shorter and follow the "directory-slash-directory" model of URL construction, they're easier to print in offline materials, recite over the phone, and remember. Web surfers—especially novices—shouldn't be expected to remember the arcane syntax of complex query strings involving questions marks, ampersands, and equals signs.

Clean web page addresses also encourage power users to go "URL fishing." If ...*mens/shoes/loafers/* works, then sophisticated visitors to your site may conclude that ...*mens/shoes/boots/*, ...*/mens/shoes/sandals/*, and a variety of other permutations will work, too. This approach to improving your site's user-friendliness can be applied to as many "aliases" to the various pages of your site as you can think of, both static and dynamic. For example, if you keep your news releases in a directory called */news*, set up rewrite rules (or a redirect) for */pr* and */press*. That way, you'll always have an answer for web surfers who "guess" their way to your site.

 Believe it or not, web surfers in the wild do not always follow your prescribed pathways to pages on your site. Many will "fish" for URLs in hopes of landing somewhere good.

Clean URLs also make your life as a web designer easier as your site grows and changes. By providing a layer of abstraction between your visitors and your site's backend technology, clean URLs allow you to rearrange and even re-engineer your site without too much trouble. For example, you might want to move your store's shopping cart from PHP to a proprietary ecommerce platform that ties into your point-of-sale and inventory system. That probably means different server-side script names (possibly not ending in *.php*) and different query strings to get the same product lists. But with a few changes to the rewrite rules, the clean URLs in your site's links and visitors' bookmarks can stay the same.

It might seem that clean URLs generated with rewrite rules can do everything but slice your crusty loaf of artisan bread. One area they do fall short in, though, is making much of an improvement in your site's search engine "indexability." That's because dynamic pages are, ultimately, still generated by the query string that the clean URL hides. The pages of thousands, if not millions, of sites lie beyond the reach of search engines—an area dubbed the *deep Web*.

Search engines were originally designed to index static pages found through links. A dynamic page on your site accessible through a hardcoded link in your HTML code—whether its clean or complex—will be found using this method. But the automated spiders and robots crawling your site are not designed to uncover the bulk of your dynamic content by guessing at other permutations of the same query string, much less enter terms in a site search form or negotiate a subscribers-only login form. Google, Yahoo!, and others are at work on the problem of indexing this hidden content, which may prove to be up to one hundred times larger than what's available through search engines today.

See Also

For other techniques that use Apache's rewriting engine, see Recipes 1.6 and 9.1.

For more on the issues surrounding permanent web page addresses, read World Wide Web inventor Tim Berners-Lee's article "Cool URIs don't change" at *http://www.w3.org/Provider/Style/URI*. For more about the problem of the deep Web, see *http://deepweb.com*.

2.9   Creating a Flowchart for Complex Site Functionality

Problem

You need to map out how visitors to your web site will interact with a complex form or tool.

Solution

Use the standard flowchart symbols (see Figure 2-7) to create a diagram for the web site process.

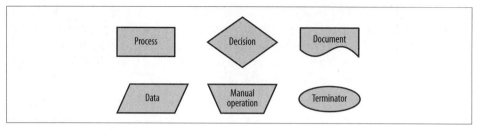

Figure 2-7. Common flowchart symbols for diagramming a process

Discussion

Time to get out your No. 2 pencils. Although software such as Visio and OmniGraffle can make your flowchart look more presentable, the place to start is with a clean sheet of paper and your favorite erasable writing implement.

Wherever you have visitors signing up, logging in, checking out, or undertaking some other interactive endeavor on your site, your planning and implementation of the process can benefit from a flowchart. Flowcharts are all about improving communication: between you and the programmer who will implement the process and between your site and its users. A flowchart helps you visualize interaction points between visitors and the site and identify places in the process where error messages and other feedback are necessary. Include the flowchart in your functional specification document (see Recipe 2.1) to augment your textual descriptions of complex processes.

A visual example will help in this Recipe, too. Figure 2-8 shows a flowchart for the subscriber login process on a site I worked on a couple of years ago. The site already had a straightforward system for authenticating visitors: after data entered on a login form is checked against a list of valid subscriber accounts, the visitor gets the requested page, or an error message if the login information was incorrect. But the high cost of a subscription led to a lot of password sharing between subscribers and nonsubscribers. The owner of the site wanted the site to check the login information supplied by a user for other active sessions with the same login, and then let the new user kick the other user off the site. The site would allow only one active session per user—"second come, second served," so to speak.

As shown in Figure 2-8, adding the additional checking required extra logic in the login routine (diamond-shaped decisions) and new system-generated messages (shown in rectangles). The visitor starts at the lozenge-shaped terminator marked "Home." Clicked links and user-input data are shown in parallelograms.

When an already logged-in visitor clicks a link for subscriber-only page, success is a straight shot down the left side of the chart. The system checks for an active session for the visitor (using a cookie set on the visitor's computer) and delivers the requested page if it finds one. If not, the visitor enters the extended logic of the login process, significantly simplified here for demonstration purposes.

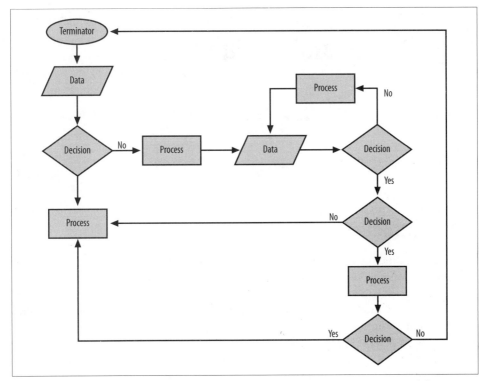

Figure 2-8. Flowcharts help you visualize complex interactions between your users and the server, such as logging in to view subscriber-only content

The user name and password entered on the login form leads to another system decision: Is the login valid? If not, the visitors gets looped back to the login form, this time with an error message. If yes, the login routine performs a second check—this time for an active session associated with the same login information. If yes, the system presents users with another choice—logout the other user? If the user clicks "Yes" she proceeds to the desired page. If no, back to the home page.

One thing to note about this (and other flowcharts you create) is that logical decisions often create the need for short bits of content that explain to users what happened. Error message or instructions are easy to overlook because they don't have a place on your site map or in your content inventory. You'll find them on a flowchart.

See Also

Microsoft's Visio (*http://microsoft.com/visio/*) and Omni Group's OmniGraffle (*http://www.omnigroup.com/applications/omnigraffle/*) are both excellent tools for putting a finer point on your pencil-and-paper flowcharts.

CHAPTER 3

Page Design and Navigation

3.0   Introduction

Color, layout, and navigation are what usually come to mind when one thinks about web design. With your web server set up and your site-building plan ready to go, you're surely ready to turn your attention to more artistic pursuits. But the path from site map and mockup to finished web site can't be followed in a blind pursuit of creative freedom. The visual impression your site projects demands careful consideration of the tradeoffs that lie at the intersection of inventive design, user satisfaction, and business needs. In this chapter, I'll explore some of those choices and present solutions that will help you balance aesthetics with usability.

3.1   Choosing Between a Flexible and Fixed Layout

Problem

You need to determine which design format will do the best job of presenting your web site's content for its audience.

Solution

Web designers have three basic options when creating a grid into which web site content can be arranged and presented: a fixed-width layout that locks page elements in place regardless of the browser window size; a flexible, or liquid, layout in which content blocks can be resized when the browser window size changes, and a hybrid layout that combines both fixed and flexible components.

Consider a hypothetical three-column web page that uses CSS-styled content blocks in <div>s for its layout. A fixed-width design specifies pixels for the three columns and their margins:

```
<html>
<head>
...other head tags...
```

```
<style type="text/css" title="text/css">
<!--
#column1 {
 float: left;
 width: 150px;
 margin-left: 5px;
 background-color: #CCCCCC; }
#column2 {
 float: left;
 width: 390px;
 margin-left: 5px;
 background-color: #FFFFCC;}
#column3 {
 float: left;
 width: 200px;
 margin-left: 5px;
 background-color: #CCCCCC;   }
-->
</style>
</head>
<body>
<div id="col1">...column 1 content...</div>
<div id="col2">...column 2 content...</div>
<div id="col3">...column 3 content...</div>
</body>
</html>
```

The code for a flexible layout looks the same, but uses a relative unit, such as percentages, rather than an absolute dimension.

```
<html>
<head>
...other head tags...
<style type="text/css" title="text/css">
<!--
#column1 {
 float: left;
 width: 20%;
 margin-left: 2%;
 background-color: #CCCCCC; }
#column2 {
 float: left;
 width: 50%;
 margin-left: 2%;
 background-color: #FFFFCC;}
#column3 {
 float: left;
 width: 20%;
 margin-left: 2%;
 background-color: #CCCCCC;   }
-->
</style>
</head>
<body>
```

```
<div id="col1">...column 1 content...</div>
<div id="col2">...column 2 content...</div>
<div id="col3">...column 3 content...</div>
</body>
</html>
```

Two coding notes: first, all together the widths and margins total less than 100 percent to account for situations when the browser rounds a percentage value up or down, depending on the window size. Also, if you want to put content beneath the columns (such as a footer), you will need to follow the last floated div in the "row" with a `<br class="clear" />` and assign a `clear` attribute (either left, right or both) to the CSS rules for the last `div`'s id. Alternatively, you can wrap all the column divs in a container div and clear that.

A hybrid layout might use percentages in the outer columns and a pixel width for the middle column to ensure a more consistent line length in the middle content block. Amazon.com is one of the best examples of the opposite hybrid approach—fixed outer columns and a stretchable middle.

Discussion

Ideally, your site layout should minimize the amount of mousing and scrolling it requires of its users and avoid hiding content beyond the right edge of the browser window. That was a relatively easy task in the early days of the Web, when a designer could more or less count on visitors seeing his site on a 640×480 pixel monitor. Now, the 800×600 pixel resolution has become the new standard. But depending on whom you ask, only about half of the surfers on the Web today browse at that resolution.

After deducting pixels for the various menus and scrollbars around the edges of the browser window, the actual space available on the web page canvas, or *viewport*, is about 740×410 pixels on an 800×600 display.

Browsing devices and screen resolutions are increasingly varied, as are the browsing skills of the people who will visit your site. Power users know the extent to which they can adjust browser windows, resize web site font sizes, and even change their monitor's resolution, but many others do not.

Ultimately, the fixed-or-flexible decision comes down to one of personal preference, filtered through as much site planning, testing, and user feedback as possible. With that in mind, let's look more closely at some of the pros and cons for the fixed and flexible layout templates presented in the Solution.

Flexible layouts

Designers who use liquid layouts assume—correctly—that they have no control over the conditions in which the site will be viewed. Whether viewed on a 1600×1200 monitor in a maximized browser window or squeezed down on an ancient public library PC, a flexible layout yields control of the browsing experience to its users. Flexible layouts succeed for the most part at being an all-in-one design approach, with some pitfalls. Flexible layouts are:

- Better for sites with lots of content, such as e-commerce sites or photo galleries (see Figure 3-1)
- Harder to execute with a complex design
- Better than fixed layouts for visitors with smaller-than-average monitors
- Better when visitors need to make type larger
- Not so good for designs that require fixed positions for page elements such as ads
- Difficult to read when maximized—stretched out pages can look very odd

Figure 3-1. Two views of the Wired.com home page: narrow (left) and wide (right)

Fixed layouts

Control is what turns many designers to fixed layouts. By gearing a site's layout toward some middle ground—say, the perceived 800×600-pixel standard—fixed layouts provide a better canvas for accurately translating a designer's mockup into HTML. On larger monitors at higher resolutions, however, locked-down layouts permit ample stretches of empty space to fill the right and bottom sections of the browser window (see Figure 3-2). An increasingly popular *faux*-flexible layout style minimizes the visual impact of unsightly white space by centering all content in a fixed-width block. When a visitor widens her browser window, the content block shifts to the right, dividing the increased empty space against the right and left edges of the window.

Beyond that, the arguments for and against fixed layouts fill a mixed bag. Fixed layouts are:

- Better at holding line lengths constant, which improves readability
- Better for designs that use fixed-width elements, such as large images or movies

Figure 3-2. The fixed-width layout of the jcpenney.com homepage fills a compact corner of a maximized browser window

- Awaiting obsolescence that will come when baseline monitor sizes and resolutions improve
- Frustrating for visitors with smaller-than-average monitors, who must scroll horizontally to see the whole page
- Space-wasters on high-resolution monitors with maximized browser windows

See Also

For more information on the actual sizes of various browser windows, read Chunky-Soup.net's article "Tracking Visitor's Browser Sizes" at *http://www.chunkysoup.net/advanced/bugged/*.

3.2   Creating a Color Scheme

Problem

You need to select colors for your site's background, text, links, and other elements.

Solution

Choosing a color scheme for a site might be the most subjective task confronting a web designer. Of the nearly infinite number of color combinations at your disposal, there are certainly more than a few right ones for your site, as well as many wrong ones.

Choosing the right colors can have a big impact on how your site is received by visitors, while the wrong combination can just as easily repel them. But differentiating right from wrong has less to do with opting for, say, a shade of light purple over a shade of light green, than it has to do with choosing a palette of colors that supports your design and the goals of your site.

With that in mind, follow this checklist when developing a color scheme for your site:

Follow the lead of the materials you already have.

Your favorite color may be flaming red-orange, but you'll have to hide your light under a bushel if your project already has an existing logo or offline material that employs an orange-free color scheme. Using a web design project to branch out visually from an established color scheme will cause credibility issues for your site. Don't shock visitors with a color scheme that bears no resemblance to the other "touch points" by which they know you—be it your catalog, your packaging, your delivery vehicles, the neon sign in your store front window, or something else.

Use a background color that does not weaken text legibility.

White wins the contest for most popular background color because usability studies have shown that white provides the best background on which to read web site content. Choosing to use black or dark text over a white background doesn't preclude the use of other colors in design elements such as borders, navigation bars, and display copy. But it does lower the level of difficulty associated with devising a complementary color scheme that doesn't sacrifice readability.

On the other hand, a non-white background offers a canvas on which to design a distinctive and visually compelling site. The hue-saturation-brightness interface to your favorite color picker is a good place to find complementary pairs of colors. Pairs of background and text colors that vary only in brightness will naturally enhance one another, while preserving readability.

Always specify colors for text and links.

To prevent a browser's default color values from clashing with your color scheme, start your stylesheet with rules for the text and link colors, as well as the background color:

```
body {
 background-color: #FFFFFF;
 color: #000000;
}
a:link
{
 color: #0000FF;
}
a:visited
{
 color: #333333;
}
```

Choose and use colors that help highlight information.

A guiding tenet of graphic design asserts that a good design works equally well with color and without. In other words, you shouldn't rely on color to validate design decisions about type sizes and layout. The color red can make a smallish headline stand out, but that headline should probably be bigger regardless of its color. However, a web site that uses color effectively obviously has an advantage over a "colorless" web site or a site that uses color indiscriminately. That's because color accentuates the context of your web site content. Bright, strong colors help visitors focus on the most important parts of your site, but if everything is strongly colored, then nothing stands out.

Discussion

Creating a color scheme requires some familiarity with how colors relate to one another, practice, and a bit of experimentation. By learning a few tricks, you'll be able to whip up beautiful, professional color schemes at a moment's notice. Don't rely on small swatches to make your color decisions, though. Mock up some text on a sample web page and take your color choices for a test drive.

First, use a *color wheel* or color picker, such as the one in Photoshop, to experiment. A color wheel displays the red-to-violet rainbow of colors wrapped back on itself in a circle. Points on the circle identify colors that harmonize with each other (see Figure 3-3). Analogous colors, like blue and teal, lie next to each other on the wheel and can work together in a low-contrast, understated scheme. Complementary colors at opposite sides of the wheel—such as purple and green—combine in more dramatic schemes. Even richer color combinations can be found by combining color *triads* from three points of a equilateral triangle on the wheel. If you don't know where to start on the color wheel, take a favorite image (or the site's logo), optimize it as a JPEG or GIF, and zoom in on it until you can see individual pixels. Adjacent pixels are usually complementary colors.

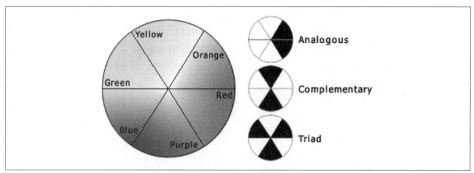

Figure 3-3. Points on a color wheel identify color combinations that go together

When you've exercised on the color wheel long enough, step away from your computer and pay attention to your surroundings. Mother Nature is the supreme color expert. A walk in the outdoors can reveal surprisingly obvious color combinations that work well on a web site, too. Everyday objects also can be a source of inspiration. Keep a clipping file of color schemes you find attractive, whether it's a cereal box or conversion van artwork. Take note of how the notable color schemes you collect complement their subject and affect your emotions.

See Also

Other design considerations are covered in Recipes 3.1 and 4.3.

There are several addictive point-and-click online tools for mixing and matching colors from a color wheel, including the Webmaster's Color Laboratory (*http://www.visibone.com/colorlab/*), ColorWhore (*http://www.colorwhore.com/*), and the Color schemes generator 2 (*http://wellstyled.com/tools/colorscheme2/index-en.html*).

3.3   Making Room for All Your Navigation

Problem

You need to make sure that all of your site navigation will fit in your design.

Solution

The deepest pages on your site often will have to display the most navigation. When considering various navigation schemes, make a mockup or sketch of one of these pages to test possible arrangements. It's always easier to take away navigation from pages higher in your site structure (where it's not needed) than to try to wedge in important navigation on a page that wasn't designed to handle it.

Discussion

Navigation plays two related roles on a web site. By arranging links in a logical hierarchy, navigation gives visitors the mechanisms they need to browse from one page on your site to another. Navigation also provides feedback to users that helps them understand where they are in your site and how the page they're looking at relates to other pages on the site.

Navigation can appear in a variety of shapes and sizes to meet its two obligations to web surfers. The primary, or global, navigation outlines the main sections of your site and should appear on every page, including the home page. Have your proposed site map handy (see Recipe 2.1) before you start thinking about what your primary navigation items should be and how they will be presented.

Don't alter the position or wording of your primary navigation from page to page, lest you drive away visitors in confusion. You can, however, vary the text or background color on a primary navigation item to signify the current section of the site in which a visitor is browsing.

Local navigation includes everything that appears only within a certain section, subsection, or small collection of pages. Sites with a deep hierarchy often have secondary navigation, *tertiary* (third-level) navigation, and even page-specific navigation that connects visitors (via "anchor" links) to subheads further down on one long page or to related material displayed over multiple pages.

Don't overload or complicate your navigation with long, hard-to-scan lists of links to make every page no more than two or three clicks away from every other page. Usability studies have shown that pages with more than a couple of dozen navigation options produce severe eye-glazing in web surfers. If your navigation is logical and hierarchical, then a site that's four, five, or even more clicks deep is OK. And remember, many visitors will skip your navigation by *deep linking* to your site from Google, your own site's search engine, or another web site.

 You can facilitate a little deep linking on your own by placing a handful of "Google links" at the bottom of your pages. These are links that reference specific web-searcher keywords and link to deeper pages of single-subject sites. For example an e-marketing consultant could augment his top-level navigation (Philosophy, Products, Services, About Me, Clients) with specific links at the bottom of each page to pages about Email Marketing, Search Engine Optimization (SEO), Search Engine Marketing (SEM) that are all deeper in the site under the Services section. Doing so can bump up a site's page rank in Google and give users one click to get to relevant subject matter.

Other components of navigation include links to pages that convey general, site-related information or pages that don't fit into any particular section. They go by a handful of names: *permanent navigation* for items such as copyright and privacy policies, *functional navigation* for visitor actions such as login or checkout, and *utility navigation* for things like site search, site map, or contact. These navigation items, which can be mixed and matched to meet the needs of your site, are usually displayed as text links and tucked away in a corner of the layout.

The primary links and the various levels of local links form the core navigation for your web site. In the Western, left-to-right reading world, the top and left edges of your design are the best places for this navigation. Carving out enough room to show all the necessary navigation on any given page often requires a bit of compromise. Starting with a modest list of concise, user-oriented navigation phrases helps.

Horizontal navigation, or tabs, are popular because they mimic the familiar GUI menu systems of modern PC operating systems and applications. But they eat into precious vertical space in your design—especially when you must leave room below the primary links for section-specific local navigation. Arranged horizontally, your primary navigation can hold only about six to eight items.

You can use the left edge of the screen instead of—or inconjunction with—horizontal navigation. By arranging links vertically, you can more easily add new links when needed, but the narrow space is less accommodating of longer navigation phrases.

Also, you might prefer to use that space for additional content or advertising (see Recipe 3.4). Using drop-down menus can save space in both horizontal and vertical arrangements.

See Also

Web usability consulting firm Adaptive Path has two excellent articles about site navigation on its web site: "A Few Helpful Definitions" (*http://www.adaptivepath. com/publications/essays/archives/000048.php*) and "Keeping it Under Control (*http:// www.adaptivepath.com/publications/essays/archives/000103.php*). For more about the art of creating page titles and link text, see Recipe 6.2.

OpenCube sells some of the best cross-browser drop-down menu systems at *http:// opencube.com*.

3.4   Designing Pages for Advertisements

Problem

You want to include advertisements on your site.

Solution

Design your pages to accommodate standard ad sizes.

Discussion

If generating income is one of your web site's goals (see Recipe 2.1), then sooner or later your might consider running advertisements alongside your content to meet it. If you've determined that your site's content and traffic will support advertising, then you'll need a page layout designed to hold the ads. If it isn't, then you'll spend unnecessary effort reworking ads to fit your design or redesigning your site to fit the accepted sizes. Or worse—you won't get any advertisers.

> Designing your pages to hold ads is only half the battle, if that. You'll find that many advertisers require specific placement on your pages. They will always want to be "above the fold" (i.e., visible without scrolling down), and balancing these requests without losing room for your content can be a real challenge.

Although there might be several hundred different sizes and shapes of "banner" ads on display on the web these days, the most common ones match the standard sizes established by the Interactive Advertising Bureau (IAB) in late 2002.

Large sites like Yahoo!, AOL, and CNET, all of whom are members of the IAB, use these sizes almost exclusively. Figure 3-4 shows the four sizes the IAB endorsed.

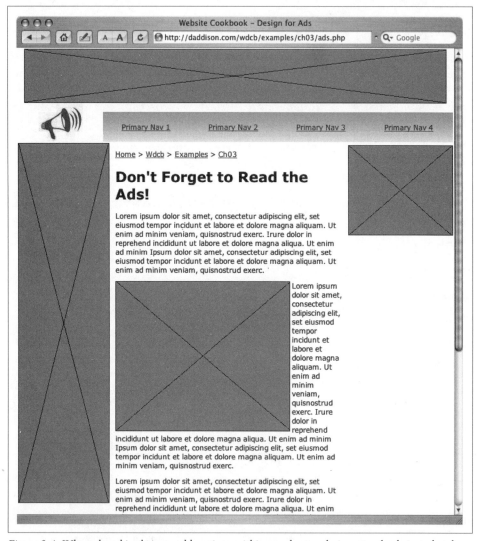

Figure 3-4. When placed in their usual locations within a web page design, standard-size ads take up a lot of screen real estate

If you think these ads have been on a supersize-me fast food diet, you're right. The 728×90 pixel size (top of the page in Figure 3-4) is almost two and half times larger than 468×60 pixel ad common five or six years ago. The vertical and button-style ads have grown, too (see Table 3-1 for details). Including the new horizontal banner, these three standard sizes are designed for placement along the edges of your pages in spaces you might otherwise use for your site's navigation or additional content. The 300×250 size, on the other hand, has no direct analog among older sizes; its TV-screen aspect ratio makes it ideal for multimedia-heavy pitches placed in close proximity to the web site's own content. You need to have pages with enough content to "wrap around" this style of ad.

Table 3-1. Many advertisers will expect your site design to accommodate the standard ad sizes approved by the Interactive Advertising Bureau in 2002

Standard Size	IAB Weight Limits	Replaces	Usage
728×90	20K (30K for Flash)	468×60, 460×55, 392×72, and others	Banner ad
180×150	15K (20K for Flash)	120×90, 120×60, and 125×125	Button ad
160×600	20K (30K for Flash)	120×240	Vertical banner, tower, or skyscraper ad
300×250	20K (30K for Flash)	Various sizes	In-line multimedia ad

Beware that advertising on your site will add extra weight (and load time) to your pages, crowd your content into peculiar spaces, and might very well be ignored by your visitors. Usability studies have shown that web surfers have a blind spot for peripheral page elements (such as ads) that flash or jiggle in a bid for attention.

Because they are generated from the content on the page, text-based ads, such as those generated by Google's AdSense program, have a much better track record for generating clicks. When browsing a site for information on, say, the care and feeding of a pet iguana, web surfers have been shown to be more receptive to text ads promoting related services, such as iguana carriers, iguana medications, and iguana psychics. Many sites run text ads interchangeably—or instead of—graphical ads in the same standard dimension spaces (Figure 3-5 shows an example).

See Also

To review the findings of the IAB's Ad Sizes Task Force, which established the standard ad sizes in widespread use today, visit *http://www.iab.net/standards/adsizes.asp*. For more about the Google AdSense program, see *http://google.com/adsense*.

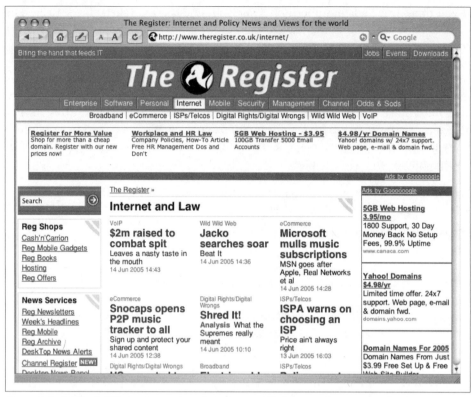

Figure 3-5. Ad blocks filled with text-based pitches can fill the same slots in your design as graphical ads

3.5   Expanding Your Web Site

Problem

You need to add pages, a new section, or a distinct subsite to your web site.

Solution

You should design your web site only once, not each time you create a new page. Follow these code and site management techniques to make sure every page on your site has a consistent look and feel:

Separate shared code blocks into include files.

When you save common elements of your site design as include files, you can be sure that the content, wording, and links are the same on every page where that include file appears. For example, if you put all the code for your primary navigation in an include file called *primnav_inc.php*, then a change to your main navigation requires editing just one file, rather than every page on your site. You can follow the same strategy for other discrete blocks of code, such as the page header and logo, other navigation blocks, and the page footer.

Isolate content from display rules using CSS stylesheets.

In the days before reliable browser support for (and widespread use of) stylesheets, web designers would specify background images, link colors, font sizes, and other display characteristics in the individual tags on every page of a web site. When an inevitable change became necessary, every page on the site had to be edited and re-uploaded to the web server. The process is tedious and introduces the risk that an inadvertent change might mangle the code. Putting the display rules in every page also increases the file's size.

Separating content from display makes sitewide changes easier, and also allows you to apply different styles to the same code used in different areas of your site. For example, you might want to create a subsite or microsite to promote a particular part of your online endeavors. The design of a subsite should be distinct but related to the design of your main site. The subsite also should retain at least a small part of the main site's global navigation, such as the logo, links to the main home page, site map, and site-wide search. By saving the global code in an include file, you can give it two different design treatments on the main site and subsite using two different stylesheets.

Learn and use a site management application's template system.

With web design applications such as Dreamweaver, GoLive, and FrontPage, you can create page templates that prevent unwanted changes to common code. When you create a new page based on a template, the unique content for that page can be added to only one of the template's editable sections. Used in combination with include files and stylesheets, templates ensure that pages remain consistent, especially when a group of site editors shares responsibility for adding new pages and maintaining a web site.

Discussion

Consistency is a key trait of a successful web site. It encourages visitors to trust your web site and facilitates a smooth, efficient browsing experience. Even subtle changes to the color, position, size, or functionality of design elements that appear on every page force a visitor to spend extra time trying to decide if the page he's viewing has the information he's seeking. Visitors should have to learn the design and navigation scheme of your site only once. Then, on that first *and* subsequent visits, your site layout should serve as a constant background that frames the content that deserves your visitors' attention.

See Also

Recipe 1.4

Recipe 4.4

The CSS Zen Garden (*http://www.csszengarden.com*) provides a powerful demonstration of using different stylesheets on the same content. Many other sites provide CSS-based layout templates for free, including the Layout Reservoir (*http://www.bluerobot.com/web/layouts/*), Intensivstation (*http://intensivstation.ch/templates/*), and inknoise (*http://www.inknoise.com/experimental/layoutomatic.php*).

3.6   Adding Background Images

Problem

You need to place stationary or tiled images as backgrounds for certain page elements or an entire web page.

Solution

Use the CSS properties `background-image`, `background-position`, `background-attachment`, and `background-repeat` to specify how you want the background to be displayed.

Background styles can be assigned to the `<body>` tag in a CSS stylesheet to display an image once in a fixed position:

```
body
{
    background-image: url(/images/backgrounds/penguins.jpg);
    background-position: 0px 0px;
    background-attachment: fixed;
    background-repeat: no-repeat;
    background-color: white;
    margin: 0px;
}
```

Or you can assign a CSS ID to other page elements, such as table cells or `<div>`'s, to display a repeating, tiled image across the item's background:

```
#topnav
{
    background-image: url(/images/backgrounds/topnav.jpg);
    background-repeat: repeat-x;
}
```

Discussion

Background images can add an extra dimension to your design, but they also can create usability problems for your visitors. A strong, busy background can make the text that appears over it hard to read. To maintain a balance between design and readability, use an image editor to fade or otherwise restrain the impact of a photo to be used as background, while strengthening the text to appear over it with extra font weight, size, and line height.

Figure 3-6 shows a web page that uses both background techniques described in the Solution. The main background (the penguins) is one large image given a fixed position at the upper left corner of the page by the stylesheet.

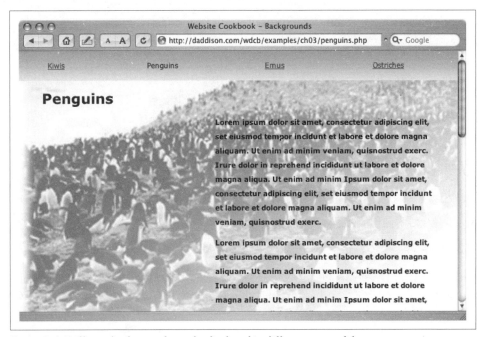

Figure 3-6. Different backgrounds can be displayed in different areas of the page

Using the CSS rule `background-attachment: fixed` the image will not move even as the visitor scrolls down the page, as shown in Figure 3-7.

 Fixed position backgrounds do not stay put in Netscape Navigator Version 4 and they never will. They also can behave poorly in older versions of Internet Explorer for Windows, but there is a JavaScript-based fix for IE. Check the link in the "See Also" section in this Recipe for more information.

For the background of the navigation bar (#topnav), I created a 1×50 pixel JPEG with a top-to-bottom, teal-to-white gradient. By default, CSS background images will repeat both horizontally and vertically. Because the row of links on my page runs along the top of the page, I used the `background-repeat` property to replicate the image only across the horizontal, x axis of the page. To repeat the background vertically but not horizontally, use `background-repeat: repeat-y`.

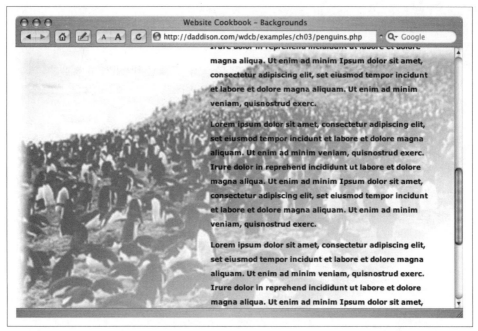

Figure 3-7. Fixed background images stay put, even as the user scrolls down the page

See Also

Andrew Clover has written a JavaScript that fixes Internet Explorer's non-compliant rendering of fixed position background images. Download it at *http://doxdesk.com/software/js/fixed.html*.

3.7   Creating Breadcrumb Links

Problem

You need to help users navigate your site by putting a chain of links, or breadcrumb, that matches your site structure.

Solution

Use a PHP script to generate the links on-the-fly from the directory names on your web site (see Figure 3-8).

Discussion

Breadcrumb links make a nifty addition to your site's navigation. Although they shouldn't replace a site's primary or secondary navigation, they give visitors an additional tool to use when browsing a deep site.

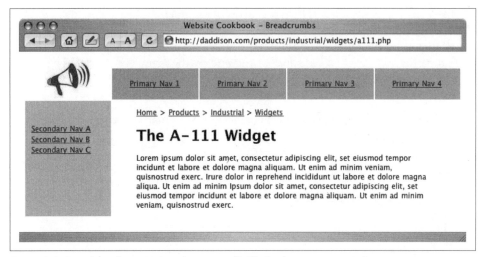

Figure 3-8. Breadcrumb navigation shows a trail of links that mirrors a site's structure

Using the names of your web site directories, this PHP script creates links to the main pages in every directory above the current page.

```
<?
$full_path = substr(getenv("REQUEST_URI"),1);
$full_path = trim($full_path,"\/");
$bc = split("\/", $full_path);
```

First, the script defines the variable $full_path as the names of the directories and the file that are part of the current page's URL (leaving out the http:// and the domain name) and trims the leading and trailing slashes from the string.

Using the split( ) function, the script turns the string value of $full_path (*products/industrial/widgets/a111.php*) into a four-value array—three directory names and a filename.

Next, the script will take a closer look at the filename (or lack thereof) of the URL that has been requested.

```
if (strstr(end($bc), "index")) {
  $j=2;
} else {
  $j=1;
}
```

The if condition tests the last value of the directories and filename array, end($bc). If it contains the text index, then the script assigns the value 2 to the temporary variable $j, which will play a role in the for loop that builds the links.

```
for ($i=0;$i<(sizeof($bc)-$j);$i++) {
```

The loop starts at the first element in the array, but the number of array elements it turns into links depends on the value of $j. We never want the script to create a link to the last value of the array.

That value is either the current filename (*a111.php*) or a directory name, meaning the visitor has requested the main page in a directory with a URL that ends with a trailing slash and no filename. When the visitor does request *index.php*, then a $j value of 2 stops the loop *two values* short of the end of the array $bc, because we don't want self-referencing links to *index.php* or the directory that contains it in the breadcrumb.

Now that we know how many of the elements in the path array we need to deal with, the script can begin to construct the links, which will be compiled in the variable $bc_path.

```
    $bc_start = strpos($full_path,$bc[$i]);
    $bc_length = $bc_start+strlen($bc[$i]);
    $bc_link = substr($full_path,0,$bc_length);
    $bc_text = ucfirst($bc[$i]);
    $bc_path .= " > <a href=".$bc_link."/>".$bc_text."</a>";
    }
```

For each element in the array—$bc[$i]—the script calculates its starting ($bc_start) and ending ($bc_length) character positions in $full_path. For *widgets*, this would be 21 and 27. Then the substr( ) function extracts the link—$bc_link—from the start of $full_path to the end of the current value of $bc[$i]. The ucfirst( ) function gives the link text $bc_text first-letter capitalization, and then its value is concatenated with the link code in $bc_path and printed on the web page.

```
    echo "<p><a href=\"/\">Home</a> ".$bc_path."</p>";
    ?>
```

See Also

Recipe 2.3

3.8   Creating a Link Menu to Other Pages

Problem

You need to create a way for visitors to quickly navigate to the most popular pages on your site.

Solution

Add a JavaScript function that accepts a URL from a form and uses it to load the new web page in the visitor's browser. Add this code to the <head> section of your web pages:

```
    <script type="text/JavaScript" language="JavaScript">
    <!--
    function goToPage(url) {
     if (url != '') {
       window.location = url;
```

```
      }
    }
    //-->
    </script>
```

The function goToPage( ) takes the parameter url from the selected value in a form menu on the page. After checking to make sure that the value of the parameter is not empty (url != ''), the function assigns the value to the location property of the window object, causing the browser to load the new page.

A select menu (shown in Figure 3-9) gives site visitors a way to choose the page to jump to and invoke the function.

Figure 3-9. Combined with a simple JavaScript, a select menu gives visitors another way to navigate your site

```
<form name="jmenu" method="post">
<select name="jchoices">
<option label="-Jump to another page-" value="" selected>-Jump to another page-
</option>
<option label="Widgets" value="http://yoursite.com/widgets/">Widgets</option>
<option label="Doo-Dads" value=" http://yoursite.com/doodads/">Doo-Dads</option>
<option label="Things" value=" http://yoursite.com/things/">Things</option>
</select>
<input type="submit" value="Go"
onClick="goToPage(jmenu.jchoices.options[jmenu.jchoices.selectedIndex].value);return
false;">
</form>
```

The onClick event handler in the submit button calls the function when the visitor clicks "Go" on the form. Both the form and the select menu have names—jmenu and jchoices—which will be needed to extract the value of the user's choice. The options property of any select menu in a form (here, jmenu.jchoices.options[]) is an array of sequential numbers—starting with zero—for each choice in the menu. The selectedIndex property is the one number from that array that matches the user's choice in the menu and the value property gives its value. So, when a user selects "Widgets," jmenu.jchoices.selectedIndex equals 1 and jmenu.jchoices.options[1] equals *http://yoursite.com /widgets/*, the value that gets sent to the function.

Discussion

Like a breadcrumb menu (see Recipe 3.7), a jump menu provides an alternative to the primary navigation that should be near the top of every page on your site. By combining your most popular pages in a menu, you can give visitors a snapshot of your site's offerings that cuts across the various sections on your site.

Jump menus can't replace traditional navigation, though, because the nature of the select menu inhibits browsing—all but one of its choices are hidden until the user clicks the menu. Also, the menu will be useless to web surfers who browse your site with JavaScript disabled.

A good place for a jump menu is at the bottom of the page. There, it can provide a useful navigation tool to visitors who know where they want to go next on your site but don't want to scroll to the top of the page to find the link.

See Also

Recipe 3.7

3.9   Creating Navigation That Does Not Link to Itself

Problem

You need to add a menu of links to several related pages, but want to leave off the link to the current page being viewed.

Solution

Use a PHP or JavaScript function on each page to match the address of the current page in a list of related pages. Then build the menu from the list, leaving off the link for the matched address.

Discussion

Some simple scripting can eliminate the need to create and maintain individual, hand-coded menus on each page. In both the PHP and JavaScript versions, you will create arrays for the page addresses and link text, and then use a for loop to compare each address value to that of the current page and build the code for the menu. The PHP code concerns three related pages titled Purple, Green, and Orange:

```
<?
$color_urls = array('/colors/purple.php',
                    '/colors/green.php',
                    '/colors/orange.php');
$color_links = array('Purple',
                     'Green',
                     'Orange');
```

First, you will assign the values you want to use for your menu in the two arrays, making sure the link paths (*$color*_urls) and link names (*$color*_links) are listed in the same order. The rest of the code contains the function makeMenu that builds the menu.

```
function makeMenu($urls,$links) {
$full_path = getenv("REQUEST_URI");
 for ($i = 0; $i < sizeof($links); $i++) {
  if (!strstr($full_path,$urls[$i])) {
   $menu .= '<p><a href="'.$urls[$i].'">'.$links[$i].'</a></p>';
  } else {
   $menu .= '<p>'.$links[$i].'</p>';
  }
 }
 echo $menu;
}
?>
```

The function expects two parameters: $urls and $links. In our example here, the values you created in $color_urls and $color_links will be sent to the function. By separating the menu making in a function, you can create a variety of other URL and link arrays, and then pass any pair of array names to the function to create the menu you need on that page.

The first line of the function uses PHP's built-in getenv( ) function to assign $full_ path a string value equal to the web page's URL minus the protocol and domain name—in other words, everything except *http://yourdomain.com*. The variable $menu will contain the code for the menu and the for loop will add a value to it for each element in the $links array. Then, for each iteration of the loop—enumerated by the variable $i—a conditional statement compares a value from the $urls array to the current page address, $full_path, using the strstr( ) function.

 PHP and JavaScript arrays are numbered starting with 0. In the first iteration of our loop (when $i=0), $urls[$i] refers to element zero in the array, or /colors/purple.php.

If the array value is *not found* in the address of the current page—if (!strstr($full_ path,$urls[$i]))—then the corresponding array value in $links gets added to $menu as a link. Otherwise, the corresponding array value in $links gets added to $menu unlinked. You can modify this script to give the unlinked text a color or other design treatment that sets it apart from the linked text, which is a good way to give "you are here" feedback to users as they browse your site.

In the spot in your web page code where you want the menu to appear, add this code:

```
<? makeMenu($color_urls,$color_links); ?>
```

The JavaScript version works largely the same, but only in browsers that have Java-Script enabled. Because the PHP code is a server-side script, the menus it creates appear regardless of browser configuration. Here is the complete JavaScript code:

```
<script type="text/JavaScript" language="JavaScript">
<!--
var colorURLs = new Array('/colors/blue/index.html',
                          '/colors/red/index.html',
                          '/colors/yellow/index.html');
var colorLinks = new Array('Blue',
                           'Red',
                           'Yellow');
function makeMenu(URLs,Links) {
var Menu= '';
 for (var i=0;i<URLs.length;i++) {
  if (location.href.indexOf(URLs[i]) == -1) {
   Menu += "<p><a href = \"" + URLs[i] + "\">" + Links[i] + "</a></p>";
  } else {
   Menu += "<p>" + Links[i] + "</p>";
  }
 }
 document.write(Menu);
}
// -->
</script>
```

Make note of a few differences from the PHP version: first, the variable Menu must be defined before the function can add values to it in the for loop. Also, the value of the current page address is derived from the href property of the location object. The indexOf method looks for a match between the current page address and the value of URLS[i], returns -1 if it doesn't find one, and adds a linked line to Menu. Call the function with code in your web pages:

```
<script language="JavaScript">makeMenu(colorURLs,colorLinks);</script>
```

CHAPTER 4

Formatting Text and Code

4.0   Introduction

The HTML code of your web pages forms the foundation for your site. Properly structured pages act as hubs, coordinating the display of the text and graphics that visitors to your site seek. We'll come back to formatting and displaying graphics in Chapter 5, focusing first on the written content that, for the majority of sites, constitute the meat and potatoes of their online offerings. We'll start by looking at the hidden components of web page code: the tags and server directives that ensure the availability of your content to the widest audience, regardless of their connection speed, physical abilities, or native languages. Then we'll look at some specific, practical strategies for getting the text onto the page in the most user-friendly manner, whether its on statically coded pages or delivered dynamically from a database.

4.1   Writing Standards-Compliant Web Pages

Problem

You need to create standards-compliant pages for your web site.

Solution

Add a DOCTYPE declaration to the first line of your HTML code, above the <html> tag:

```
<!DOCTYPE HTML PUBLIC "-//W3C//DTD HTML 4.01//EN"
 "http://www.w3.org/TR/html4/strict.dtd">

<html>
  <!-- Other HTML content -->
</html>
```

Then validate your code using tools available online or built in to your HTML editor to check your code's conformity to the W3C specification.

Discussion

Document Type Definitions (DTDs) for web pages are published lists from the World Wide Web Consortium that declare to later versions of common web browsers the valid structure for a web page. Modern browsers use DTDs to determine how a page should be rendered. The vocal supporters of best practices in web design have elevated these W3C recommendations to standards in a virtuous effort to advance web design from the late 1990s age of proprietary tags and inconsistent page rendering among various browsers to an era when web pages look more or less the same in every browser on every platform. Universal compliance with web standards requires that web pages declare a DOCTYPE and follow the DTD's HTML markup rules to the letter to achieve the noble goal of uniform browser rendering. Web pages without DOCTYPEs—and there are millions of them with more going online every day—are just prolonging the days of the browser wars.

Hypertext Markup Language (HTML) was created in the early 1990s as an extended subset of the older Standard Generalized Markup Language (SGML), which has been used since the mid 1980s to standardize the exchange, management, and publishing of all types of electronic documents, not just web pages. Since then, the HTML specification has been revised and expanded numerous times: to HTML 2.0 in late 1995, HTML 3.2 in 1997, HTML 4 in 1999, XHTML 1.0 in 2000, and XHTML 1.1 in 2001. Each revision to the specification came with a new DTD that added to or amended those that came before it, but did not end the use of older DTDs. The most common DTDs used for new web sites these days are HTML 4.01 and XHTML 1.0, although many web sites still use HTML 3.2 as their DTD, while others don't use one at all. Table 4-1 shows a list of common DTDs and the declaration code to be included on the first line of a web page's source code.

Table 4-1. Common DTDs used in new web pages include HTML 4.01 and XHTML 1.0

Name	Web page Code
HTML 3.2	`<!DOCTYPE HTML PUBLIC "-//W3C//DTD HTML 3.2 Final//EN">`
HTML 4.01 Strict	`<!DOCTYPE HTML PUBLIC "-//W3C//DTD HTML 4.01//EN"` `  "http://www.w3.org/TR/html4/strict.dtd">`
HTML 4.01 Transitional	`<!DOCTYPE HTML PUBLIC "-//W3C//DTD HTML 4.01 Transitional//EN"` `  "http://www.w3.org/TR/html4/loose.dtd">`
HTML 4.01 Frameset	`<!DOCTYPE HTML PUBLIC "-//W3C//DTD HTML 4.01 Frameset//EN"` `  "http://www.w3.org/TR/html4/frameset.dtd">`
XHTML 1.0 Strict	`<!DOCTYPE html PUBLIC "-//W3C//DTD XHTML 1.0 Strict//EN"` `  "http://www.w3.org/TR/xhtml1/DTD/xhtml1-strict.dtd">`
XHTML 1.0 Transitional	`<!DOCTYPE html PUBLIC "-//W3C//DTD XHTML 1.0 Transitional//EN"` `  "http://www.w3.org/TR/xhtml1/DTD/xhtml1-transitional.dtd">`
XHTML 1.0 Frameset	`<!DOCTYPE html PUBLIC "-//W3C//DTD XHTML 1.0 Frameset//EN"` `  "http://www.w3.org/TR/xhtml1/DTD/xhtml1-frameset.dtd">`
XHTML 1.1 DTD	`<!DOCTYPE html PUBLIC "-//W3C//DTD XHTML 1.1//EN"` `  "http://www.w3.org/TR/xhtml11/DTD/xhtml11.dtd">`

Among the many changes from HTML Version 3.2 to HTML Version 4.0, the most notable shift came with the W3C's official phase out, or *deprecation*, of presentation-oriented tags—such as the once ubiquitous `<font>` tag—in favor of presentation rules defined using Cascading Style Sheets (CSS).

Web designers suffering from `<font>` tag withdrawal should note that they can use `<span>` with a style attribute to do almost anything they used do with `<font>`. For example, instead of `<font color="red">` use `<span style="color:red">`.

The XHTML specifications further build on HTML 4.0, and also move HTML toward a future marriage with the eXtensible Markup Language (XML), with which web builders can extend the functionality and interactivity of web pages.

A web page with a proper DOCTYPE declaration can be validated using online tools from the W3C (see the "See Also" section in this Recipe). Some web page editors have built-in validators that will check your source code against the W3C's rules.

A common validation error occurs when a URL in a web page's code contains unencoded ampersands (or other reserved characters defined by the W3C) in a query string, like this:

```
<a href="search.php?f=t&arg=doug&p=1&c=0&sr=10&tf=75">More
search results</a>
```

The ampersand characters should be replaced with the HTML entity `&amp;`, like this:

```
<a href="search.php?f=t&amp;arg=doug&amp;p=1&
amp;c=0&amp;sr=10&amp;tf=75">More search results</a>
```

The server will decode the request and pass the correct query string—with ampersands instead of entities—to the script or CGI for processing.

If you're new to DTDs or have a lot of legacy pages to check, prepare for lengthy validation reports that point out line by line where your web page code falls short of web standards. Try not to take it personally. (Instead, try a transitional DOCTYPE with a more lenient standard that's more likely to validate.) If you're new to web design, using a validator can be a great way to learn the latest HTML specification and make your pages perfect from the start.

For the most part, a web page with *no* DOCTYPE tag—or a malformed one—or tags that violate the declared DTD standard will not fail to load or be rendered as unintelligible gibberish. By and large, newer browsers can handle a page with a few invalid tags or DTD violations. They will, however, render the page in what's called "quirks" mode, through a process called a DOCTYPE switch.

Microsoft's Internet Explorer 5.0 for Mac was the first to do the DOC-TYPE switch. Now, all major browsers—Mozilla, Internet Explorer 6.0 for Windows, and Opera 8, among others—ship with a split personality: "standards" mode when the web page correctly declares its DOCTYPE (and follows its rules) and "quirks" mode when it does not.

Basically, quirks mode means the browser reverts to its own notion of how to render HTML code, standards be damned. Each browser has its own rules for entering quirks mode, as well as its own quirks. For more about Internet Explorer, Mozilla, and Opera quirks, see the links in the "See Also" section of this Recipe.

Among the most notable examples of rendering inconsistencies in quirks mode are Internet Explorer's non-standard implementation of padding and margins—the so-called "box model" problem—and Mozilla's imperfect rendering of inline images in table cells.

Standards mode is the ideal, but quirks mode is reality. And add to that the limited time and budget of most web design projects, as well as the particular needs and browsing requirements of a web site's audience, and you'll get a pretty good idea why standard design is not yet part of that reality. Even some of the most well-known sites on the web do not conform to standards. A random sample of ten of the Web's most popular sites, from Amazon to The Weather Channel, found that four don't even declare a DOCTYPE on their home page! A majority of the rest used a transitional DTD, which in some cases can trigger quirks mode as well.

Should you declare a DOCTYPE on your web pages? Yes. Defining a DTD is first step in creating a standards-compliant web site. But ultimately, the proof is in the pudding. Validate your web page markup, but don't consider it a means to an end. Test your pages in common browsers and fix real rendering problems that detract from your audience's ability to use your site.

See Also

For a concrete example of how a web page's DOCTYPE can affect the way it gets rendered, see Recipe 5.3.

The major browser makers all have pages describing their product's handling of the DOCTYPE switch and rendering idiosyncrasies in quirks mode: Mozilla (*http://www.mozilla.org/docs/web-developer/quirks/*), Internet Explorer (*http://msdn.microsoft.com/workshop/author/css/overview/cssenhancements.asp* and *http://msdn.microsoft.com/workshop/author/dhtml/reference/properties/compatmode.asp*), and Opera (*http://www.opera.com/docs/specs/doctype/*).

World Wide Web Consortium's list of valid DTDs is at *http://www.w3.org/QA/2002/04/valid-dtd-list.html* and the W3C's HTML validator is at *http://validator.w3.org/*.

4.2   Displaying Foreign and Special Characters

Problem

You need to display words, or entire pages of text, in a language other than the primary one used by your site and audience.

Solution

Use a `<meta>` right after the `<head>` tag to declare a character set on all the pages on your site:

```
<meta http-equiv="Content-Type" content="text/html; charset=utf-8">
```

Or, alternatively, override or modify your server's default character sets with an *.htaccess* file that specifies a different character set for a particular file:

```
<Files "russian.html">
 AddCharset windows-1252 .html
</Files>
```

Discussion

It's safe to assume that your web site and its audience have a primary language, whether its English, Greek, Japanese, or something else. You create the pages in that language and web surfers view those pages without giving much thought to how the site appears in their language.

Behind the scenes, though, character sets enabled on your web server and on your visitors' browser are making sure everything looks as it should. Offering basic, multilingual site information—for example, "About Us" pages in Russian, Japanese, and Arabic—presents a problem to sites that are otherwise served and intended to be viewed with a character set that does not include the required characters for the other languages. Only one character set can be used on a web page, and it can't be changed mid-page. Before getting into the problem of mixing words and pages from other languages and alphabets into your web site, though, let me give you a quick overview of how character sets work on the Web.

The first widely used character set for electronic documents was American Standard Code for Information Interchange (ASCII), created in the late 1950s and formally defined for the first time in 1963. It assigned machine-readable codes to the upper- and lowercase Roman alphabet, punctuation marks, and control characters such as line feeds and tabs. There are 128 characters in what is now called the US-ASCII character set.

In the mid 1980s, the European Computer Manufacturer's Association (ECMA) expanded and improved ASCII with the introduction of a handful of 256-character sets that cover the languages and alphabets of Europe and the Middle East, from Iceland to Yemen and everything in between. Endorsed by the International Standards

Organization (ISO), each character set from what has come to be known as the ISO-8859 family, retains the first 128 characters of ASCII while adding special characters unique to languages such as Arabic or Cyrillic in the second half of the set. Many, if not most, English-language web sites use the ISO-8859-1 character set, also known as Latin 1. Characters from the latter half of any ISO-8859 set, which include symbols and accented characters, should be encoded as named or numerical entities to ensure their proper display. For example, an "é" would be represented in HTML code as é or é.

> The ampersand character (&) marks the beginning of special named or numerical entity codes for special characters in HTML. The number sign (#) precedes the numerical code for a character entity (and follows the &). Both named and numerical entities end with a semicolon. To show a literal ampersand character on a web page, convert it to its numerical (&) or named (&) entity to prevent browsers from misinterpreting it as the start of a character entity.

Unicode represents a great leap forward in the internationalization of electronic communication. As the Unicode web site (*http://www.unicode.org*) puts it, "When the world wants to talk, it speaks Unicode." At nearly 100,000 characters in the recently released Version 4, Unicode incorporates all the characters from the various ISO-8859 sets, and then some. And, conveniently, the first 256 characters are a one-to-one match with the Latin 1 character set.

All of these character sets and several others are available to web browsers and web servers. Your Apache web server may have one or more character sets enabled in its configuration file. Web browsers use the default character set defined in their preferences settings, although most can switch to another available character set when instructed to do so by the Content-Type HTTP header sent to the web browser by the web server before the rest of the page.

That's how it's supposed to work—ideally. But in shared hosting environments from which sites in a variety of languages may be served, the web server may not send the correct Content-Type header. Or it may not send one at all. You can play it safe, though, by specifying the character set with a <meta> tag on every web page.

Here is the structure of a <meta> tag for displaying a page's contents using the Latin 1 (ISO-8859-1) character set:

```
<meta http-equiv="Content-Type" content="text/html; charset=iso-8859-1">
```

If you need to mix languages on every page, say, by displaying "About Us" links translated to the various languages for which you offer content in the site's main navigation, then you should use the Unicode character set.

Given Unicode's vast repertoire of characters from nearly all the world's languages, plus its overlap with Latin 1, your English language content will not need any special treatment when you specify Unicode for your pages. Special characters from other languages can be encoded as Unicode decimal entities for proper display. Your web page editor may offer a function for encoding characters as Unicode entities. If not, online resources listed in the "See Also" section in this Recipe are there to help. The Unicode character set <meta> tag looks like this:

```
<meta http-equiv="Content-Type" content="text/html; charset=utf-8">
```

However, two problems—one big, one small—can occur using the <meta> tag method for specifying Unicode content. First, the web server character set configuration (if the web server actually does send one in the HTTP header) trumps a document's setting, so a browser might not shift its character set to display the page properly, even when told to do so by a <meta> tag.

If your <meta>-tagged pages don't look right, you might need to override your server's default character set for a directory or specific file in a directory with an *.htaccess* file. Add this line to the *.htaccess* file you create or modify in your site's root directory:

```
AddType 'text/html; charset=utf-8' .html
```

Alternatively, you also can modify the server character set for specific files in a directory. For example, your directory of "About Us" pages might have an *index.html* file in English, and translated versions named *russian.html*, *japanese.html*, and *arabic.html*, along with an *.htaccess* file that instructs the server to change the character set for a given file based on its name, like this:

```
<Files "russian.html">
 AddCharset windows-1252 .html
</Files>
<Files "japanese.html">
 AddCharset Shift_JIS .html
</Files>
<Files "arabic.html">
 AddCharset iso-8859-6 .html
</Files>
```

The <meta> tag method also can cause a small problem in older browsers when they've already received a character set from the web server for a page. The second character set setting (in the <meta> tag) can cause older browsers to draw the page twice, which appears to visitors as an annoying screen flicker.

To minimize this glitch, the <meta> tag declaration of a web page's character set should always be on the first line following the <head> tag:

```
<head>
<meta http-equiv="Content-Type" content="text/html; charset=utf-8">
```

Declaring a document's character set with a <meta> tag also can be useful when the web server is out of the picture, such as when pages are to be viewed offline, either from a CD or locally from a user's hard drive.

Finally, bear in mind that pages that mix languages and alphabets may require some effort on the part of your visitors to display correctly. Even if your pages include properly encoded entities for special characters—for example, a &#224 for the aleph character in ISO-8859-8—a web browser may not be able to display those characters if the font to display Hebrew characters is not enabled on the user's system. Similarly, site visitors may need to manually override their browser's default character set to see the content as you intend it to be viewed. If access to the multilingual content is critical to your web site or its audience, consider creating a help page showing a screenshot of the properly rendered page with instructions for users on how to configure their browsers and systems to achieve the same result.

See Also

The Unicode organization has several FAQs about using its vast character repertoire on web pages at *http://www.unicode.org/faq/unicode_web.html*. At FileFormat.info you can search for character entities in a number of different sets: *http://www.fileformat.info/info/charset*.

4.3   Choosing Type Sizes for Display and Body Text

Problem

You need to make sure that the text on your web pages displays readably, with headlines, subheads, body text, and other content appropriately sized relative to one another.

Solution

Use a stylesheet rule to define a base type size:

```
<style type="text/css">
<!--
body {
    font-size: 100%;
}
-->
</style>
```

Then add rules for headings (<h1>, <h2>, etc.), paragraphs (<p>), and other block elements that will contain text to increase or decrease their size relative to the base size:

```
h1 {
    font-size: 2em;
}
h2 {
    font-size: 1.5em;
}
p {
    font-size: 1em;
}
```

If you specify a typeface for your body, you'll also need to reiterate it for all block elements, including those listed above as well as table cells (<td>) and list elements (<ul>, <ol>, etc.).

Discussion

Web pages that display written content need a scheme for organizing and displaying different types of text so visitors can quickly determine if the page they're looking at has the information they're seeking. Generally speaking, web page content falls into two broad categories: *display copy*—such as headlines, subheads, captions, and other short scannable text blurbs—and the *body copy*, which constitutes the bulk of rest of the text on the page. Web designers that make no distinction among these two categories of content on their pages are setting up their visitors for frustration (see Figures 4-1 and 4-2).

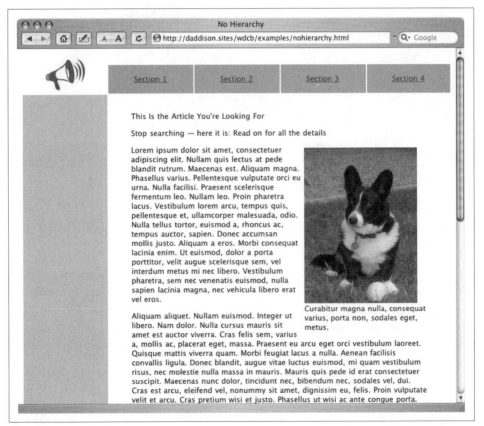

Figure 4-1. A page that doesn't distinguish one type of content from another can frustrate visitors to your site

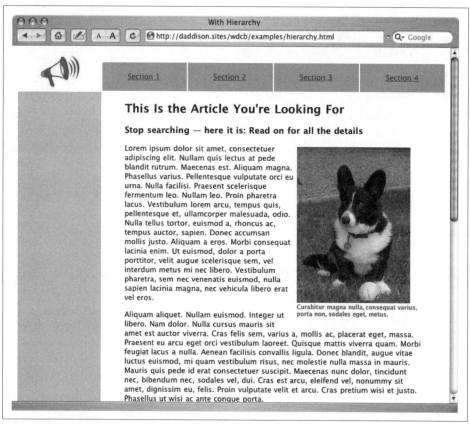

Figure 4-2. Using varying sizes and colors for display and body copy makes for a more user-friendly page

HTML offers a variety of methods for specifying type size on a web page. In the early days of the Web, heading tags (<h1> through <h6>) and <font> tags were the common approach for specifying type size. With these tags, web designers could alter the weight and size of text on the page between 50 and 200 percent (or more, depending on the browser) of a visitor's default text size. CSS are now the preferred—and far more powerful—method for setting type sizes. Heading tags remain an integral partner in CSS-enabled web sites, but <font> tags are out, having been officially deprecated—retired from use—by the W3C in its most recent HTML and XHTML specifications (see Recipe 4.1).

CSS introduces a much finer level of control over type size and a smorgasbord of unit choices that promise something for everyone. With CSS you can size type in pixels, points, or picas, millimeters, centimeters, or inches, by percentage, or in ems or exs.

Using points or pixels, however, leads us back into the land of browser inconsistencies. Even though <font> tags add extra weight to web page file sizes and make site-wide design changes difficult, they had one thing going for them: Web surfers could use their browser's built-in commands to enlarge or reduce on-screen type sized with a ⟨font⟩ tag to a size they could read. Not so with pixel- or point-based CSS rules, especially in Internet Explorer for Windows. The world's most popular web browser will not enlarge or reduce the type size of page elements given fixed point- or pixel-size rules in a style sheet. For that reason, avoid absolute type sized in pixel or point in favor of relative type sized using percentages and ems for text elements on your web page.

You might be wondering why it matters—aren't all browsers set to display web pages at 72 pixels, or *dots per inch* (dpi)? If only it were that easy! The original Mac came closest, with its 72 dpi display neatly mimicking a WYSIWYG display for graphic designers accustomed to 72 points in a vertical inch of printed type. Internet Explorer, on the other hand, wants to display web pages at 96 dpi. But the wide variety of computer monitor sizes and screen resolutions means that neither 72 dpi nor 96 dpi resolutions are guaranteed.

For example, my 19-inch CRT display set to a resolution of 1600×1200 pixels for my Mac yields almost 115 dpi. On my Windows XP box hooked up to the same monitor—and set to 800×600 pixels for testing—displays at only 58 dpi. I have to increase the resolution in Windows XP to 1280×1024 to get 96 dpi in Internet Explorer. The wide variety in actual screen resolutions is one reason why the type in some sites designed on a Mac look huge on Windows and the type in sites designed on Windows looks tiny on a Mac. Not to mention the fact that users can tweak their default font size in their browser, from say, medium to smaller in Internet Explorer, or from 12 point to 10 point or 14 point in Mozilla. In the end, determining the right size relationships among body copy, headlines, subheads, captions, and other type particular to your site requires not just a well thought-out design decision, but a process of experimenting with various permutations and testing them in the browsers commonly used by your site's visitors.

Fortunately, someone has done a lot of that testing for you. A couple of years ago, a tenacious web designer named Owen Briggs set about to discover what base percentage yields the most consistent type sizes among various browsers, new and old, Mac and Windows.

 I highly recommend reading Owen Briggs' complete description of the cross-browser type sizing process, linked in the "See Also" section of this Recipe.

Borrowing from Briggs' method, a sample stylesheet might set the base type size for a web page at, say, 76 percent, and then add a rule making headlines (⟨h1⟩) two times larger, subheads (⟨h2⟩) one and a half times larger, and body copy (⟨p⟩) equal to the default size:

```
<style type="text/css">
<!--
body {
    font-size: 76%;
}
h1 {
    font-size: 2em;
}
h2 {
    font-size: 1.5em;
}
p {
    font-size: 1em;
}
-->
</style>
```

With this stylesheet, you can add rules for other elements and adjust the size of everything on the page by changing just the base percentage.

See Also

For more information and screenshots about Owen Briggs' quest for consistent cross-browser type sizing, see his article, "Sane CSS Typography" at *http://www. thenoodleincident.com/tutorials/typography/*. For even better choices and font control, check out the Scalable Inman Flash Replacement, which allows web designers to use any typeface with no web standards or accessibility compromises (see *http:// www.mikeindustries.com/blog/archive/2004/08/sifr*).

4.4   Including Dynamic Content in Static Pages

Problem

You need to include dynamic content in the body of a static HTML page.

Solution

Use your server's built-in SSI parsing of `<!--#include -->`, `<!--#echo -->`, and `<!--#exec -->` tags in the body of your static pages.

For example, server-side include tags can print the current date and time, or a file's last modification date on an HTML page. Here is the tag for displaying the date:

```
<!--#echo var="DATE_LOCAL" -->
```

With this tag, you'll get the server's default date format, which might look something like this:

```
10-May-2005 16:09:53 CDT
```

Discussion

In Recipe 1.4, I explained how, by saving small files containing text and HTML code in one location on your server, you can embed their contents on other pages throughout your web site by placing simple server-side include tags in your web page code. Using SSIs for common, frequently updated content facilitates fast site updates, since you only have to update one file for the change to take effect everywhere the SSI appears on the site. With SSIs, though, you can embed much more than included text in otherwise static web pages.

Server-side includes are great for small, time-saving tasks, but I'm of the opinion that date stamps on web pages are redundant, since anyone at a computer should have ready access to a clock and calendar. But that doesn't mean date tags are useless. Automating the display of the current month or year can be a real time-saver when used in the small, easily forgotten corners of your site. For example, add an SSI tag to display the current year in the copyright notice for your site, and you'll never have to remember to update that bit of web page code by hand again. Likewise, if you have links throughout your site to a regularly updated calendar of events, use the SSI date code for the month to keep that link current.

An SSI also can print the last modification date for a web page. The variable uses the same formatting codes as the DATE_LOCAL variable. The code to print the variable looks like this:

```
<!--#echo var="LAST_MODIFIED" -->
```

More so than date stamps, modification dates have great value for web surfers. Knowing when a page was last changed augments their impression of a site's legitimacy and reliability.

 If you can crow about how often you update pages on your web site, add the LAST_MODIFIED variable to your pages. Leave it out if you can't.

You can tweak the format with another SSI tag placed *above* the command to echo a date, like this.

```
<!--#config timefmt="%D" -->
```

Table 4-2 shows a handful of the many date format codes that can be included in this tag. Others are available for displaying the time down to the second or the time zone. Codes can be combined, so that this:

```
<!--#config timefmt="%B %d, %Y" -->
<!--#echo var="DATE_LOCAL" -->
```

yields this:

```
May 10, 2005.
```

Table 4-2. A selection of date formats for use with server-side includes.

Date format code	Displays
A	Day of the week, i.e., Tuesday
B	Month name, i.e., May
D	Numerical date as month/day/year, i.e., 05/10/05
F	Numerical date as year-month-day, i.e., 2005-05-10
Y	Just the four-digit year
d	Just the day of the month, i.e., 10

You also can use SSIs to embed the results of a Perl, PHP, shell, or other script in a web page. Everything from simple hit counters to the results of complex database queries can be placed in a static HTML file with the `<!--#virtual -->` or `<!--#exec -->` SSI tags.

Include a simple script with a tag like this:

```
<!--#include virtual="/cgi-bin/hello.cgi"-->
```

or this:

```
<!--#include virtual="/includes/nav/script.php" -->
```

The SSI tag also can pass arguments to a script. Say, for example, you have a script that returns a list of items from your online catalog based on criteria you specify. This hypothetical include tag would query the catalog for five sale items, which could then be displayed on an otherwise static page:

```
<!--#include virtual="/cgi-bin/catalog.cgi?items=sale&show=5" -->
```

See Also

The Apache Software Foundation has a server-side include introduction and tutorial at *http://httpd.apache.org/docs/howto/ssi.html*.

4.5   Adding a Discretionary Hyphen to Long Words

Problem

You need to specify a grammatical break in an extremely long word or group of words that frequently appears on your web pages.

Solution

The web page in my mock example (see Figure 4-3) extols the virtues of Dr. Chandrasekhar's interdenominational electroencephalograph.

Imagine having this or other long words and phrases popping up all over your web site, pushing your layout around and otherwise wreaking havoc. The soft hyphen—­ or ­—can help rein it in. Here's the code I used for the main headline:

```
Chan&shy;dra&shy;sek&shy;har's
E&shy;lec&shy;tro&shy;en&shy;ceph&shy;a&shy;lo&shy;graph
```

The HTML soft hyphen will appear when needed and remains hidden when not.

Figure 4-3. A sample web page that uses the soft hyphen to indicate optional hyphens in log words at the end of a line

Discussion

Print publishers have long relied on the powerful auto-hyphenation features of their layout programs to give the text in their finished work a smooth, even appearance. The knowledge of the natural grammatical breaks in words that was once the sole domain of experienced typesetters now ships standard with programs such as QuarkXPress, Adobe InDesign, and others. Modern-day Gutenbergs working on documents to be printed have another powerful tool: by inserting a discretionary hyphen, they can indicate where a long word can be broken, or hyphenated, at the end of a line when fitting copy into their page layouts.

HTML has few, if any, of the copy-fitting conveniences of desktop publishing programs. As any experienced web designer can attest, web surfers have a lot more control over the way the page looks than, say, a magazine reader has over the design of his favorite periodical. Visitors to your site can view, enlarge, reduce, copy, and print the contents of your web site in ways not possible with traditional print media.

You can bring a little of that control over the display—just a little—in situations when long words have to fit in small spaces. Use the HTML equivalent of the discretionary hyphen, called a *soft hyphen*, denoted in your code as either a numerical (­) or named (­) entity.

When the time comes to employ this technique, consult a good reference, such as *Webster's New World Dictionary*, for guidance on where to insert the breaks each time the word appears on a page, and you can start calling yourself a cyber-typesetter.

Two notes of caution: use this Recipe sparingly. Flexibility in the way your content gets displayed is a good thing. Becoming a control freak with soft hyphens everywhere...not so good. Also, support for the soft hyphen among web browsers varies. Internet Explorer for Windows and Safari for Macs treats them as expected—there when you need them, gone when not. Mozilla, Firefox, and recent versions of Netscape Navigator do not show the soft hyphen at all. Long words either appear in their entirety at the end of one line or jump completely to the beginning of the next line when the page is squeezed and the text gets reflowed. Navigator Version 4 and Internet Explorer Version 5 for Mac, unfortunately, can't hide its dislike for the soft hyphen. It appears as an ugly box "glyph" all the time, regardless of its position on the line.

4.6   Dividing a Text Block into Multiple Pages

Problem

You want to display long articles stored in a database over multiple pages.

Solution

Add logic to your web page code that breaks text into chunks based on word count or some other parameter.

Discussion

Woe is the modern-day Melville or Proust trying to hone their craft online at 72 dots per inch. Nothing turns off an online audience faster than an eye-glazing block of text that scrolls on and on and on (see Figure 4-4). The conventional wisdom of online publishing contends that no one *reads* web pages. Web surfers browse, scan, and pick through online content—so the thinking goes—and then print what they want to give it their full attention in a more comfortable reading environment.

Sometimes, though, long articles are not only central to your web site's mission, they're what your visitors are seeking. Everything from essays to technical white papers require every last word to serve their readers. And breaking up articles over multiple pages offers the bottom-line benefit of increasing advertising impressions for sites that generate revenue in that way. Remember, it was newspapers—not web sites—that first came up with the idea of giving readers a taste of many articles on the front page, and then forcing them to flip inside to the conclusion displayed alongside the lingerie ads. Let's look at some ways to add one or more "jump pages" to your online articles by automatically breaking up long articles into two or more linked pages.

This Recipe makes a couple of assumptions. Since it uses PHP scripting to manipulate the text, you'll need some familiarity with the use of variables and functions in that language. Also, the solution described below assumes that you don't need to exercise any fine-grained editorial measures to keep lines or words together on the same page that might otherwise be separated automatically by the scripting logic.

First, you will need to load all the text from long article into a PHP variable. The text can come from a record in an articles table in your web database or from a static file on your web server (that, in turn, might be opened and read into the variable by PHP's built-in file-handling functions). Call the variable with the article $text.

Then you'll need to add a function for performing a variety of formatting routines on the text. For now, you'll limit this function's action to replacing line breaks in the $text variable with opening and closing <p> tags. In Recipe 4.7, you'll learn ways to expand this function to handle other inline HTML code in your stored text.

Assuming each paragraph of stored text is separated by two line breaks—each represented by \n—the basic text-processing function looks like this:

```
function processText( $texttoProcess )
{
    $texttoProcess = str_replace("\n\n"," </p>\n<p> ",$texttoProcess);
    return $texttoProcess;
}
```

You may need to tweak this function, depending on how paragraphs in your stored text are separated. For the function to work reliably, though, the separating characters should be consistent between all blocks of text.

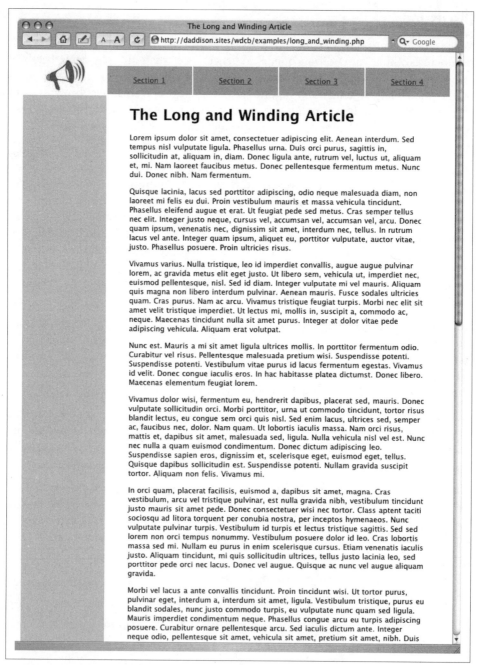

Figure 4-4. Long articles can be divided into multiple pages for easier reading

Now define a new variable to tell PHP how many words of the article to display on each page:

```
$text_limit = 275;
```

Now, you need to add the logic to count the number of words in the article and load that value into a new variable, keep track of the start and end of each article chunk, and add links to the top and bottom of the page to navigate forward and backward among the pages.

First, use PHP's built-in explode( ) and count( ) functions to create an array of individual words in the article and tally the total number of words:

```
$text_array = explode(" ",$text);
$text_total_words = count($text_array);
```

Next, you'll introduce the variables needed to keep track of the currently displayed article section: $start and $step. Eventually, the previous and next links on the page will pass these variables as arguments back to the PHP script to display other sections. If no arguments are passed, then this part of the script instructs PHP to display the first section of the article, up to the limit you defined above as the variable $text_limit:

```
if (!isset($step)) {
  $start = 0;
  $step = $text_limit;
}
```

Now, add a for loop to the script by using the $start and $step variables to create a new variable—$text_display—that contains just the number of words you want to display per page:

```
for ($x=$start;$x<$step;$x++) {
  $text_display .= $text_array[$x]." ";
}
```

And pass the $text_display variable to the function you defined at the top of the script to swap line feeds with paragraph tags:

```
$text_display = processText($text_display);
```

For the previous and next page links, you'll need to add a couple of conditional statements to the script that prepend or append the previous and next page links—if they're needed—to the text block to be displayed. Because you're using the $start variable as a marker to define where an article section should start, the page will need a previous or back link if $start's value is greater than zero, like this:

```
if ($start > 0) {
  $pstart = $start - $text_limit;
  $pstep = $step - $text_limit;
  $text_display = "<a href = \"article.php?start=".$pstart."&step=".$pstep."\">&#60;
  Prev page</a> ... ".$text_display;
}
```

The conditional statement uses two new variables—$pstart and $pstep—to deduct the word limit value from the current values of $start and $step and build a link to the previous block of article text.

The next page link operates in a similar fashion, with new variables $nstart and $nstep defined as additions to the current text block markers. Here, the condition compares the total word count of the article—$text_total_words—to the end-point marker of the currently displayed block—$step. If the former is greater than the latter, there's more text to show and a next page link is needed:

```
if ($text_total_words > $step) { //still more text to read
  $nstart = $start + $text_limit;
  $nstep = $step + $text_limit;
  $text_display = $text_display."... <a href =
  \"word_break.php?start=".$nstart."&step=".$nstep."\">Next page &#62;</a>";
}
```

Finally, print the text block on the page wrapped in paragraph tags to ensure the proper display of the first and last paragraphs not formatted by the function.

The full script is shown in Example 4-1.

Example 4-1. This script splits lengthy text over multiple pages and creates links between the pages

```
<?
$text = "Some long-article text gets loaded from a database record or file into this
variable.";

function processText( $texttoProcess )
{
  $texttoProcess = str_replace("\n\n","\n</p>\n<p>\n",$texttoProcess);
  return $texttoProcess;
}

$text_limit = 275;

$text_array = explode(" ",$text);
$text_total_words = count($text_array);

if (!isset($step)) {
  $start = 0;
  $step = $text_limit;
}

for ($x=$start;$x<$step;$x++) {
  $text_display .= $text_array[$x]." ";
}
$text_display = processText($text_display);

if ($start > 0) { //we're beyond the first page
  $pstart = $start - $text_limit;
  $pstep = $step - $text_limit;
```

Example 4-1. This script splits lengthy text over multiple pages and creates links between the pages

```
$text_display = "<a href = \"word_break.php?start=".$pstart."&step=".$pstep."\">&#60;
Prev page</a> ... ".$text_display;
}
if ($text_total_words > $step) { //still more text to read
  $nstart = $start + $text_limit;
  $nstep = $step + $text_limit;
  $text_display = $text_display."... <a href = \"word_break.php?start=".$nstart.
"&step=".$nstep."\">Next page &#62;</a>";
}
  echo "<p>\n".$text_display."\n</p>";
?>
```

The displayed text looks like Figure 4-5.

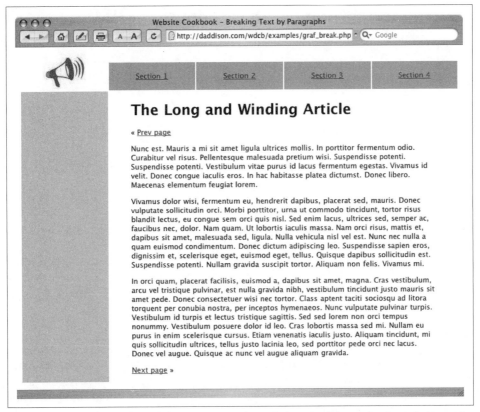

Figure 4-5. The segmented article has previous and next links to lead the reader through the article over multiple pages

You can alter this Recipe to divide articles by paragraph, rather than by word, if you like. Using word count offers a more consistently sized chunk of text per page, but the page breaks will fall arbitrarily in the middle of sentences. On the other hand, a newspaper editor will tell you that mid-sentence page breaks are good for maintaining reader interest and preventing readers from thinking an article has ended before it actually has. Pages of paragraph-based chunks will vary more in length, but the breaks will be neater.

To split the text by paragraph, change the `explode( )` statement near the top of the script to build your article array out of paragraphs, rather than words (splitting on line endings, rather than spaces between words):

```
$text_array = explode("\n\n",$text);
```

And reduce the value of the block limit to a much lower number:

```
$text_limit = 3;
```

4.7   Reformatting Database Content as HTML

Problem

You need to convert characters in text stored in or retrieved from a database to their proper HTML entities.

Solution

Use PHP's built-in string formatting functions, such as `htmlentities( )` and `str_replace( )`, to build your own an on-the-fly reformatting function:

```
function processText( $text )
{
    $text = str_replace("&gt;",">",$text);
    $text = str_replace("&lt;","<",$text);
    $text = str_replace("\r\n\r\n"," </p>\n<p> ",$text);
    $text = str_replace("\r\n "," </p>\n<p> ",$text);
    $text = str_replace("\n\n"," </p>\n<p> ",$text);
    $text = str_replace("\n "," </p>\n<p> ",$text);
    return $text;
}
```

Discussion

The articles and other content displayed on a dynamic or template-driven web site are stored in database tables on the web server in which each bit of a page—headline, subhead, byline, and main text—likely has its own field, or slot, in an individual article record. The logic of the template file, written in PHP or another server-side scripting language, then retrieves a specific article based on a browser request and formats the contents of the article record as an HTML web page. A template may be designed to display just a handful of different articles, or thousands of different entries.

PHP has some built-in tools for handling the special requirements of text that moves from a database to a web page and back again. Combining these tools into one master function that meets the specific needs of your database-driven site ensures that all the content on your site gets formatted the same way. When you need to make a change, editing this single function does the trick.

addslashes( ) and stripslashes( ) are two built-in PHP functions that escape and unescape single-quote, double-quote, and backslash characters in text strings inserted and retrieved from a database. PHP will prevent those characters from being misinterpreted as delimiters between records by adding a slash before them. For example, addslashes( ) changes "St. Patrick's Day" into "St. Patrick\'s Day", while stripslashes( ) reverses the process.

 If your PHP installation has magic_quotes_gpc enabled, then you *should not* use either of these functions. PHP will do it for you. You can easily check this and other PHP configuration settings by uploading a file to your web site called *test.php* containing this one line:

```
<?php phpinfo( ) ?>
```

Then request the file through your web browser (*http:/domain.com/ test.php*); the status of magic_quotes_gpc should be listed as "On" or "Off."

Beyond that convenience, PHP makes no assumptions about how the text coming and going from your database should be formatted. But it provides a handful of built-in functions that you can use to do it yourself, such as converting new line characters—\n—to HTML line break characters—
—via the nl2br( ) function.

But using <br> tags to create line breaks after text blocks is an obsolete technique. In fact, the <br> tag has been retired from use by the WC3 in the latest HTML DTDs (see Recipe 4.1). Instead, you should be using block element markup—typically the paragraph tags <p> and </p>—along with a stylesheet to define styles for text blocks between them. If you've got the rest of your site formatted this way (and you should), then text converted with nl2br( ) may not get formatted correctly.

PHP's all-purpose find-and-replace function, str_replace( ), offers a way to wrap text blocks in paragraph tags:

```
$text = str_replace("\n\n"," </p>\n <p> ",$text);
```

Here, the str_replace( ) function replaces all double new line characters with closing and opening paragraph tags and retains one new line character to make the resulting code more readable. So this:

```
The quick brown fox jumped over the lazy dogs\n\nNow is the time for all good men and
women to come to the aid of their country.
```

Becomes this:

```
The quick brown fox jumped over the lazy dogs</p>
<p>Now is the time for all good men and women to come to the aid of their country.
```

When you print the text block in the PHP template, enclose it in paragraph tags, since the first and last paragraphs of the text block likely were not preceded or followed by new lines:

```
echo "<p>".$text."</p>"
```

So, the result would be:

```
<p>The quick brown fox jumped over the lazy dogs</p>
<p>Now is the time for all good men and women to come to the aid of their country.</p>
```

The str_replace( ) function looks for an exact match, so you may need to include some alternate searches, depending on how text is stored in your database. Paragraphs may be separated by just one new line character, or as many as two new line characters and two return characters (\r), or more. Here's a function that handles a few likely scenarios. When combining searches, always start with the most complex pattern and work toward the simplest to avoid double replacements. First, add this function to your PHP template:

```
function processText( $text )
{
    $text = str_replace("\r\n\r\n"," </p>\n<p> ",$text);
    $text = str_replace("\r\n "," </p>\n<p> ",$text);
    $text = str_replace("\n\n"," </p>\n<p> ",$text);
    $text = str_replace("\n "," </p>\n<p> ",$text);
    return $text;
}
```

Then apply the function to your text:

```
$text = processText($text);
```

PHP also has a couple of functions for converting special characters to their HTML entities. For more about entities, see Recipe 4.2. One—htmlspecialchars( )—converts only ampersands, greater than (>) signs, and less than (<) signs (by default), as well as double and single quotes in a user-specified extended mode. The other—htmlentities( )—converts any character for which there is an HTML entity, including the ones that htmlspecialchars( ) converts.

 Support for characters outside the Latin 1 (ISO-8859-1) repertoire varies depending on the character set installed on your web server and your installed version of PHP.

If you or your web site's visitors submit content to a database that is then displayed on the site, you can create a function to format and encode that text before it is saved in the database.

This function includes the addslashes( ) function to demonstrate how two built-in functions can be combined into a custom function:

```
function processInsert( $text )
{
    $text = addslashes($text);
```

```
      $text = htmlentities($text);
      return $text;
   }
```

If the content submitted to the database includes inline HTML tags, such as <em> Important</em> for italics, htmlentities( ) will change it to <em>Important</ em>. And that will be rendered on the page as:

```
<em>Important</em>
```

The tags are showing, but without the emphasis the author intended. You can modify the text-processing function I described above to undo a little of what htmlentities( ) has done so tags display properly. Two calls to str_replace( ) restore the greater than and less than sign to the tags:

```
$text = str_replace("&gt;",">",$text);
$text = str_replace("&lt;","<",$text);
```

The complete function now looks like this:

```
function processText( $text )
{
   $text = str_replace("&gt;",">",$text);
   $text = str_replace("&lt;","<",$text);
   $text = str_replace("\r\n\r\n"," </p>\n<p> ",$text);
   $text = str_replace("\r\n "," </p>\n<p> ",$text);
   $text = str_replace("\n\n"," </p>\n<p> ",$text);
   $text = str_replace("\n "," </p>\n<p> ",$text);
   return $text;
}
```

See Also

The online PHP Manual has detailed information on all the built-in functions described in this Recipe:

- addslashes (*http://us2.php.net/manual/en/function.addslashes.php*)
- stripslashes (*http://us2.php.net/manual/en/function.stripslashes.php*)
- htmlspecialchars (*http://us2.php.net/manual/en/function.htmlspecialchars.php*)
- htmlentities (*http://us2.php.net/manual/en/function.htmlentities.php*)
- nl2br (*http://us2.php.net/manual/en/function.nl2br.php*)

4.8   Optimizing Web Page Code

Problem

You need to optimize your web pages to improve load time.

Solution

Remove whitespace, hidden characters, and other unnecessary tags from your code using simple regular expression searches, or a full-fledged code optimization utility.

Discussion

Even though high-speed Internet access has a firm foothold in U.S. homes and offices, everyone still likes a fast-loading web page. Unnecessarily large files also consume disk space and bandwidth resources on your web server, which can cost you if your web site starts to exceed the limits of your account quotas.

 Web site file optimization usually calls to mind the compression and color management techniques used to strike an acceptable balance between fidelity to a high-resolution original image and the smallest acceptable file size for the web version. See Recipe 5.1.

There's some slack in your HTML code, too, and the good news is that getting rid of some or all of it won't affect how the page looks in a browser. Depending on the coding techniques you used in creating the original file, and the extent of the optimization techniques you use, the size of an optimized web page can be 5 to 25 percent less than the original. The one downside: Fully optimized HTML code is noticeably not user-friendly to the hand-coder, since all line feeds, extraneous spaces and tabs, and even comments are stripped away. Scanning over a dense, unformatted block of HTML code looking for the place to make a change can be maddening.

To make a modest impact on the file sizes of your web pages, you can use regular expressions in the find-and-replace dialog of your web page editor to remove extra spaces between tags, after tag attributes or punctuation, or at the beginnings of lines. Using an HTML editor capable of performing regular expressions, or grep, searches (such as BBEdit, HomeSite, or Dreamweaver) , type >\s+< into the search field and >< into the replace field to push all your tags up close together. Using just this technique on what I thought was a well-coded page of my own reduced its file size more than 5 percent. For a full list of special characters and wildcards that can be used in a regular expression search, see the tutorial site in the "See Also" section of this Recipe.

You can also use Perl to execute regular expression searches directly on a batch of files on your web server, or combine a bunch of Perl find and replace commands in a shell script:

```
perl -pi -e 's/>\s+</></g' /full/path/to/your/files/*.html
```

 The asterisk in this command tells Perl to perform the search on all files in the directory you specify that end in *.html*.

Combine more than one Perl command, each on its own line, and save them in a file on your server called *optimize_files.sh*:

```
#/bin/bash

perl -pi -e 's/>\s+</></g' /full/path/to/your/files/*.html
```

```
perl -pi -e 's/.\s\s/.\s/g' /full/path/to/your/files/*.html
perl -pi -e 's/\t+/\t/g' /full/path/to/your/files/*.html
perl -pi -e 's/\r+/\r/g' /full/path/to/your/files/*.html
```

Then run the script from the command-line prompt to your web server:

```
sh optimize_files.sh
```

 The first line of your shell script, as well as the command to execute it, varies depending on the default shell for the account on the machine on which you plan to run the script. To find out the shell your account uses, type env at the command prompt.

To squeeze every last byte out of your HTML files, there are numerous PC applications and online tools that will cut the fat out of your web pages. I tried one of each on the original file mentioned above and got an overall file size reduction of about 12 percent with each of them. But in both cases, the code bore only a scant resemblance to its former self (see Figures 4-6 and 4-7).

Both procedures approached file optimization more or less the same way: remove everything that's not absolutely necessary. The online tool (links are in the "See Also" section of this Recipe) offers no way to tweak its routine. Just enter the URL of the page in the form, and it returns the optimized code. The PC application (also mentioned in "See Also" section of this Recipe) will optimize one file, a batch of files, or an entire site, and offers a long list of settings that let the user dictate what stays and what goes.

Heavy-duty optimization complements the model of web sites as software. By that, I mean you as the designer work on a version of the site with easy-to-read formatting and comments, and then deliver an optimized version to your customers, which in this case are your site's visitors.

 Makers of proprietary software often call file optimization *compiling* the code. They do it not just to optimize the software's performance, but to prevent end users from reverse engineering their products. Despite the many source code protection and encryption tricks available to web designers, there's not much you can do to protect your HTML code once it's published on the Web.

Web page optimization is all about speed and visitor satisfaction. After all, the comments and neatly aligned tags are for your benefit, not the web surfer's. If you want to go as far as you can with optimization and keep a version that's easy to edit, you could maintain two versions of your site—an offline version that's easy to edit by hand and an optimized "live" version that is uploaded to the web server. (Software mentioned in the "See Also" section of this Recipe can help you set this up.)

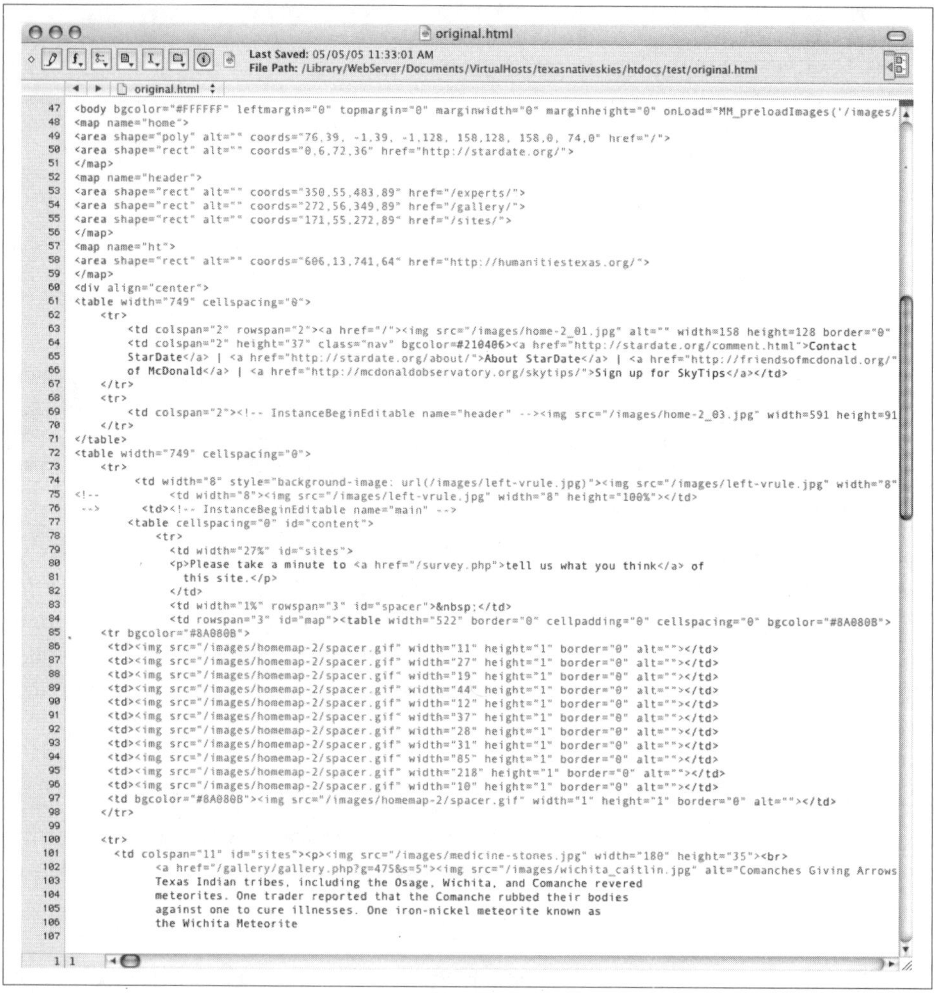

Figure 4-6. My original, pre-optimization file; maybe a few too many line feeds and tab indents, but easy to read for a hand-coder

The amount of optimization you'll want to do depends on your work habits and web site needs. If you prefer to edit HTML code by hand (and you have to do it frequently), then you'll probably want to pick and choose how and what to optimize. For example, you might want to get rid of unneeded spaces, tabs, and tag attributes that specify a default setting, but leave your comments and line feeds so the files remain more manageable. Or, you could get the best of both worlds by structuring your pages as optimized shell files, while leaving the content you edit most often in a more-readable, lightly optimized include file. You can optimize to the fullest extent possible if you don't edit the pages very often or you do most of your site editing in the WYSIWYG or design view of your web page editor, rather than in code view.

Figure 4-7. Post-optimization; a smaller file…but a bigger headache?

See Also

For a good tutorial on using regular expressions see *http://www.anybrowser.org/ bbedit/grep.shtml*. The two heavy-duty optimization tools I used for this Recipe are HTML Code Cleaner (online form at *http://www.yook.de/webmaster/clean/*) and HTML-Optimizer Pro (download from *http://www.tonbrand.nl/products.htm*). Port80 Software also offers a full-featured web page optimization application called w3compiler (*http://www.w3compiler.com/*).

CHAPTER 5

Formatting Graphics

5.0   Introduction

Along with text, graphics comprise the bulk of your web site's content. Graphics can convey specific information (logos and charts) or set a tone for the site (photos and illustrations). Even though visitors may not linger over your site's visuals the way they do the written word, graphics have a subtle effect on the perceived quality of your web site. Graphics also make up the majority of a web page's overall file size. Although your HTML code itself may total just 15 or 20 KB, a half-dozen graphics files on the page at 5 or 10 KB each quickly add up to a weighty download. In this chapter, I'll cover a few of the most common issues surrounding the use of graphics on a web site, including how to choose the right ones and optimize them for fast download.

5.1   Optimizing Your Images

Problem

You need to minimize the file size of images to be used on your site while retaining as much image quality and color integrity as possible.

Solution

The Web's main image formats, JPEG and GIF, along with their oft-forgotten stepsister PNG, complete a trio of optimization methods for web designers. You may already know the basic rule of thumb for choosing among the three:

> Use GIFs (or 8-bit PNGs) for logos and simple graphics; use JPEGs for photographs.

Discussion

Why optimize? About half of all U.S. households have some kind of broadband Internet access, and many of those users don't have high-speed access at the office, school, public library, or Wi-Fi hotspot. Even a low-end cable or DSL connection can pull down about 85 Kbps. The Internet has come a long way since CompuServe commissioned the creation of the Graphics Interchange Format in 1987 to speed up the delivery of images to its members (most of which were using 2400 baud modems).

First, since the most common browser image formats are compressed formats, you don't have much choice. There's no convenient way to put your EPS, TIFF, and native Photoshop files on a web page. Sure, you can leave the compression options pegged to the top end of the scale when optimizing, but your images will still get compressed to some degree before they end up on your web site.

The second, more serious reason is conservation of bandwidth—your visitors' and yours. As I mentioned in Recipe 4.8 optimizing web page code and images ensures that no one who visits your site waits too long for the page to load. An Internet filled with poorly optimized sites would quickly eat up most of that high-speed access and leave those without it frustrated and looking at partially loaded pages. Also, large image files can quickly consume most or all of your web server disk quota and bandwidth limit, adding extra charges to your hosting account.

Once you know you need to optimize, it's largely a matter of choosing the right file format.

Graphics Interchange Format (GIF)

GIF is a 256-color, lossless compression format that predates the Web by a few years. All graphical web browsers can display GIF files inline on a web page. GIFs are best for images that depict text, drawings, or graphics with large, flat areas of color.

GIF's lossless compression algorithm means that every pixel of the original image remains in the optimized version. Photoshop and other graphics editors allow users to increase the "lossy" setting for non-interlaced, non-dithered GIFs (see Table 5-1 for more about optimization terms), but a high amount of compression will leave the images looking grainy (see Figure 5-1).

Table 5-1. Some important image optimization terms

Term	Definition
Dithering	A GIF option that simulates colors outside the palette in continuous tone sections of an image. Not necessary for images for which the GIF format typically excels—such as logos and flat-tone artwork—but good for photographs that must be saved as GIFs.
Interlace	Creates a GIF file that displays at a lower resolution first while the high resolution version finishes downloading.
Progressive	Similar to interlaced GIFs, a progressive JPEG displays at lower resolution while the rest of the file loads.

Contrary to common web designer belief, the 256-color limit does not mean there is a magical, fixed palette of colors that can be used in a GIF. The format supports 8-bit color, meaning that there are two to the eighth power, or 256, "slots" for color codes in the optimized file. You can use a graphics editing application such as Adobe Photoshop to choose from preset color palettes, choose individual colors to be included in the optimized file, and/or reduce the color palette to as few as two colors, before saving it.

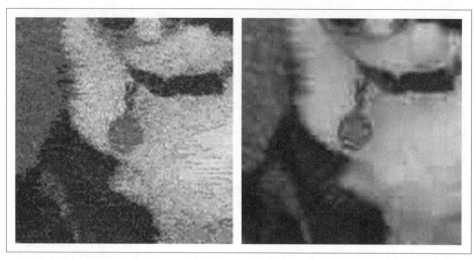

Figure 5-1. A highly compressed GIF (left) becomes grainy; a highly compressed JPEG (right) becomes pixilated

One color in a GIF's palette can optionally be set as transparent, giving web designers a way to "knock out" an area of an image so a web page's background color or image can show through. PNG also supports transparency, but JPEG does not.

Unlike the other two formats, GIF files can easily be combined into modestly sophisticated, yet lightweight animations that can be displayed inline on a web page in all major browsers.

Joint Photographic Experts Group (JPEG)

JPEGs can include more than 16 million colors—more than the human eye can distinguish—which makes them best for detailed, realistic images, such as photographs and paintings, or images with drop shadows or other finely gradated detail. Colors in a JPEG are true colors, not chosen from a (limited color) palette.

The JPEG format uses a more complicated, "lossy" algorithm that replaces selected pixels and remixes areas of an image with colors already in use elsewhere in the compressed file (see Figure 5-2). JPEG compression can yield a smaller file size faster than GIF optimization, but a highly compressed images becomes *pixilated* (see Figure 5-1).

The JPEG format does not offer a transparency or animation option.

Figure 5-2. GIFs are better for logos and graphic artwork; a JPEG (above) shows compression artefacting around the lettering that would not appear in a GIF

Portable Network Graphic (PNG)

The PNG format came about in the mid-1990s when GIF creator Unisys began asking for royalty fees from companies using its compression algorithm. Most major browsers (Version 4.0 or greater) handle PNGs just like GIFs and JPEGs. Like GIF, PNG optimizes images with a lossless compression. Photoshop offers the option of optimizing images either as 8-bit PNGs—with a 256-color palette—or as full-color 24-bit PNGs. The limited palette PNG often beats a similarly optimized GIF in file size by 5 percent or more, while the 24-bit option usually can't beat a JPEG. But since both PNG formats support transparency, full-color PNGs can have a place in certain design situations.

See Also

Recipe 4.8

5.2   Creating a Web-Friendly Logo

Problem

You need a graphical representation of your company or organization to display on your web site.

Solution

Whether you're converting an existing graphic for online use or starting from scratch, keep these guidelines in mind when creating a logo for your web site:

Make sure the logo matches your business.
   Your web site logo should closely resemble the logo from your offline materials, such as your storefront sign, business cards, or letterhead (see Figure 5-3).

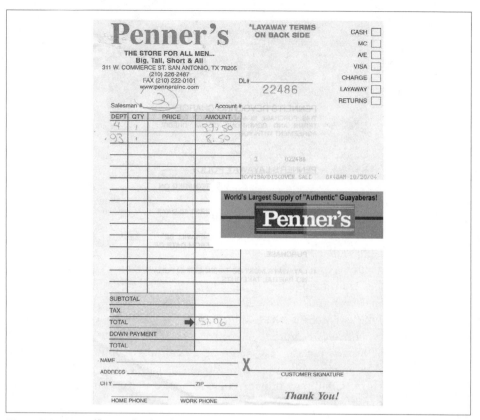

Figure 5-3. Keep offline and online logos consistent, like those found on the receipt and web site (inset) for this San Antonio clothing retailer

Keep it simple.

Straightforward web logos that combine small, plain glyphs or graphics with a stylized text treatment of the name of the site work best (see Figure 5-4).

Figure 5-4. Deceptively simple text treatment and color usage combine to make one of the best web site logos

Keep it small.

Both the dimensions and file size of your web logo are crucial. The logo has to load fast, but as the most important graphic on your site, it has to look good in a small space, too.

Use a domain suffix for distinctiveness.

Although it's not absolutely necessary, adding a graphical *.com*, *.biz*, or other domain identifier to your logo can be a key part of your online marketing and branding strategy. It also offers an outlet for design cleverness, such as those shown in Figure 5-5.

Figure 5-5. Putting the whimsy in dot-com

Discussion

Your logo builds your brand everywhere it appears, but online it has a more specific role. Visitors to your site—especially first-timers—want visual confirmation that they've come to the right place. Putting a fast-loading logo graphic in the upper left corner of your home page helps in that respect. You can make some minor modifications to optimize an existing logo for the web, but don't start over with a new logo unless you plan to use it everywhere (offline and online). Avoid adding photographic elements, color gradients, and animation to your logo, since those effects will make optimization more complicated, or force you to save a larger file than should be necessary.

Creating a web-friendly version of your logo will put your image optimization skills to the test. First, try to fit your web site logo into a horizontal space no more than about 150 pixels wide and 75 pixels tall. Then—since you'll likely be outputting a GIF or PNG—experiment with different palette and lossy settings to get the best balance between fidelity to the original and file size.

See Also

GotLogos.com sells custom logos for $25 (*http://gotlogos.com*). Image compression and optimization is detailed in Recipe 5.1.

5.3   Slicing and Recombining Complex Images

Problem

You need to align several images in a complex table to appear as one seamless image.

Solution

If you are creating new web pages or have upgraded older web pages to use a strict DOCTYPE (described in Recipe 4.1), then you may find that your tried-and-true method for slicing and recombining images in a table does not end up looking the way it once did. Images that are supposed to butt up against one another have an annoying space beneath them, as seen in Figure 5-6.

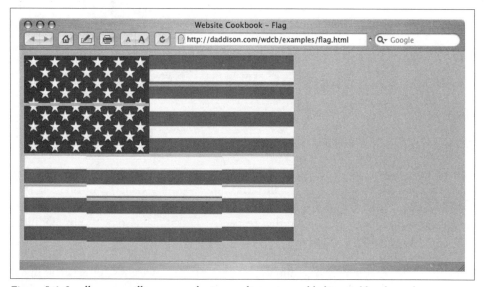

Figure 5-6. Small spaces will appear under image slices reassembled in a table when a browser renders the page using a strict DOCTYPE definition

To fix the problem, add a CSS rule to your page or master stylesheet that changes how the browser renders images in a table cell on a web page using a strict DOC-TYPE:

```
td img {
    display:block;
}
```

Or use an older or transitional DOCTYPE declaration tag (or no DOCTYPE at all) to prevent the problem. The DTD tag appears in the web page code above the <html> tag, like this:

```
<!DOCTYPE HTML PUBLIC "-//W3C//DTD HTML 4.01 Transitional//EN"
        "http://www.w3.org/TR/html4/loose.dtd">
```

Discussion

Slicing up a large image into several small images, and then rejoining those parts in a table, has several advantages. Working with small pieces of what would otherwise be a monolithic download, web designers can apply different optimization schemes, rollover effects, and <alt> attributes to the individual images that together speed download time and improve usability for web graphics such as page headers.

Site builders have long relied on the browser behavior that shrinks table cells up against the edges of images inside the cell. But newer DTDs—beginning with HTML 4.01—treat images in table cells differently than did older DTDs, such as HTML 3.2. Images in web pages using strict DTDs are rendered as inline content, like text.

A line of text sits on an imaginary line called a baseline. The letterforms of a typeface appear mostly above the baseline, but some space is reserved below the baseline for letters that have *descenders*, such as "p" and "j." When rendered as inline content, images—even in table cells with no adjacent text—are placed on the baseline and given the same breathing room above and below that a line of text would get (allowing for descenders, even though an image will never have one). The actual amount of space varies depending on the typeface, but even a GIF 1 pixel tall and 10 pixels wide gets both ascender and descender space (see Figures 5-7 and 5-8).

Figure 5-7. Even a short 1×10 pixel graphic gets space above and below in a table cell

Figure 5-8. Text next to the 1×10 pixel graphic in a table cell shows where the extra space comes from

Without the stylesheet fix offered in the Solution, multi-slice web page graphics that are supposed to appear as one contiguous image instead look like they've been dropped and hastily glued back together (see Figure 5-9).

Figure 5-9. Who broke the web page header? Images displayed by default as inline content get a little space below in a table cell

Applying a blanket CSS rule to all images in table cells will fix the rendering problem in Figure 5-9, but may have unforeseen consequences for other images that you want to be aligned on a baseline with real adjacent text in a table cell. If that's the case for you, then apply a unique class name, such as headergraphic, to the images that you want to display without extra space and then modify the stylesheet entry like this:

```
td img.headergraphic {
    display:block;
}
```

Netscape Navigator image display quirks

Finally, a note about Netscape Navigator 4.x. The rendering quirks of modern browsers presented with images in table cells probably seems familiar to any web designer who has ever torn his hair out trying to figure out why Netscape's once-popular browser put the same mysterious spaces between images. The DOCTYPE was not the culprit in this case. Turns out that Netscape puts visible whitespace in the rendered web page wherever whitespace characters—tabs, returns, and spaces—occur in the actual source code for the page.

A table full of cells formatted like this will results in a jagged image:

```
<td>
 <img src="images/sunset_01.jpg" width="71" height="50" alt="">
</td>
```

Closing up the code for the cell fixes the problem:

```
<td><img src="images/sunset_01.jpg" width="71" height="50" alt=""></td>
```

If your server logs indicate significant Netscape Navigator 4.x users, be sure to test with this browser.

See Also

The W3C may introduce additional methods of fixing the inline content mode of rendering images in table cells with Version 3 of the CSS specification, which is still under development. You can follow along at home: *http://www.w3.org/Style/CSS/current-work*. See Recipe 4.1 for more about DTDs. For further discussion of the benefits of tightening up your web page code, see Recipe 4.8.

5.4 Choosing Clip Art and Stock Photos

Problem

You need to liven up your web site design with professional looking photos or illustrations.

Solution

The right photo or illustration can support your web site's design and convey its message with visual impact. Consider this checklist when browsing through the myriad sources of artwork that you can add to your design.

Copyright and usage restrictions

Your first consideration should be what rights you have to use an image on your site. As you'll see in more detail in Recipe 5.5, there's little to be done to prevent web surfers from taking an image from one site and using it on another. Images you find on someone else's site typically belong to someone, so take the time to find the owner and ask for permission to use the image on your web site. Even public domain images from government sites, though copyright free, usually require some acknowledgement of the source.

Images from subscription-based sites such as ClipArt.com and EyeWire may come with usage restrictions. For example, you may need to pay a higher price for an image that you can use online *and* in a printed newsletter, or for a version of the image that you can manipulate significantly from the original. Spend some time thinking about your graphics needs before downloading the first great image you find.

Stylistic consistency

Combining graphics or photos of two or more artistic styles is one of the most common mistakes novice designers make. When you use icons or standalone images to set the tone for your web pages, consistent style is important—but it's also hard to manage (see Figure 5-10). Using a watercolor-style graphic for one icon and a pen-and-ink style for an adjacent will give your web pages an unprofessional look. One way to avoid this is to look for plain black and white graphics to which you can apply your site's color scheme.

Figure 5-10. Varying styles of clip art is a warning sign of novice web design

Strive for uniqueness

Try to avoid the graphical clichés that plague the web these days. The acrobatic envelopes that invite email communication and tireless construction workers on unfinished web pages have lost their distinctiveness. And although the inclusion of human faces have a timeless quality in all sorts of design, the visual tropes of ladies with headsets and men shaking hands need to be retired—along with the older couples staring expectantly at brandless laptops.

Choose the right file format and resolution

Graphics for web site use are typically offered at 72 dpi, although only the overall height and width in pixels truly matters. (See Recipe 4.3 for more about the surprisingly wide variety of screen resolutions on your visitors' computers.) If the image you've download is already in a compressed format, such as GIF or JPEG, then you're limited in how much you can resize or otherwise customize the image. A 100 pixel by 100 pixel graphic can't become a 200 pixel by 200 pixel graphic without significant loss in image quality. Higher resolution or uncompressed files can be more easily manipulated. You can add or remove backgrounds, enlarge the image or crop in on details, or change colors in specific areas before you optimize the image.

Discussion

Anyone who has browsed through a clip art or stock photo collection looking for the right image to add to a publication or web site knows that the signal-to-noise ratio is pretty high. Outdated hairdos and "Schoolhouse Rock"–style caricatures seems to be more the norm than the exception, especially in the budget bin. Use a "less is more" approach when adding images from these collections to your site. Make sure each addition is just that—a way to extend and enhance your web site's design, not detract from it.

See Also

Search several online stock photo catalogs at one time with Fotosearch (*http://www.fotosearch.com/*). Recipe 5.1 discusses various image file formats, and Recipe 4.3 will help you match image text to your web site's text.

5.5   Disabling Image Download

Problem

You need to prevent visitors to your web site from downloading proprietary images displayed on your site.

Solution

JavaScript, DHTML, and other sneaky coding tricks can be used to discourage, if not completely prevent, visitors to your web site from copying images from your web pages. None of the free options are impenetrable, but together they may be enough to ward off the less dogged online poachers. Consider these methods the equivalent of a cheap bike lock—it works great until the thief with bolt cutters finds it.

- Disable the right-click (and therefore Save Image) feature
- Disable Internet Explorer's Image Toolbar

- Place invisible layers over your images
- Store images in a protected directory

Discussion

The Internet has a love-hate relationship with stealing. Viewing the source code of a nifty-looking web page is by far the most popular method for learning about web design (after reading this book, of course). By borrowing a snippet of code from one site and adapting a bit from another, web designers have been advancing the state of their art for years—and few of their "victims" would consider what they're doing stealing. But then there's the whole Napster thing...

To be sure, the fruits of an artist or photographer's labors have more in common with music than HTML. Web page code—the structural part, not the content—is a commodity. There are only so many ways you can make a page look the way it does. If you find a new approach, you're almost obligated to share it. Many of the methods of protecting source code fail, and for the same reasons listed for the methods described above: the available schemes are fairly rudimentary and easy to circumvent. The Web is just not the greatest medium for exhibiting—without giving away—digital content of any real value. Once something is out there on the Internet, it's free for the taking unless you go out of your way to prevent it. Unless, of course, you work at making your images less accessible.

Disable right-click with JavaScript

There are a handful of scripts available on the Web that will display an error message in a visitor's browser when he right-clicks anywhere on the page. Just search Google for "javascript disable right click" to find one to download for your web site.

 I'd love to put the contents of the script that I use in this book; however, it's copyrighted, and I'm not a fan of legal action (especially when it's aimed at me). You can find the same script via Google, though.

Most work by rerouting the onMouseDown event handler of the Document object of a web page from the default—a browser-generated menu that usually includes an option for downloading an image—to a custom warning or error message (see Figure 5-11).

Savvy web surfers can skirt this tactic by disabling JavaScript in their browser. No JavaScript, no warning message. And later versions of Mozilla and Firefox give advanced users a finer level of control over what JavaScript can and can't do—such as controlling contextual menus—without completely disabling it.

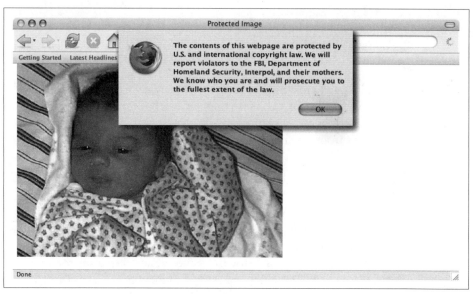

Figure 5-11. JavaScript can display a message when a visitor tries to right-click on an image to download it; the more threatening the warning, the better, since this technique can be easily circumvented

Disable the Internet Explorer image toolbar

The following `<meta>` tags will hide the little toolbar widget the pops up over an image in Internet Explorer (see Figure 5-12). However, this one's only good for protection from grandmas and least-competent criminals—no offense, grandmas.

Figure 5-12. The Internet Explorer image toolbar—I copied this image from the Microsoft web site!

```
<meta http-equiv="imagetoolbar" content="no">
<meta http-equiv="imagetoolbar" content="false">
```

Use layers to put a transparent force field over your images

This cunning method uses the z-index attribute of a <div> to place a fake transparent image over the real one.

```
<div id="L2" style="position:absolute; z-index:10">
  <img src="daddison_img_60128.gif" width="503" height="353">
</div>
<div id="L1" style="position:absolute; z-index:5">
  <img src="protected_img.jpg" width="503" height="353">
</div>
```

The z-index is the third dimension of a web page, allowing you to layer an item over another by giving it a higher z-index value. In my example, *daddison_img_60128.gif* is just a devious name for a 1×1 pixel transparent GIF sized up in the browser to match the dimensions of my real image, *protected_img.jpg*. Because the protected image is in a <div> with a lower z-index, visitors who are able to right-click will be right-clicking on the fake image above it. Bwahahahahahaha!

Downsides? A couple. This method requires at least four times as much HTML code as a simple inline image. Using it for multiple images on a page will lead to some really weighty pages. And, as with other methods mentioned above, anyone with the time and knowledge of HTML can view your page's source code to find the real image and download it that way. Or they can just take a screenshot of the page, and then crop out what they don't want to get their own copy of your "protected" image.

Limit listing and linking

Finally, you'll want to keep your "protected" images in a separate directory that Apache can't auto-index. You can ensure this by adding one line to an *.htaccess* file in the directory of protected images:

```
Options -Indexes
```

If no default web page exists in a directory—which is usually the case with a directory full of GIFs and JPEGs—Apache will show a list of files in the directory (see Figure 5-13).

Turning off indexing keeps the file list private (see Figure 5-14)

A couple of rewrite rules in the same *.htaccess* file will limit links to files in the directory to those that come from your web site:

```
Rewriteengine on
RewriteCond %{HTTP_REFERER} !^$
RewriteCond %{HTTP_REFERER} !^http://domain.com/.*$ [NC]
RewriteCond %{HTTP_REFERER} !^http://www.domain.com/.*$ [NC]
RewriteRule .*\.(gif|GIF|jpg|JPG|png|PNG)$ - [F]
```

This will prevent an unscrupulous free-loader from stealing your images—and your hosting account bandwidth—by adding links on his web site that point to files on your web site. This one doesn't generate a scary message, just a broken image on the offender's site.

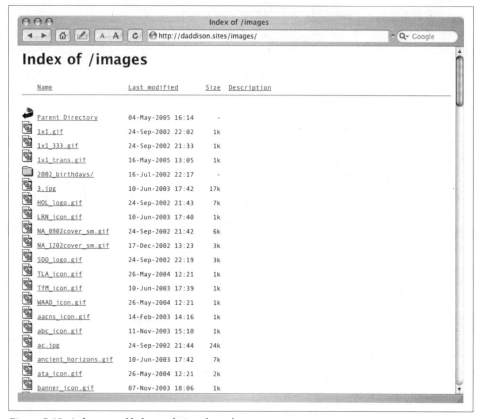

Figure 5-13. A directory file list with Apache indexing

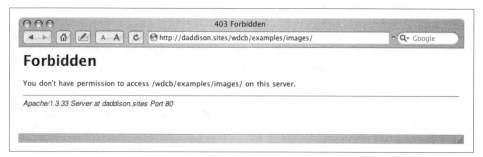

Figure 5-14. Disabling Apache indexing keeps the file list private

Commercial solutions

A couple of commercial solutions can help: digital watermarking and file encryption.

Watermarking valuable images with copyright information and usage terms will not, by itself, keep people from downloading them from your web site. Unlike watermarks on fine stationery, digital watermarks may be invisible to the viewer, but they can be read and even tracked on the Internet even if a file is copied and moved several times. DigiMarc Corporation (*http://digimarc.com/*) offers a digital watermarking technology that's available as a plug-in for Adobe Photoshop and other image editors. The watermark even remains readable on images captured from a site via screenshot. The company's subscription-based tracking service will scan web sites for unauthorized use of watermarked images.

Artistscope (*http://artistscope.net*) sells a variety of applications for copy protection of online content. With its popular Secure Image Pro application, you can encrypt image files and run Artistscope's proprietary Java applets on your web server to display the images for visitors.

5.6   Creating Watermarked Images on the Fly

Problem

You want to visibly mark images downloaded from your site with a logo or copyright information to dissuade people from using them as their own.

Solution

Use the PHP image-generating functions that are part of Thomas Boutell's GD Graphics Library to merge a transparent watermark image with your original downloadable images.

First, create the image you want to use as a watermark as a 24-bit transparent PNG. The opacity on the watermark image should be reduced to about 25 to 40 percent. The watermark image can be any size, but you may want to tweak it depending on the dimensions of the original images it will appear over.

Then upload the original images you want to watermark to your web server. If you want to control how visitors to your site download images from it, put the originals in a directory outside of the web root (see Recipe 1.7), and then define that location in your watermarking script.

Then upload the script that will open the watermark image and the protected, high-resolution original, merge the two, and output the new image file to the browser as a download.

Finally, add linked thumbnails to a gallery page of thumbnail images that when clicked will download the watermarked large version of the file (as shown in Figure 5-15):

```
<a href="download.php?src=dog_hires.jpg"><img src=" dog_thumbnail.jpg"
    width="75" height="100" align="none"></a>
```

Figure 5-15. Watermarking images on the fly with PHP's image-handling functions allows you to overlay usage information on images downloaded from your site, while preserving the unmarked original on the server for authorized use

Discussion

I wrote this script to merge the file referred to by src with the watermark image. The script begins with some variable definitions:

```
<?
$src_path="/path/to/hires/images";
$src_file = $src_path."/".$src;
$wm_file = "watermark.png";
```

For this script, I've decided to save the images to be watermarked outside the web site's root directory. Placing the images in a directory outside the root ensures that visitors don't have any way to access your non-watermarked originals. Only the *download.php* script (which also applies the watermark) can access the files.

The $src_path variable defines the full server path to the images. By combining the filename in the variable $src with the value of $src_file, the script gets a file handle to pass to the GD library image functions. The watermark image is saved in same directory as the script, so no path is necessary in its file-handling variable ($wm_file).

The script uses the GD functions imagecreatefromjpeg( ) and imagecreatefrompng( ) to create image identifiers for the original and watermark images to be manipulated by the rest of the script:

```
$src_file = imagecreatefromjpeg($src_file);
$wm_file = imagecreatefrompng($wm_file);
```

For information about using the GD function library for other image types, see the PHP web site manual page listed in the See Also section of this Recipe.

Passing the image identifiers to the functions imagesx( ) and imagesy( ) gives us the width and height of the original image and the watermark image:

```
$src_w=imagesx($src_file);
$src_h=imagesy($src_file);
$wm_w=imagesx($wm_file);
$wm_h=imagesy($wm_file);
```

The imagecopy( ) function requires three pairs of numeric parameters to merge the watermark image ($wm_file) with the original image ($src_file): the placement coordinates ($output_x and $output_y) on the destination file, the starting coordinates (0,0) in the source file, and the size of the image to be placed ($wm_w, $wm_h):

```
$output_x = ( $src_w / 2 ) - ( $wm_w / 2 );
$output_y = ( $src_h / 2 ) - ( $wm_h / 2 );
imagecopy($src_file, $wm_file, $output_x, $output_y, 0, 0,$wm_w, $wm_h);
```

The PHP header( ) function sets the HTTP headers for content type, as well as the filename for the merged image, and the imagejpeg( ) function outputs the file to the browser:

```
header("Content-type: image/jpg");
header("Content-disposition: filename=".$src);
imagejpeg ($src_file);
```

Finally, the script calls the imagedestroy( ) function twice to clear the image file handlers from memory:

```
imagedestroy($src_file);
imagedestroy($wm_file);
?>
```

See Also

Recipe 6.11 discusses another use for the GD Graphics Library.

The PHP manual pages for the GD Graphics Library is online at *http://www.php.net/manual/en/ref.image.php*.

CHAPTER 6

Displaying and Delivering Information

6.0   Introduction

Most everyone who comes to your web site wants to take away an answer to a specific question as result of their visit. It's your job as web designer to build a site that fulfills that desire in an efficient and uncomplicated manner. Although you may see your site as a well-structured collection of pages—containing just the right words and images—your visitors, especially first-timers, might see it more as a haystack hiding the needle they want. In this chapter, we'll look at some techniques for using visual cues—such as link text, link titles, and pop-up windows—and delivery mechanisms—such as printable versions, downloadable files, and RSS feeds—that will help your site visitors find, understand, and acquire the information they came to your site to find.

6.1   Explaining Who's Responsible for Your Site

Problem

You need to make sure that your site visitors understand who you are, how to contact you, and how the information that is exchanged over your site is created and managed.

Solution

Be ready with answers to visitors' questions about your web site by creating the following components:

- A page listing the name, mailing address, phone number, and legal name of the entity responsible for the site

- An email address for *webmaster@yourwebsite.com*

- Auto-responders for emails sent to *webmaster@yourwebsite.com* and other generic addresses set up for fielding specific questions or complaints

- Names of third-party content sources and destinations of offsite links
- A privacy policy
- A copyright or terms of use statement

Discussion

Web surfers will visit your site seeking specific information. Sometimes their questions pertain to the area of expertise espoused on your site. At other times they want to know more about the site itself and the enterprise or individual who runs it. Making this type of information clear and easy to find will greatly improve how visitors perceive your site.

First, list your complete contact information on a "Contact Us" or "About Us" page. A contact form works great for quickly delivering messages from web site viewers to the appropriate staff person, but some visitors will want to know how to contact you by mail, phone, and fax. Don't hold this information back just because you think the email form serves as an adequate substitute—it doesn't.

Also, double-check that your site provides a way for visitors who eschew email forms to contact you by email. Even if you don't list it anywhere on your site, some people will try sending email to *webmaster@yourwebsite.com*. Your webhosting account may be set up to forward every email sent to your domain to a default address if the actual address does not exist. If that's the case, make sure that emails sent to *webmaster@yourwebsite.com* get through to someone who will read them regularly. Or, just go ahead and set up a mailbox or forwarding alias for *webmaster* and designate someone to read and respond to them. You may, however, find it impossible to respond personally to every email sent to the webmaster. In that case, set up an *auto-responder* that confirms the receipt of the email, lists your full contact information, and answers other common questions about your site.

In addition to divulging all *your* information, you also need to explain to visitors how you plan to use the information *they* might be asked to provide while using your site. To explain how a site interacts with its visitors and their personal information, a good privacy policy should:

- Acknowledge that the server collects traffic statistics about their visit
- Identify site features that use cookies and how those cookies are used
- List the types of personal information that the site collects and stores, as well as how (or if) it will be used, sold, traded, or disclosed
- Provide instructions to visitors for opting-out of mailing lists and for changing the personal information the site has collected from them
- Explain any security measures the site uses to protect personal information, such as digital certificates and secure sockets layer (SSL) connections between browser and server

- Contain a disclaimer that the terms of your site's privacy policy do not extend to other sites that visitors may access through offsite links they follow from your site

- Notify visitors about how other laws or policies may affect the terms of the privacy policy

Your site also should clearly state how (and if) visitors can reuse site content. You (or your lawyers) may wish to go a step further with a "terms of use" statement that covers, among other things, the legal disclaimers and visitor obligations for the site, as well as copyright information. At the very least, a simple copyright page should grant visitors the right to link to the site, explain the terms of republishing content from the site (and how to request permission to do so, if necessary), and list the required credit line to use. Also, be sure to make it clear where your copyright or usage terms do not apply because the content was provided by another site (for example, via an RSS feed; see Recipe 6.7 for more on RSS).

 Links to your privacy policy and usage terms pages should be listed on every page on your site, preferably out of the way in the footer near the bottom of the page.

See Also

Many visitors will attempt to contact you after encountering a problem with your site (see Recipe 9.1). For more information about SSL protocol and digital certificates, see Recipe 8.5.

The Platform for Privacy Preferences Project (*http://www.w3.org/P3P*) is an effort by the W3C to standardize, simplify, and automate the way web sites notify their visitors about what they do with their personal information.

6.2   Writing Meaningful Link Text

Problem

You need to guide visitors to the page they're looking for with well-written link text.

Solution

When building a hypertext experience on your web site, follow this checklist to ensure that your links require as little effort from your visitors as possible to make them useful:

- Links should be formatted to stand out from other text.
- Followed links should look different than links that are not followed.
- Links should describe their destination.

- Links should be succinct.
- Link text should be straightforward. Avoid riddles, sarcasm, and culturally specific references.

Discussion

The words and phrases you place in `<a href="...">` tags are by far the most important bits of text on your site. Web surfers, by their nature, are scanners. After determining that the page he's viewing does not have the information he wants, a visitor to your site will scan the page looking for the link that will take him closer to his goal.

A visitor's first job when scanning a page is to visually distinguish text that *is* a link from text that *is not* a link. As the designer, you should have already done the work to make this an easy task. In your site's stylesheet, you should define colors for text, links, and followed links, like this:

```
body {
color: #000000;
}
a:link {
color: #0000FF;
}
a:visited {
color: #660099;
}
```

These styles will create blue, underlined links on black text. When the visitor returns to a page from which he has followed a link, that link will appear purple (#660099) rather than blue. Conservative usability experts advocate close adherence to the blue-then-purple link-coloring scheme, allowing for some flexibility in the shade of blue and purple that can be used. The argument for doing so is strong. When a page contains no specification for its link colors, most browsers will use blue and purple. This design convention is prevalent enough that you'll be doing your visitors a favor by using it, rather than making them learn your custom color scheme.

On the other hand, some web designs (and designers) yearn to break the mold. As long as your link text stands out from the non-link text and the followed links can be differentiated from links without fading into illegibility, then you can indulge yourself with a little creative freedom. But a license to experiment should not lead you to remove the underline from links, despite the many alternate text decoration rules you can specify with CSS. Whether you use the standard blue and purple scheme, or something more complementary to your site's color scheme, keep the underline. It's a core part of what makes a link look like a link. Likewise, avoid underlining any text in your web pages that *is not* a link.

You might be tempted to use CSS to give links extra styling that identifies their purpose. For example, you might use standard underlined text for links to other pages on your site, text over a background color for pop-up windows, and dotted underline text for offsite links. Not only will this create visual clutter that will confuse your visitors, few, if any, will spend the time to learn and understand your system. If you have a small, well-defined audience—say, for an intranet or web application—you may be able to educate your visitors about the intricacies of your link-formatting system. But in most situations, you're better off using link titles and well-written text to convey the action that results from clicking a link.

Color change is just one of the ways links convey information to your visitors. The actual content of the link is the other. Lazy web writers often fall into the bad habit of thinking like a link-seeking surfer—or not thinking at all—when they enclose the infamous phrase "click here" in the their <a> tags rather something more informative.

The "click here" scourge has proliferated because it makes writing for the web easy. Yes, web surfers will visit as many pages as they can in search of the answer to their question. And yes, most will click to get there. So, web designers construct their pages like a laboratory maze, with blind corners that they hope will lead their mouse-wielding subjects to their reward: "To get the piece of cheese, **click here**." But when scanning a page full of "click heres," most visitors will wonder where their cheese went!

Writing (or rewriting) your links without "click here" takes some practice (and an appreciation for the web surfer's mindset), but your visitors will thank you when you do. Let's consider some before and after examples:

Before: Please **click here** to download your certificate as a Portable Document Format (PDF) file.

After: **Download your certificate** as a Portable Document Format (PDF) file.

Before: To report problems with this web page, **click here**.

After: **Report a problem** with this web page to the webmaster.

Before: For information on where to stay and eat in the area, **click here**.

After: Consult our **lodging and dining guide** for more information.

The "after" versions in these examples demonstrate a couple of common improvements over the "click here" versions. The link itself has moved closer to the beginning of the sentence that contains it. When "click here" dangles off the end of a sentence, visitors must scan *backward* over the text to ascertain the purpose of the link. When a well-written link hooks a surfer at or near the beginning of a sentence, she can read the rest of the sentence to put the link in context more easily.

Mimicking your search engine keywords in your link phrases can also improve your page rank.

The improved versions also use action words or highly informative phrases: "Download," "Report," and "lodging and dining guide." In the last example, I chose not to extend the link to include "Consult our" for the sake of brevity. The two extra words might actually detract from, rather than improve, the scannability of the link for visitors looking for a "lodging and dining guide." In general, concise links are better than wordy ones. With links longer than 25 to 30 characters (including spaces), you run the risk of them wrapping onto a second line where they might be compete with links above or below them on preceding or subsequent lines or be misinterpreted as two separate links.

See Also

Recipe 6.3 discusses another way to improve your links. Page titles become link text when viewed on search results. For more information on this often-overlooked page element, see Recipe 2.5. Recipe 3.2 explores the aesthetic choices that web designers face when building a site. In his article "Reviving Advanced Hypertext" (*http://www.useit.com/alertbox/20050103.html*), Jakob Nielsen describes some proposed features that browsers and web designers could use to make links easier to manage and use.

6.3   Adding Preview Information to Links

Problem

You need to give site visitors extra information about a link, or provide a textual preview of a link's destination.

Solution

Use the `title` attribute of the `<a>` tag to display additional information when a user mouses over a link:

```
<a href="/index.html" title="Return to the home page">...text or image to be linked...</a>
```

Discussion

The `title` attribute for links works similarly to the `alt` attribute of the `<img>` tag. When the user passes her mouse over a linked phrase or image, the browser displays a small text tag (see Figure 6-1). The latest versions of Internet Explorer for Windows and Mac, Firefox, Safari, Opera, and Netscape Navigator will display the tag. Navigator Version 4 will not.

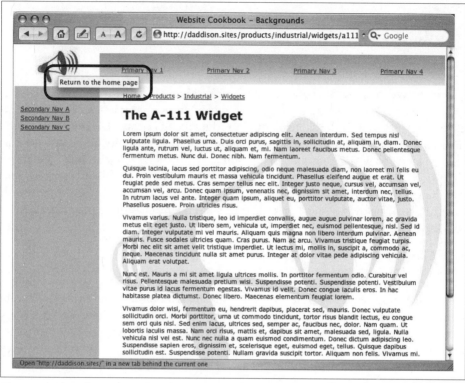

Figure 6-1. The title attribute of an <a> tag appears as floating box in most newer browsers when a user holds her cursor over a linked image or bit of text

Web site links can create anxiety for web surfers who aren't sure what will happen when they click the link. Linked words and phrases have the advantage of explaining themselves to web surfers (that is, if they're well-written—see Recipe 6.2). When you add a link to an image, your site visitors often can benefit from additional information that explains the results of clicking the link. A title attribute can be useful for identifying offsite links (even text-based ones), links that open in a new browser window, links that enlarge an image in a pop-up window, and links that create a new email message, among other things. Combined with code for an image map, title attributes also can be used to annotate a complex image or group photo.

See Also

Recipe 6.2

6.4   Creating Effective Pop-up Windows

Problem

You want to display information that supplements the current page in a second, smaller window that opens when a visitor clicks on a link.

Solution

Add this JavaScript function to the <head> section of your web page:

```
function openWindow(address, name, width, height) {
        window.name = "main";
        var features = "width=" + width + ",height=" + height + ",";
        features += "resizable=yes,scrollbars=yes,status=yes,";
        features += "menubar=no,toolbar=no,location=no,directories=no";
        var newWindow = window.open(address, name, features);
        newWindow.focus();
}
```

Then call the function using the onClick( ) event handler in a link on your page, like this:

```
<a href="popup.html" target="_blank" title="New Window - Short Explanation"
onClick="openWindow('popup.html','popup','480','360');return false;">
```

Before adding the link, make sure that:

- The link explains that it creates a pop-up window.
- Visitors that have JavaScript disabled can get to the page, too.
- The content of the pop-up window supplements or extends the information on the page that generates it.
- The size of the pop-up window minimizes or eliminates the amount of scrolling necessary to see its contents.
- Your main site navigation *is not* part of the pop-up window layout.
- Search engines cannot index the pop-up window.

Discussion

Pop-up windows are a well-known and often reviled fact of life on the Web. Marketing experts, however, swear by the effectiveness of advertisements presented in windows that pop up over or under the main browser window. Many savvy web surfers, intent on preserving the integrity of their browsing experience, block automatic pop-up windows using built-in browser settings or add-on utilities. Others just dismiss the offending pop ups as quickly as they appear and get on with the reason they came to the site.

In a typical setup, a user's pop-up blocker will not prevent additional windows from opening when she *requests* the action by clicking a link. In this scenario, a pop-up window provides an ideal forum for presenting ancillary information about the content on the originating page without leading the visitor away (possibly forever) from the page. Potential uses include FAQs related to a sales-oriented landing page, enlarged or alternate views of products, glossary terms, or context-sensitive technical support for a complex web application. Pop-up windows that contain an "Email this page" form, a real-time web chat interface, or other useful tools also are fairly common (see Figure 6-2). But the sketchy reputation of pop-up windows demands that you use them judiciously and be explicit about when and why a link opens a pop up.

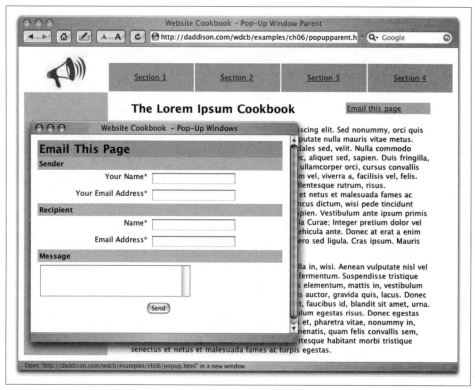

Figure 6-2. Pop-up windows are welcome guests in the browsing experience when they are invited and do something useful

There are two tried and true methods for opening additional browser windows with HTML and JavaScript. One uses the target attribute of the <a> tag, like this:

```
<a href="popup.html" target="_blank" title="New Window - Short Explanation">Pop-Up
Window</a>
```

The title attribute displays a small hovering annotation of the link's purpose or destination when a visitor mouses over the link. For more information, see Recipe 6.3.

The _blank value is one of four reserved target values. Using it ensures that the link will open in a new window. You also can specify a custom value, such as popup, but if a window with the name popup is already open, the link will load in that window.

The JavaScript method offers more control over the properties, and more importantly, the size of the window into which the link gets loaded. Small pop-up windows reinforce the perception that its contents are supplemental to the main window. To create a 480×360 pixel pop up with a link, use the open( ) method of JavaScript's window object. The method takes three parameters—url, name, and features:

```
<a href="#" title="New Window - Short Explanation"
onClick="window.open('popup.html','popup','width=480,height=360');">Pop-Up
Window</a>
```

The link code presented in the Solution includes both the target attribute and the JavaScript onClick() event handler methods to ensure that it works for users with JavaScript disabled. Adding return false; to the function call prevents the same window from opening twice when a visitor clicks the link.

The openWindow( ) function shown in the Solution uses the window.open( ) command and improves on it with additional code. The first line:

```
window.name = "main";
```

gives the originating window a name to which links and forms in the pop-up window can refer. For example, you can code links in your pop-up window to open back in the main window, like this:

```
<a href="anotherpage.html" target="main" title="Another Page - Loads in Main
Window">Another Page</a>
```

The next three lines define a variable containing a string of pop-up window options that will be passed to the actual window.open( ) command. First, the width and height parameters that are passed to the openWindow( ) function from the link:

```
var features = "width=" + width + ",height=" + height + ",";
```

Then additional features grant the user some control over the pop-up window:

```
features += "resizable=yes,scrollbars=yes,status=yes,";
```

while other features eliminate most of the window's frame to restrict the functionality of the pop up:

```
features += "menubar=no,toolbar=no,location=no,directories=no";
```

In addition to presenting your pop up in a stripped-down browser window, you should take steps to make sure that visitors can't get to or leave the page except by the link that creates it. First, design your pop-up windows without any of the site navigation that you would include on the other, *main* pages of your site. Add a <meta> tag to the <head> section of your pop-up page code to exclude it from search engine indexing:

```
<meta name="robots" content="noindex, nofollow">
```

See Also

Recipe 6.3 explains how to use the title attribute in links.

6.5   Randomizing Text or Images

Problem

You need to display a different text block, image, or other type of content on a page every time it gets viewed.

Solution

Use JavaScript's Math.round( ) and Math.random( ) functions to select and print one random element from an array of content items that can be displayed on the page.

First, define the array of content items and variables that will define one random selection from the array in the <head> section of your web page:

```
<script type="text/JavaScript" language="JavaScript">
<!--
randContent = new Array();
randContent[0] = "...item 0...";
randContent[1] = "...item 1...";
randContent[2] = "...item 2...";
randContent[3] = "...item 3...";
randContent[4] = "...item 4...";
var numb = randContent.length-1;
var mathRandom = Math.random();
var mathRound = Math.round((mathRandom*numb));
var randDisplay = randContent[mathRound];
//-->
</script>
```

Then use JavaScript to print one element from the array by adding this code to the <body> of the page where you want the content to be displayed:

```
<script type="text/JavaScript" language="JavaScript">
<!--
document.write(randDisplay);
//-->
</script>
```

Discussion

Content items listed in the `randContent` array can be almost anything you want: testimonials from your best customers, sale items from your online store, work samples from your portfolio, Flash movies, or even advertisements and sponsor logos.

The variable `mathRound` defines the element in the array that will be displayed.

 Remember, JavaScript array elements are numbered starting at zero.

To get that value, the script generates a random number between 0.0 and 1.0 with the `Math.random( )` function, and then multiplies that number by the number of elements in the array—less one—to ensure that the product of `Math.round((mathRandom*numb))` never exceeds the last element number in the array, which in this example is 4.

You also can randomize an array with a PHP script using the built-in `shuffle( )` function. After passing the array to the function, echo element number 0 on the page:

```
$randContent[0] = "...item 0...";
$randContent[1] = "...item 1...";
$randContent[2] = "...item 2...";
$randContent[3] = "...item 3...";
$randContent[4] = "...item 4...";
shuffle($randContent);
echo $randContent[0];
```

6.6   Highlighting the Search Term

Problem

You want to make it clear to site visitors what they searched for when they view a results page.

Solution

Combine a stylesheet rule with a PHP text-processing function to make the search term stand out.

For this Recipe, let's assume you have a search form that queries a database for articles, like this:

```
<form action="/search/search.php" method="post">
<input name="arg" type="text" value="" size="10" maxlength="20">
<input type="submit" value="Go">
</form>
```

The value of the `<input>` field `arg` gets passed to the *search.php* script and becomes the variable $arg. First, add a rule to your stylesheet that will highlight this block of text, as shown in Figure 6-3:

```
.arg {
    background-color: #00CCCC;
    font-weight: bold;
}
```

Then add a line to the results page that simply prints the search term, wrapped in the style:

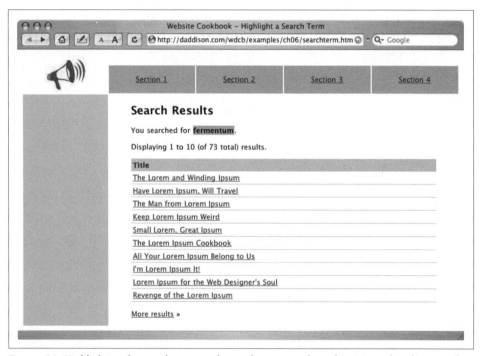

Figure 6-3. Highlighting the search term on the results page confirms for visitors that they got what they requested

```
echo "You searched for <span class=\"arg\">".$arg." </span>";
```

You also can create a custom PHP function (or modify one you've already made to handle other text-processing tasks) to highlight the search term in the body of the article that the visitor requests from the results page:

```
function processText($text,$arg) {
...other text-processing commands...
$text = str_replace($arg,"<span class=\"arg\">".$arg."</span>",$text);
return $text;
}
```

This processText( ) function takes two parameters: the full text of the article to be displayed and the search term. In the article links on the results page, you'll need to pass the $arg variable on to PHP template that displays articles. Figure 6-4 shows how it might look to a visitor.

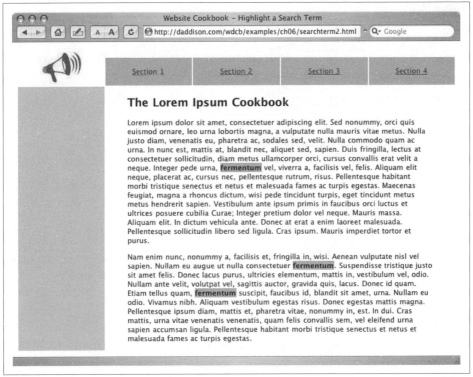

Figure 6-4. You can extend the feedback mechanism by highlighting the search term on pages linked from a results page

Discussion

Web surfers fall into two behavior groups: there are browsers and there are searchers. Both groups have one thing in common, though. When they get to your site, they almost always have a specific goal in mind—a question in search of an answer. Many web surfers will dutifully follow your navigation in hopes it will lead them to what they're seeking. Others go straight to your search box to cast about for the page that will give them what they came for.

Small details separate a frustrating—or even just average—web site experience from a great one. Whether they know it or not, web surfers take comfort in a web site that strives to establish continuity while they use the site to get what they want. Like well-written link phrases and page titles, highlighting the search term on your results page makes it easy for visitors to your site to understand what they asked for and what they got. When visitors can make quick decisions about the relevance of the information they're viewing, they leave satisfied in knowing that the site can meet their needs.

See Also

Recipe 2.5 explains the importance of establishing a naming convention.

Recipe 4.7 describes ways to convert characters in text stored in or retrieved from a database to their proper HTML entities.

Recipe 6.2 explains how to guide visitors to the page they're seeking.

6.7 Embedding RSS Feeds on Your Site

Problem

You want to add another web site's content, such as news headlines, to your web site.

Solution

Get the URL of the RSS feed you want to syndicate, and then use one of the many feed parsing tools to reformat the entries in the feed as HTML for display on your site.

Discussion

RSS, which stands for Rich Site Summary or Really Simple Syndication, is a file format that facilitates the sharing and syndication of web site content. RSS files typically contain 10 to 25 entries, each with a headline, short description, and a link to more information about the entry on the parent web site. RSS files are structurally similar to web pages, but use XML tags instead of HTML. The RSS file format is discussed in more detail in Recipe 6.8.

 Always make sure you have the publisher's permission to syndicate their feed on your site. And never pass off someone else's content as your own—lest you be accused of "feed hijacking" or "blog plagiarism."

The number of RSS feeds has grown rapidly during the last couple of years. Nearly every major news operation, blog, and high-traffic specialty site offers its frequently updated content as a feed. RSS feeds are popular because of their potential: they have been anointed as an antidote to spam and heralded as a way to harness the Web's daily deluge of information. Feeds also scale down nicely for display on small-screen mobile devices. And, of course, they provide a new vehicle for driving traffic to the publisher's web site.

Web surfers can subscribe to one or more feeds using a variety of online aggregators and PC newsreader applications that can open a feed file and parse the XML code into a human-readable format. Your web site also can subscribe to a feed using a script to reformat the feed as HTML. Feed2JS (which uses JavaScript) and Caching RSS Parser (CaRP) (which uses PHP) are just two of the many scripts you can download and use on your web site for this purpose.

To use Feed2JS, you enter the feed URL and information about how you want the feed to be displayed into a form on the Feed2JS web site. You can specify options such as the number of entries to display at one time, the length of the description (or none at all), and a CSS "hook" that lets you tweak the display using your own style sheet. The form then generates customized JavaScript code that you can copy into the body of your web page where you want to display the feed. The script itself is stored on the Feed2JS web server (or one of its mirror sites), and, like all client-side scripting, requires that the visitor's browser have JavaScript enabled for it to work.

The server-side script CaRP is a commercial RSS feed parser written in PHP (a free-ware version also is available). To use CaRP, you have to download the scripts and copy them to your web server. The extra effort pays off in the form of many more configuration options, compared to Feed2JS. With CaRP, you can specify all the display options available with Feed2JS, as well as aggregate multiple feeds into one list, cache feed information to speed download time, filter feed entries by their subject, and censor offensive words. And unlike JavaScript solutions, there is no browser-side requirement for viewing the HTML feeds created with CaRP (see Figure 6-5).

See Also

For more information about the RSS feed converters discussed in this Recipe, visit their web sites: Feed2JS (*http://jade.mcli.dist.maricopa.edu/feed*) and CaRP (*http://www.geckotribe.com/rss/carp*). For a tutorial on installing and using a Perl script to convert feeds to HTML, see *http://webreference.com/perl/tutorial/8*. Universal Feed Parser is RSS parser written in Python (*http://feedparser.org*). Several sites provide directories of RSS feeds, including Feedster (*http://www.feedster.com*), Bloglines (*http://bloglines.com*), and 2RSS.com (*http://www.2rss.com*)

6.8   Creating an RSS Feed from Database Content

Problem

You want to notify the world about updates on your web site with an RSS feed.

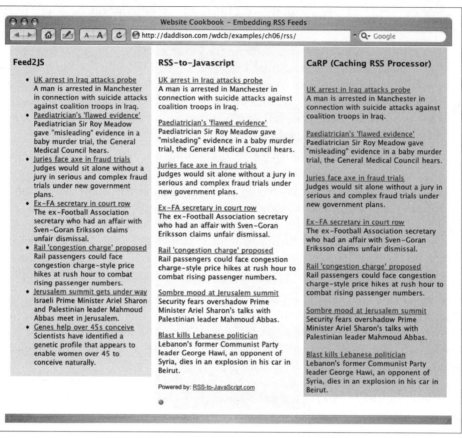

Figure 6-5. Three easy-to-use feed-parsing tools—Feed2JS, RSS-to-JavaScript, and CaRP—can reformat RSS feeds from other sites and display them on your site

Solution

Use a PHP script to get your web site content from a SQL database, format the records as valid RSS feed entries, and save the complete feed file to your web server.

First, define a connection to your SQL database:

```
$dbName = "mydatabase";
$conn = mysql_connect("dbhost","dbuser", "dbpassword") or die("Couldn't Connect.");
$db = mysql_select_db($dbName, $conn) or die("Couldn't select database.");
```

Then define a function to generate the RSS code for individual items:

```
function createItem ($title, $description, $link, $pubdate) {
  $item  = "  <item>\n";
  $item .= "    <title>".$title."</title>\n";
  $item .= "    <description>".$description."</description>\n";
  $item .= "    <link>http://yourwebsite.com/".$link."</link>\n";
  $item .= "    <pubDate>".$pubdate."</pubDate>\n";
```

```
  $item .= "  </item>\n";
  return $item;
  }
```

To save the feed file on your web server, define the full server path to the file in the variable $feedfile:

```
$feedfile = "/full/path/to/rss.xml";
```

 Your web server must have write privileges for the directory the feed file will be saved in.

Also, define a variable for a properly formatted last-modified timestamp for the feed using the PHP date( ) function:

```
$lastBuildDate = date("D, j M Y H:i:s");
```

The $lastBuildDate variable will have the format Tue, 29 Mar 2005 09:58:08.

The content of the feed file will be stored in the variable $feedcontent. First, the script needs to add the RSS tags to $feedcontent that provide a general description of the feed:

```
$feedcontent = "<?xml version=\"1.0\"?>\n";
$feedcontent .= "<rss version=\"2.0\">\n";
$feedcontent .= " <channel>\n";
$feedcontent .= "  <title>title</title>\n";
$feedcontent .= "  <link>link</link>\n";
$feedcontent .= "  <description>description</description>\n";
$feedcontent .= "  <lastBuildDate>".$lastBuildDate."</lastBuildDate>\n";
$feedcontent .= "  <language>en-us</language>\n";
$feedcontent .= "  <copyright>copyright</copyright>\n";
$feedcontent .= "  <webMaster>webmaster@yoursite.com</webMaster>\n";
$feedcontent .= "  <ttl>1</ttl>\n";
```

Most of these tags are self-explanatory. The latest version of the RSS specification is 2.0, although some feeds are published using old versions. Links to specifications and RSS file validators are in the "See Also" section of this Recipe.

The <language> element allows feed aggregators to group feeds published in the same language. The <ttl> element stands for *time to live* and defines the number of minutes that must pass before a cached feed can be refreshed from the source.

Next, the script queries the database for 15 records:

```
$sql ="SELECT id, title, description, pubDate FROM table ORDER BY id DESC LIMIT
0,15";
$result = @mysql_query($sql, $conn) or die("Error #". mysql_errno() . ": " .
mysql_error());
```

Depending on the structure of your database, you will likely want to tweak the query with a WHERE statement that checks an RSS_publish field for *yes* or *true* to make sure that the set of found records includes only the content you want to publish in your RSS feed.

With a while loop, the script uses the createItem( ) function to add a new item entry to $feedcontent for every found record:

```
while ($row = mysql_fetch_array($result))
{
 $id=$row['id'];
 $title=$row['title'];
 $description=$row['description'];
 $link = "feeds/ ".$id."/";
 $pubDate=$row['pubDate'];
 $pubDate = date("D, j M Y H:i:s", $pubDate);
 $feedcontent .= createItem($title, $description, $link, $pubDate);
}
```

Two more additions to $feedcontent close the file:

```
$feedcontent .= " </channel>\n";
$feedcontent .= "</rss>\n";
```

Finally, save the feed in a static file, using this code:

```
$file = fopen($feedfile, "w+");
fwrite($feedfile,$feedcontent);
fclose($file);
```

To generate your feed file, you can request the PHP script manually by requesting its URL in a web browser as often as you care to. Or, make your life a little easier and set up a cron job to automate the process using the Unix utility wget. A cron task that generates the feed file at the top of every hour would look like this:

```
0 * * * * /usr/local/bin/wget http://yourwebsite.com/path/to/feed.php
```

Discussion

RSS files are XML documents, so they must conform to the W3C specification. A valid RSS file generated from the script presented in this Recipe will look something like this:

```
<?xml version="1.0"?>
<rss version="2.0">
 <channel>
  <title>Web Site Cookbook Daily Feed</title>
  <link>http://daddison.com/wscb/</link>
  <description>Late-breaking news and updates.</description>
  <lastBuildDate>Thu, 18 Aug 2005 17:10:00 -0500</lastBuildDate>
  <language>en-us</language>
  <copyright>Copyright 2005</copyright>
  <webMaster>webmaster@daddison.com</webMaster>
  <ttl>1</ttl>
  <item>
   <title>A Little RSS Goes a Long Way</title>
   <description>Lorem ipsum dolor sit amet, consectetur adipiscing elit, set
```

```
eiusmod tempor incidunt et labore et dolore magna aliquam. Ut enim ad minim veniam,
quisnostrud exerc. Irure dolor in reprehend incididunt ut labore et dolore magna
aliqua. Ut enim ad minim Ipsum dolor sit amet, consectetur adipiscing elit, set
eiusmod tempor incidunt et labore et dolore magna aliquam. Ut enim ad minim veniam,
quisnostrud exerc.</description>
    <link>http://daddison.com/wscb/post20050818171000.php</link>
    <pubDate>Thu, 18 Aug 2005 17:10:00 -0500</pubDate>
</item>
  </channel>
  </rss>
```

The code elements are arranged hierarchically, similar to HTML. The first two lines define the document type (XML) and the RSS version. The entire body of the feed goes between one channel element. The lines before the first item list the feed's meta-information. Only title, link, and description are required (the bolded elements in the example). The other elements, such as language and copyright, are for the benefit of subscribers and aggregators.

All of the elements that can be placed within an item are optional, but either the title or the description must be present for the entry to appear in the feed. For a complete list of optional channel and item elements, check out the RSS specification web site listed in the "See Also" section in this Recipe.

The enclosure element allows feed publishers to attach a media object, such as an MP3 file, to a feed entry. For example, feeds that include a *podcast*—a syndicated, periodic audio-based feed distributed via RSS—use the enclosure element. The enclosure element must include attributes for the file's URL, size, and type:

```
<enclosure url="http://yourwebsite.com/podcast.mp3" length="2038879"
type="audio/mpeg"/>
```

Making sure your feed file validates before unleashing it on the world might involve setting or overriding the web server's notion of the content type for the feed file. RSS feeds should be served as *application/rss+xml* or *application/xml*. You can do this by creating an *.htaccess* file in the same directory as the feed file and adding this instruction to the web server:

```
AddType 'application/rss+xml; charset=utf-8' .xml
```

For more information about web server content types and character sets, see Recipe 4.2.

See Also

Recipe 1.8 explains cron in more detail. Recipe 2.7 explains wget in more detail. The W3C specification for XML documents is online at *http://www.w3.org/TR/REC-xml*. Feed Validator has an overview of the latest RSS specification at *http://feedvalidator.org/docs/rss2.html* and a web-based feed validating utility on the home page. Feeds also may be formatted according to the Atom specification.

Build It with a Blog

An alternative way to generate an RSS feed for your web site is with a blog. While the popular stereotype for a "blogger" tends toward either the self-styled political pundit or late-night diarist, you don't need to be either to benefit from this nearly ubiquitous form of web publishing.

Taken out of its pigeonhole in the public consciousness, blogging is nothing more than a new solution to the longstanding problem of managing web site content. And blogs do it in a way that's ideal for web surfers, allowing an author to publish short, categorized, time-stamped entries that can—if the author chooses—be commented on or even updated by the audience.

Nearly all blogs are accompanied by an RSS feed. Simply put, the blog is the HTML view of the posts published on the author's web site (or on a free blogging service site such as Blogger) and the feed is a stripped-down version in XML format that can be viewed with news reader software or syndicated and formatted back into HTML on other web sites.

If you don't want or need to set up your own database to generate a customized RSS feed, there are several varieties of blog software and services at your disposal. With the aforementioned Blogger, you can be blogging within minutes of setting up a free account. Blogger blogs are hosted on owner Google's servers, but you can self-syndicate a feed onto your own site. You can exercise more control of your blog if you host it on your own site using software such as WordPress (*http://wordpress.org*) or Movable-Type (*http://movable.org*). A link to a site with a side-by-side comparison of all the popular blogging services and software is listed in the "See Also" section of this Recipe.

Finally, a word of caution about setting up a blog, especially if it's only for the purpose of generating a feed to display or syndicate elsewhere. Most blogging platforms allow readers to add comments to posts, a feature that both enriches and plagues the web. When left unattended, blog comments can quickly devolve into a new form of spam, as malicious web surfers and their automated minions fill the comments section with links to their own sites in an attempt to boost their own search engine rankings. If you don't want comments or don't have time to monitor the comments you will get on your blog, disable the commenting feature.

For more information on this method, see *http://www.atomenabled.org*. For a thorough comparison of several varieties of blog software and services, see Blog Software Breakdown at *http://www.asymptomatic.net/blogbreakdown.htm*.

6.9   Adding a Poster Frame to a QuickTime Movie

Problem

You want to display a still image preview of a QuickTime movie placed on a web page.

Solution

Create a single-frame poster movie and specify it in the src attribute of the QuickTime code on your web page:

```
<object classid="clsid:02BF25D5-8C17-4B23-BC80-D3488ABDDC6B"
        codebase="http://www.apple.com/qtactivex/qtplugin.cab"
        width="640" height="496">
  <param name="src" value="poster.mov">
  <param name="href" value="movie.mov">
  <param name="target" value="myself">
  <param name="autoplay" value="true">
  <param name="controller" value="false">
  <param name="pluginspage"
         value="http://www.apple.com/quicktime/download/indext.html">
  <param name="type" value="video/quicktime">
  <embed src="poster.mov" href="movie.mov" target="myself"
         width="640" height="496" autoplay="true"
         controller="false" border="0"
         pluginspage="http://www.apple.com/quicktime/download/indext.html"
         type="video/quicktime"></embed>
</object>
```

 To ensure cross-browser capability, you should use both the object and embed tags to display a QuickTime movie on a web page.

Ordinarily, the value of the src attribute would be the path and filename of the full movie. When you want to display a poster frame first, you specify its path and filename with the src attribute and use two other attributes—href and target—to load the full movie when the user clicks the poster frame image (as shown in Figure 6-6).

Creating a poster frame

For best results, I recommend using Adobe ImageReady and QuickTime Pro to create a poster frame, although you may be able to complete the required steps with other tools.

The poster frame is actually a single-frame QuickTime movie. To start, open the full movie in ImageReady, where you will immediately see the "Range to Import" dialog box. Move the slider under the movie preview to select the scene you want to use as a poster frame, then choose Selected Range Only and click OK.

Figure 6-6. Using a QuickTime poster frame prevents the full movie from downloading until the visitor is ready to view it

You don't have to use a frame from the full movie for the poster frame. Any properly sized and formatted image will do.

Save the imported image as a Photoshop (*.psd*) file. If you plan to show the Quick-Time controller on the full movie, add 16 pixels to the bottom of your still image. In other words, a 320×240 pixel movie with the controller takes up 320×256 pixels of space on the page, so size your poster frame to match. The bottom 16 pixels are a good place to put the "Click to Play Movie" text over a black or colored bar. Add the instruction text, then flatten the image into one layer, and save the file.

In QuickTime Pro, open the image you just created and select Export from the File menu. Use the Movie to QuickTime Movie export scheme to save the poster frame movie. You may adjust the Options as you see fit to adjust the export quality; you also can tweak several other settings to create a smaller file.

The full movie and poster movie must be saved in the same directory on your web server.

Discussion

Poster frames make displaying multimedia content on your web site user friendly. Instead of presenting visitors with a page that requires an immediate download of a large movie file, poster frames give visitors the ability to see what the movie is about and choose whether they want to download it.

See Also

Apple Computer has a tutorial on all the tags and attributes you can use to display a QuickTime movie on a web page at *http://www.apple.com/quicktime/tutorials/embed.html*.

6.10   Creating a Printer-Friendly Version of Your Site

Problem

You want to offer a printable version of all your web pages without creating separate, specially coded versions of every page, or by using complex scripting.

Solution

Add a new style sheet to the <head> section of your web pages that will reformat your existing code into a printer-friendly format:

```
<link href="print.css" rel="stylesheet" type="text/css" media="print">
```

Discussion

The desire to read web pages on paper, rather than on a low-resolution computer screen, hasn't diminished much at all in the 10-plus years of the Web's existence. When visitors find something on your site they want to read, many will print the page and retire to a more comfortable offline venue to fully absorb your content. Fortunately, the techniques for facilitating this common web surfer behavior have evolved to make life easier on the web designer.

In the early days of the Web, site builders often would create separate versions of web pages that closely mimicked—page for printed page—their on-screen counterparts. (How many pixels wide is an 8.5"×11" sheet of paper? Anyone?) Others were savvy enough to install and configure a script or CGI that would strip a page of its HTML eye-candy and return a printer-friendly version.

Along the way, some browser makers added a Print Preview feature that would allow web surfers to tweak the web page layout that was sent to their printer. But the wasted effort (not to mention ink and paper) involved in getting the output "just right" caused many to throw up their hands (and their lunch) in disgust.

Enter the power of CSS, where one web page can have multiple formatting "personalities." The media attribute of the stylesheet tag specifies which CSS rules to use depending on the device on which the page will be rendered or output. For example, here is the code for two stylesheets, one for the computer screen and one for printing:

```
<link href="screen.css" rel="stylesheet" type="text/css" media="screen">
<link href="print.css" rel="stylesheet" type="text/css" media="print">
```

The pages shown in Figures 6-7 and 6-8 are based on the same HTML code, which uses `<p>`, `<div>`, and heading tags to format and position the various elements on the page.

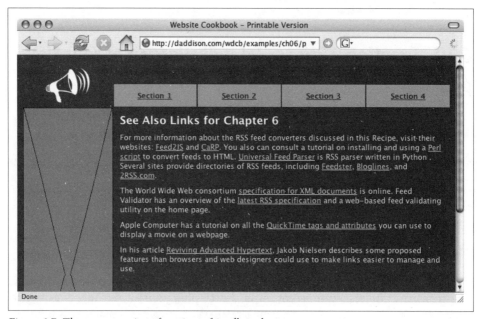

Figure 6-7. The screen version of a printer-friendly web page

The screen stylesheet has rules for the background, text, link, and primary navigation colors, as well as placement settings for the logo and advertisement (left column). The print version of the stylesheet specifies serif type and reverses the text colors to white on black:

```
body {
    background-color: white;
    color: black;
    font-family: serif;
    font-size: 12pt;
}
```

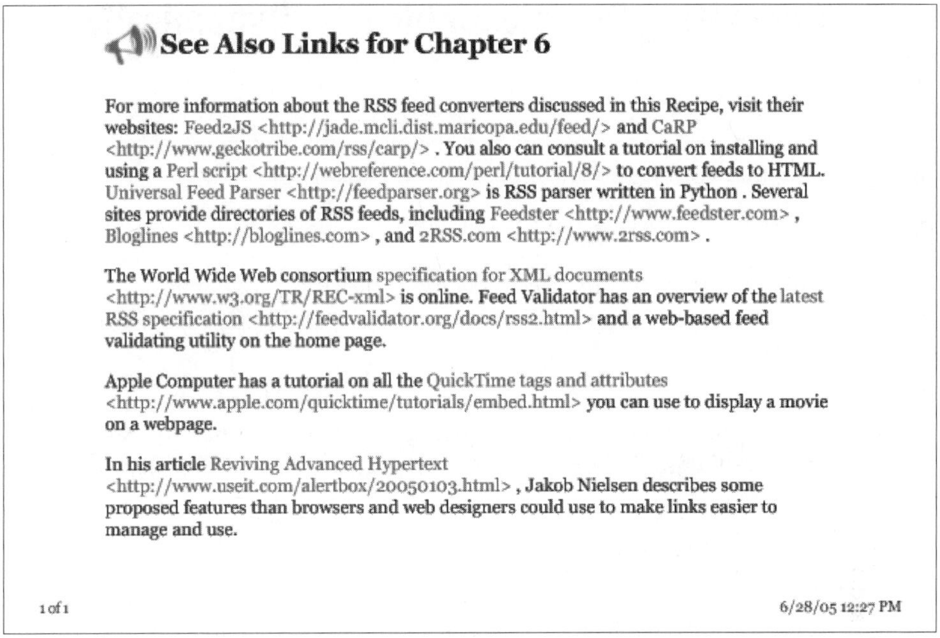

See Also Links for Chapter 6

For more information about the RSS feed converters discussed in this Recipe, visit their websites: Feed2JS <http://jade.mcli.dist.maricopa.edu/feed/> and CaRP <http://www.geckotribe.com/rss/carp/> . You also can consult a tutorial on installing and using a Perl script <http://webreference.com/perl/tutorial/8/> to convert feeds to HTML. Universal Feed Parser <http://feedparser.org> is RSS parser written in Python . Several sites provide directories of RSS feeds, including Feedster <http://www.feedster.com> , Bloglines <http://bloglines.com> , and 2RSS.com <http://www.2rss.com> .

The World Wide Web consortium specification for XML documents <http://www.w3.org/TR/REC-xml> is online. Feed Validator has an overview of the latest RSS specification <http://feedvalidator.org/docs/rss2.html> and a web-based feed validating utility on the home page.

Apple Computer has a tutorial on all the QuickTime tags and attributes <http://www.apple.com/quicktime/tutorials/embed.html> you can use to display a movie on a webpage.

In his article Reviving Advanced Hypertext <http://www.useit.com/alertbox/20050103.html> , Jakob Nielsen describes some proposed features than browsers and web designers could use to make links easier to manage and use.

1 of 1 6/28/05 12:27 PM

Figure 6-8. Using the same HTML code, but a different stylesheet, the printer-friendly version of the same web page is ready to be committed to paper

Then it uses the `display:none` rule to hide page elements that I don't want on the printed version, such as the navigation and the advertisement:

```
#weblogo {
   display:none;
}
#primnav {
   display:none;
}
#sidead {
   display:none;
}
```

Finally, the stylesheet includes rules for removing the underline from links and including the URL of the link after link text in paragraphs:

```
a:link {
   text-decoration: none;
}
p a:after {
   content: " <" attr(href) "> ";
}
```

See Also

For more information about how screen resolution affects the display size of text on your pages, see Recipe 4.3.

6.11 Generating Downloadable Files Dynamically

Problem

You want to offer a frequently updated or customized document, such as a coupon or application, that visitors to your site can download and print out.

Solution

Set up a PHP script that dynamically generates a file using code libraries that allow you to build and output custom PDFs, PNGs, JPEGs, and other types of files using built-in functions.

The functions associated with PDFlib library, created by Thomas Merz, have been available to PHP since Version 3. Image-generating functions that are part of Thomas Boutell's GD Graphics Library have been a common PHP installation option since Version 4.3.

 The PDFlib and GD functions must be enabled with PHP when it is installed on your web server. If you're unsure about the availability of either function library, check with your system administrator or web hosting provider.

If you want to create PDFs on the fly, but don't have access to PDFlib, you can use a third-party PHP class that replicates most of the functionality of PDFlib; refer to the "See Also" section in this Recipe for more information.

Discussion

For this Recipe, I'll use the example of creating a coupon (see Figure 6-9) with an expiration date one week from the date the visitor downloads it. Coupons are a great way for a brick and mortar establishment to get regular visitors to its web site. Setting up a script that keeps the coupon up to date, and offers some flexibility about the terms of the offer, will relieve you or your client from the tedium of generating and uploading a new coupon every week.

Regardless of the graphics library you use, the steps for creating a dynamically generated coupon are the same:

1. Define any variables to be plugged into the contents of the file.
2. Create the canvas.
3. Add any borders, graphics, or text to be displayed in the file.
4. Output the file to the browser.

For our coupon, I will define two variables—$discount for the percentage discount and $duration for the length of time in weeks that it will be valid—and then use

Figure 6-9. A downloadable coupon can be generated on the fly with a PHP script

PHP's built-in time( ) and date( ) functions to create a third variable—$expiry—for the human-readable expiration date:

```
$discount = "50";
$duration = 1; //weeks
$expiry = time( );
$expiry = $expiry+($duration*604800);
$expiry = date("F j, Y",$expiry);
```

The PHP function time( ) creates a timestamp in seconds. By adding 604800 to the timestamp value (the number of seconds in one week), the scripts will then format the expiration date variable ($expiry) in "Month Day, Year" format for one week from the current date.

You could also leave these variables out of the script itself and instead pass them from a form on a web page.

Using PDFlib

For the PDFlib script, I also have defined the variables $file for the megaphone logo (which will be uploaded to the same directory as the script) and $fontdir for the path to the font I want to use in the coupon:

```
<?
$discount = "50";
$duration = 1; //weeks
$expiry = time( );
$expiry = $expiry+($duration*604800);
$expiry = date("F j, Y",$expiry);

$file = 'logo.jpg';
$fontdir = $DOCUMENT_ROOT."/path/to/your/fonts";
```

The canvas will be a letter-size sheet of paper, measured in pixels; this coupon is 612 wide and 792 tall:

```
$pdf = pdf_new( );
pdf_open_file($pdf);
pdf_set_info($pdf, "Author","Web Site Cookbook");
pdf_begin_page($pdf, 612, 792);
```

 The coordinate system for PDFlib begins at the lower left corner of the document, which takes some getting used to. I find it useful to sketch my PDFs on a blank sheet of paper, and then note the X and Y positions of elements with a ruler. One inch equals 72 pixels.

With these next three lines, I specify a border width, as well as the origin and dimensions for its placement on the document. Then the pdf_stroke ( ) function draws the coupon, as shown in Figure 6-10:

```
pdf_setlinewidth($pdf, 2);
pdf_rect($pdf, 72, 504, 346, 216);
pdf_stroke($pdf);
```

The first pair of values passed to the pdf_rect function (72, 504) define the rectangle's starting point; the second pair of values (346, 216) are the X and Y values for its width and height.

Next, the script will take the filename (stored in $file) and create an object to be placed in the document with the pdf_place_image( ) function. The three numeric parameters in the function are the X- and Y-axis start points, and the amount to scale the image (1 equals 100 percent):

```
$graphic = pdf_open_image_file($pdf, "jpeg", $file);
pdf_place_image($pdf, $graphic, 90, 540, 1);
```

These next two lines load the font. I copied the TrueType file for Verdana (*VERDANA.TTF*) from my Windows PC, uploaded it to the same directory as the script, and point to it using the $fontdir variable defined at the top of the script:

```
pdf_set_parameter($pdf, "FontOutline", "Verdana=$fontdir/VERDANA.TTF");
$font = pdf_findfont($pdf, "Verdana", "host", 1);
```

Using the pdf_setfont( ) and pdf_show_xy( ) functions together, the script specifies font sizes (20, 30, and 9) for the three text blocks to be displayed on the coupon. The numeric parameters in pdf_show_xy( )specify the X- and Y-axis start points for the text:

```
pdf_setfont($pdf, $font, 20);
pdf_show_xy($pdf, "C O U P O N", 252, 648);
pdf_setfont($pdf, $font, 30);
pdf_show_xy($pdf, $discount."% off", 252, 612);
pdf_setfont($pdf, $font, 9);
pdf_show_xy($pdf, "Not valid with other offers. Void where prohibited.", 90, 522);
pdf_show_xy($pdf, "Expires: ".$expiry, 90, 511);
```

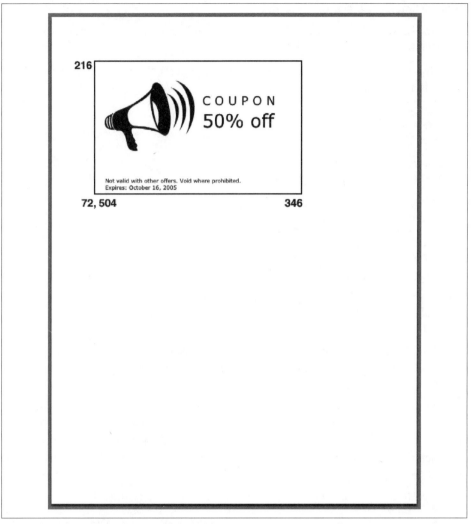

Figure 6-10. On a letter-size canvas, the pdf_rect function draws a rectangle starting at the lower-left corner

Finally, the script closes the documents and sends the data to the browser. Depending on the user's browser settings, the file might be displayed directly in the browser window or downloaded to the user's hard drive:

```
pdf_end_page($pdf);
pdf_close($pdf);
$data = pdf_get_buffer($pdf);
header('Content-type: application/pdf');
header('Content-disposition: inline; filename=coupon.pdf');
header('Content-length: ' . strlen($data));
echo $data;
?>
```

Using GD Graphics Library

With the set of functions available in the GD Graphics Library, you can create PNGs, JPEGs, GIFs, and other image files on the fly.

For our coupon example, I'll use this script to create a PNG that will display directly in the user's browser:

```
<?
$discount = "50";
$duration = 1; //weeks
$expiry = time();
$expiry = $expiry+($duration*604800);
$expiry = date("F j, Y",$expiry);

$width = 346;
$height = 216;
$im = ImageCreate($width, $height);
$white = ImageColorAllocate ($im, 255, 255, 255);
$black = ImageColorAllocate ($im, 0, 0, 0);
```

First, define a canvas 3 inches tall and approximately 4.75 inches wide; also define the colors $white and $black to be used later in the script:

```
ImageFill($im, 0, 0, $black);
ImageFilledRectangle($im, 2, 2, 343, 212, $white);
```

Two lines create a black border. First, the script fills the canvas with black, then the ImageFilledRectangle( ) function fills with $white a rectangle two pixels shy of the full canvas size on each side.

To add the text, the script uses the ImageTTFText( ) function and the TrueType Verdana font file (also used in the PDFlib script). Unlike the PDFlib script, the GD image functions draw on the canvas from the upper-right corner. The numeric parameters sent to the function are the size, angle, and X- and Y-axis starting points for the text:

```
ImageTTFText ($im, 20, 0, 172, 60, $black, "VERDANA.TTF", "C O U P O N");
ImageTTFText ($im, 30, 0, 164, 100, $black, "VERDANA.TTF", "50% OFF");
ImageTTFText ($im, 10, 0, 20, 184, $black, "VERDANA.TTF", "Not valid with other
offers. Void where prohibited.");
ImageTTFText ($im, 10, 0, 20, 196, $black, "VERDANA.TTF", "Expires: ".$expiry);
```

Two lines place the logo, too. With the file itself stored in the variable $graphic, the ImageCopy( ) function requires three pairs of numeric parameters: the placement coordinates (8,8) on the destination file ($im), the starting coordinates (0,0) in the source file ($graphic), and the size of the image to be placed (144,144):

```
$graphic = ImageCreatefromPNG("logo.png");
ImageCopy($im,$graphic,8,8,0,0,144,144);
```

Finally, the script outputs the image to the browser and removes the file from PHP's memory:

```
header ("Content-type: image/png");
header("Content-disposition: inline; filename=coupon.png");
```

```
ImagePng ($im);
ImageDestroy($im);
?>
```

Using R&OS PDF class

This PHP class provides a powerful alternative for creating dynamic PDFs if the
PDFlib functions are not available:

```
<?
$discount = "50";
$duration = 1; //weeks
$expiry = time();
$expiry = $expiry+($duration*604800);
$expiry = date("F j, Y",$expiry);

include ('class.ezpdf.php');
```

The required code and fonts for this PHP class can be downloaded from the author's
web site listed in the "See Also" section in this Recipe.

The code that does all the heavy lifting is in the file class.ezpdf.php. For this example, I have uploaded it to the same directory as the script that will generate the coupon.

These next two lines create a letter-size PDF canvas and set 1-inch margins:

```
$pdf =& new Cezpdf('LETTER','portrait');
$pdf->ezSetMargins(72,72,72,72);
```

For the border, I specify the style, and then use the $pdf->line command to draw the
four sides. The four numeric parameters define the X- and Y-axis start and end
points for each line in this order: X1, Y1, X2, Y2. The 0,0 point in this coordinate
system is at the lower-left corner of the canvas:

```
$pdf->setLineStyle(1,'','',array(3));
$pdf->line(72,531,72,720);
$pdf->line(418,531,418,720);
$pdf->line(72,720,418,720);
$pdf->line(72,531,418,531);
```

A single line places the logo at the X,Y coordinates of 18,144.

```
$pdf->ezImage($DOCUMENT_ROOT.'/path/to/logo.jpg',18,144,none,left);
```

As with the other two scripts, placing text requires selecting the font, setting placement coordinates, and writing the copy onto the canvas. Unlike its counterparts, the
R&OS PDF class comes with a few fonts, sparing you the trouble of tracking down
your own:

```
$pdf->selectFont('fonts/Helvetica.afm');
$pdf->ezSetY(684);
$pdf->ezText("C O U P O N",
    18,array('justification'=>'center','aleft'=>'252','aright'=>'400'));
$pdf->ezSetY(648);
$pdf->ezText($discount."% off",42,
```

```
        array('justification'=>'left','aleft'=>'252','aright'=>'400'));
$pdf->ezSetY(567);
$pdf->ezText("Not valid with other offers. Void where prohibited.\n".
    "Expires: ".$expiry,10,
    array('justification'=>'left','aleft'=>'90','aright'->'400'));
```

Finally, send the completed file to the browser:

```
$pdf->ezStream(array('Content-Disposition'=>'coupon.pdf'));
?>
```

All three options described in this Recipe are well documented and can be extremely powerful tools after you become familiar with the library's more advanced techniques. The GD image library can be used to create complex graphical representations of many types of data or perform manipulations on image files already stored on your server (see Recipe 5.6). With a script that generates a dynamic PDF, you can create up-to-date downloadable product sheets from database content, or printable and faxable forms for situations where applicants must sign or have their application notarized before sending them to you.

See Also

The PHP manual pages for the two function libraries are at *http://www.php.net/manual/en/ref.pdf.php* and *http://www.php.net/manual/en/ref.image.php*. The R&OS PDF class can be downloaded from *http://www.ros.co.nz/pdf*.

6.12   Offering Your Site on Mobile Devices

Problem

You want to see how your site looks on PDAs and cell phones.

Solution

First, create a mobile device-friendly stylesheet and add it to the pages you want people to be able to access while on the go. Use the attribute/value pair media="handheld" in a linked stylesheet to define separate formatting rules for pages when viewed on a mobile device, like this:

```
<link href="/styles/handheld.css" rel="stylesheet"
    type="text/css" media="handheld" />
```

Then, use a mobile-browser emulator to preview your pages and tweak them as necessary.

Discussion

If you think creating standards-compliant, cross-platform sites for large-screen browsers is a challenge, then prepare to lose some hair, some sleep, and possibly your lunch when trying to sort out the truly mind-boggling world of web browsing on the myriad wireless devices available today. Screen widths vary from as little as

120 pixels on the smallest cell phones to 320 pixels or more on the latest Palms and Pocket PCs. Although there is a version of Internet Explorer that runs on Pocket PCs, and Opera's mobile browser ships in many devices, other handset browsers (of which there are many) share little in common with their large-screen counterparts.

When faced with this amount of complexity, your best bet is to simplify. Fortunately, your mobile web surfers will be in agreement with this approach. No one wants to spend a long time navigating a web site on a handheld device. Users want to get in, get what they want, and move on. For that reason, you only need to provide stripped-down mobile versions of your highest trafficked pages, such as your contact page, a page with directions, and your home page and the frequently updated sub-pages that it links to.

If your site is already coded with valid XHTML syntax and CSS for formatting, then you've got a fairly clear path to creating a mobile version of those pages. (For more information about XHTML, see Recipe 4.1.) If your site design still uses tables, font tags, and other deprecated markup elements, then you might want to consider setting up XHTML- and CSS-compliant versions of the pages that will be most useful to mobile browsers—or redesigning your entire site to bring it up to snuff with the latest HTML specifications.

 Many mobile devices also support Wireless Markup Language (WML) over Wireless Application Protocol (WAP). Using these technologies offers the promise of better compatibility across all devices, but will require you to learn WML (which differs somewhat from HTML) and maintain a separate set of pages for your mobile content.

As you saw in Recipe 6.10, CSS gives web designers the ability to specify different stylesheets depending on the output device that will view or render the page. The CSS rule you should be using most often in your handheld stylesheet is display:none. With it, you can hide CSS id- or class-tagged navigation, images, advertisements, and other page elements that will be superfluous to the mobile browsing experience—and can drag out the load time, too.

Reorient your layout vertically, either by hiding sidebar columns or rewriting their positioning rules to stack them one atop another. Remember that content blocks and images wider than about 120 pixels will require the surfers with the smallest small screens to scroll horizontally, a web design no-no regardless of the medium.

Finally, make your mobile pages as lean as possible by streamlining your code and removing (or hiding) any Java applets, Flash movies, or other plug-in dependent eye-candy. (For more information, see Recipe 4.8.)

When reviewing your CSS-based mobile design, the Opera web browser is a good place to start. With its small-screen viewing mode, you can see on your PC how your handheld stylesheet will render a page on a mobile device. Download links for specific device and browser emulators are listed in the "See Also" section of this Recipe. If you're designing a site for users with a specific mobile device, then you'll want to invest in an actual handset for testing.

See Also

For more information on the web design techniques that apply to mobile devices, see Recipes 4.1, 4.8, and 6.10.

Emulators are available for Palm (*http://www.palmos.com/dev/tools/emulator*), Black-Berry (*http://www.blackberry.com/developers/downloads/simulators*), and Windows Mobile for Pocket PC and Smartphone (*http://www.microsoft.com/windowsmobile/downloads*). The OpenWave Mobile Browser is installed on many newer phone handsets, and a simulator can be downloaded at *http://developer.openwave.com/dvl/tools_and_sdk/openwave_mobile_sdk/phone_simulator*. Check wireless service providers and handset, manufacturer web sites for other web-based or downloadable emulators. To get the Opera browser, visit *http://opera.com*.

CHAPTER 7

Interacting with Visitors

7.0 Introduction

Even though the Web is an interactive medium, you probably can't (and don't want to) be on hand all day, every day, to guide visitors through the site or respond to errors. Likewise, you probably don't want to spend all your waking hours maintaining your site and personally leading each loyal visitor back to your site on a regular basis. Fortunately, there are many techniques for defending against unnecessary errors automatically. And when your site operates smoothly, you can focus on ways to get to know your visitors and build relationships with them with things like surveys, polls, webcasts, web chats, and webinars. In this chapter, I'll go over some of the little details that make a web site visit successful and enjoyable.

7.1 Preventing Blank Form Fields

Problem

You need to make sure visitors to your site fill in all the required fields in your web site form.

Solution

Use the onBlur, onClick, or onSubmit JavaScript event handlers in your form to check for empty fields before the form data is sent to the server.

Discussion

A well-written PHP or CGI script will check the data it gets from a web form before it performs its actions on it. If required fields are missing, the script should show the user an error page, rather than saving incomplete information in a database.

Error-checking in your server-side scripts requires a hit on your web server and causes your user to wait; you can head off an unnecessary connection by checking form data before it gets sent. Testing required fields for a value with JavaScript will save time and processing resources on your server:

```
<form action="form.php" method="post">
<fieldset>
<legend>&#x260E; Contact Information</legend>
 <h3>Name *</h3>
  <input name="name" type="text" size="20" maxlength="20" tabindex="1"
   onBlur="if(this.form.name.value=='')
      {alert('Please fill in your first and last name.')};">
 <h3>Email Address *</h3>
  <input name="email" type="text" size="20" maxlength="20" tabindex="2"
   onBlur="if(this.form.email.value=='')
      {alert('Please fill in your email address.')};">
 <h3>Phone Number *</h3>
  <input name="phone" type="text" size="12" maxlength="12" tabindex="3"
   onBlur="if(this.form.phone.value=='')
      {alert('Please fill in your phone number.')};"><br>
  <input name="Send" type="Submit" value="Send"
   onClick = "if (this.form.name.value == '' ||
               this.form.email.value == '' ||
               this.form.phone.value == '')
       {alert('Please fill in the required fields marked with an
        asterisk (*).');return false;};"/>
  <input name="f" type="hidden" value="send">
</fieldset>
</form>
```

This simple form code uses JavaScript embedded in the input and submit button elements to display alert messages (see Figure 7-1) if fields are left blank.

HTML form fields have *focus* when the cursor is in the field and they are *blurred* when the user clicks or tabs away from the field. The onBlur event handler in each text input in this form activates a warning when the form respondent leaves the field blank.

The Submit button has an onClick event handler that tests all three required fields. If any are blank, the warning message appears when the user selects the Submit button. (In JavaScript, as well as PHP, two vertical bars (||) are shorthand for *or*, so the condition expressed in the Submit is true if the name, email, *or* phone fields are blank.) This effectively disables the submit button until the three required fields in the form have been filled in. You also can put the JavaScript code in a function, like this:

```
<script type="text/JavaScript" language="JavaScript">
<!--
function checkForm(name,email,phone) {
 if (name == '' || email == '' || phone == '') {
  alert('Please fill in the required fields marked with an asterisk (*).');
 }
}
//-->
</script>
```

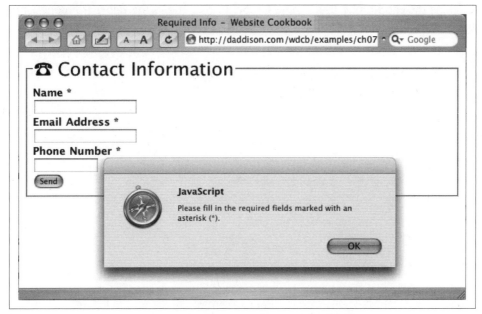

Figure 7-1. A warning message pops up when a user skips a required field

Then call the function using the onClick event handler in the submit button:

```
<input type="Submit" value="Send"
onClick="checkForm(this.form.name.value,this.form.email.value,this.form.phone.
value);return false;"/>
```

See Also

Recipe 7.4 explains how to actually change the user's entered information on the fly.

7.2   Duplicating Form Field Data

Problem

You need to give visitors to your site an easy way to enter the same information twice.

Solution

Use an onClick event handler in a form input, such as a checkbox:

```
<input type="checkbox" name="billingasshipping" value="1"
      onclick="BillingAsShipping(this.form);">
```

Clicking the checkbox runs a simple JavaScript that copies the values from one set of form fields to another set of form fields:

```
<script language="JavaScript">
<!--
function BillingAsShipping (form) {
 form.sfname.value = form.bfname.value;
 form.slname.value = form.blname.value;
 form.saddr.value = form.baddr.value;
 form.scity.value = form.bcity.value;
 form.sstate.value = form.bstate.value;
 form.szip.value = form.bzip.value;
 form.sctry.value = form.bctry.value;
 form.semail.value = form.bemail.value;
return true;
 }
//-->
</script>
```

Discussion

With a simple JavaScript function, you can give your web site visitors an easy way to copy information they have entered in one section of a form to fields in another section. E-commerce sites often offer this as an option so their customers can avoid retyping a shipping address that is the same as their billing address.

Figure 7-2 shows an example of a form that puts this feature into action.

A checkbox immediately under the "Shipping Information" heading offers customers the option of populating the shipping address fields with the same information entered under "Billing Information." The checkbox itself has no intrinsic value as far as the order form is concerned. It merely acts as a trigger for a simple JavaScript activated by the onClick event handler in the checkbox tag.

The BillingAsShipping function takes one argument: the name of the form to process. Since the form in this example does not have a value in its name attribute, the shorthand this.form works. If you assign names to your forms, you may need to tweak the code to get it to work.

In this Recipe, I've distinguished the billing fields from the shipping fields by prepending a "b" or "s" to their names—such as blname and slname for the last names on each address on the order form.

Using a specific naming convention is not required; the function will work regardless of the field names as long as each one is unique.

When the visitor clicks the checkbox, the function replaces the values of all the shipping fields (starting with "s") with the values of analogous fields starting with "b" (the billing fields).

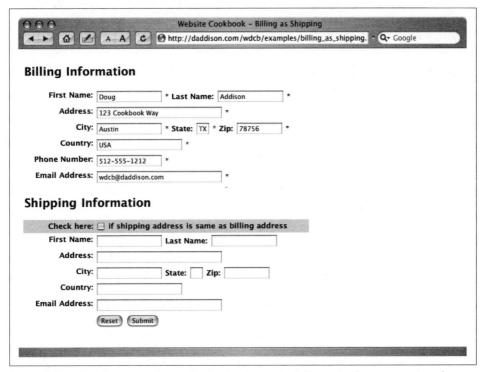

Billing Information

First Name: `Doug` * Last Name: `Addison` *

Address: `123 Cookbook Way` *

City: `Austin` * State: `TX` * Zip: `78756` *

Country: `USA` *

Phone Number: `512-555-1212` *

Email Address: `wdcb@daddison.com` *

Shipping Information

Check here: ☐ if shipping address is same as billing address

First Name: [   ] Last Name: [   ]

Address: [   ]

City: [   ] State: [ ] Zip: [   ]

Country: [   ]

Email Address: [   ]

(Reset) (Submit)

Figure 7-2. A checkbox can activate a JavaScript that copies information from one section of a form to another

7.3 Using Sample Input to Reduce Errors

Problem

You need to give visitors visual cues that illustrate the correct way to fill out a form on your web site.

Solution

You can use specially formatted sample data to demonstrate to visitors exactly what and how you want them to fill in a form. A simple, subtle label beneath a form field guides users as they type their personal information into a form. You also can pre-fill the form fields with a description of what to type in, and then use JavaScript to erase the guide text when users click in the field to begin typing.

The form in Figure 7-3 uses both methods.

First, set up a style for the sample data that appears beneath the form fields. I used the <cite> tag and gave it special properties within this form, which I tagged with a CSS ID named comments.

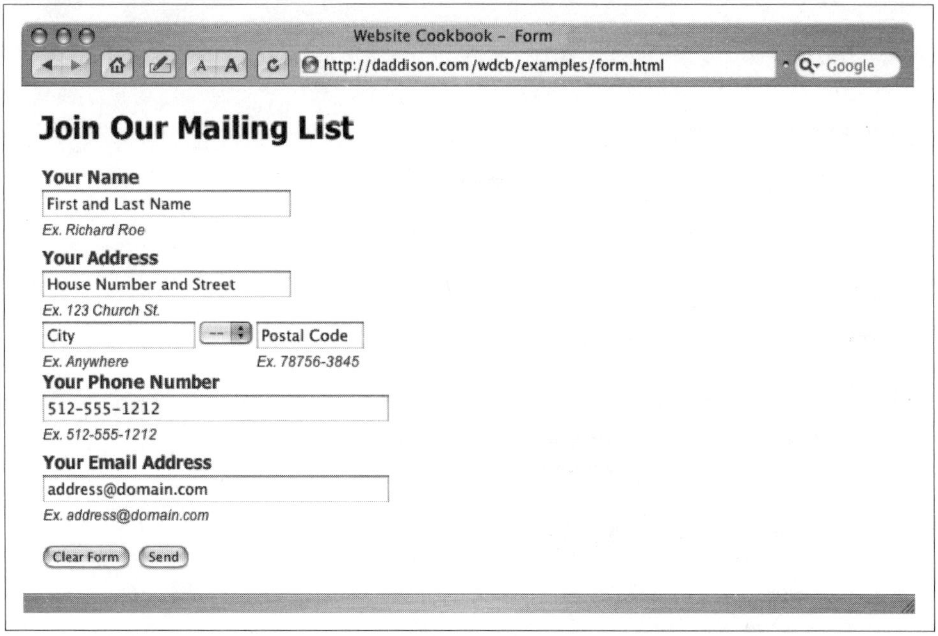

Figure 7-3. A form with sample data guides users through the information they need to enter. The gray italic labels indicate how information such as phone numbers and email addresses should be formatted. The mock data in the actual fields disappears automatically when a respondent clicks in the field

The stylesheet rule looks like this:

```
form#comments cite {
    font-size: 0.9em;
    color: #333333;
}
```

Then just wrap any sample input you want in the `<cite>` tag like this:

```
<cite>Ex. 512-555-1212</cite>
```

This form also uses the JavaScript event handler `onFocus` to wipe out the data already in the field when the visitor begins typing in it. The pre-filled information, such as "First and Last Name" or "House Number and Street," disappears automatically when the users clicks her mouse, or focuses, on the form field. The required JavaScript goes right in the `<input>` tag, like this:

```
<input name="name" type="text" value="First and Last Name" size="25"
    onFocus="if(form.name.value=='First and Last Name')form.name.value='';">
```

The JavaScript includes a condition that keeps the field from self-erasing more than once. The `if` statement checks the value of the name field in the form. If its value is the default value ("First and Last Name"), then the script sets the value to nothing, indicated by the two single quotes near the end of the script. If the user already has typed her name into the field, and then goes back to fix a typo, the script will leave her earlier entry intact as she types in her correction.

The full code for the form looks like this:

```html
<form method="post" action="/cgi-bin/formmail.cgi" id="comments">
 <h2>Your Name</h2>
  <input name="name" type="text" value="First and Last Name" size="25"
   onFocus="if(form.name.value=='First and Last Name')
             form.name.value='';">
  <br>
  <cite>Ex. Richard Roe</cite>
 <h2>Your Address</h2>
  <input name="address" type="text" value="House Number and Street"
       size="25"
   onFocus="if(form.address.value=='House Number and Street')
             form.address.value='';"><br>
  <cite>Ex. 123 Church St.</cite><br>
 <div id="ipt">
  <input name="city" type="text" value="City" size="15"
   onFocus="if(form.city.value=='City')form.city.value='';"><br>
  <cite>Ex. Anywhere</cite>
 </div>
 <div id="ipt">
  <input name="state" type="text" value="" size="2"><br>
  <cite>State/Province</cite>
 </div>
 <div id="ipt">
  <input name="pcode" type="text" value="Postal Code" size="10"
   onFocus="if(form.pcode.value=='Postal Code')form.pcode.value='';"><br>
  <cite>Ex. 78756-3845</cite>
 </div>
 <h2>Your Phone Number</h2>
 <input name="phone" type="text" value="512-555-1212" size="35"
  onFocus="if(form.phone.value=='512-555-1212')form.phone.value='';"><br>
 <cite>Ex. 512-555-1212</cite>
 <h2>Your Email Address</h2>
 <input name="email" type="text" value="address@domain.com" size="35"
  onFocus="if(form.email.value=='address@domain.com')form.email.value='';"><br>
 <cite>Ex. address@domain.com</cite><br><br>
 <input name="Reset" value = "Clear Form " type="reset">
 <input name="Submit" value="Send" type="submit">
</form>
```

 In this and other examples throughout the book, there are extra line feeds inserted for printing. For example, there would be no line feed between onFocus="if(form.address.value=='House Number and Street') and form.address.value='';">
 in your actual HTML.

Bear in mind two caveats when employing the JavaScript method described in this Recipe. First, JavaScript is case-sensitive; fields named email and Email are different animals as far as JavaScript is concerned. When I encounter a misbehaving script, that's the first thing I check. Also, if you're using JavaScript to test for missing form information, a field with a preset value can slip through the script's checking routine even if the user has not entered any meaningful information into it.

Discussion

Regular web surfers encounter dozens of web site forms every year, so every bit of guidance you can give about using yours speeds up their visit to your site. It will save *you* time, too.

The techniques described in this Recipe apply to all sorts of information you may solicit from visitors via your web site, not just simple name and address fields. Every question you can eliminate from a visitor's mind as they fill in your web site form improves the impression they have about the company or organization behind your web site. For example:

- Should I enter the year as two digits or four?
- Should I put spaces or hyphens in my credit card number?
- Should I include the leading zeroes in my account number?

Properly formatted information from a web site cuts down your workload. By reducing (or even eliminating the need) to fix and reformat information you collect from site visitors, you can concentrate on improving other aspects of your site, not on fixing what should have been right the first time.

See Also

Recipe 7.4 for actually modifying the user's data to fit into the correct format for your site.

7.4 Formatting User-Entered Information

Problem

You need to change names, phone numbers, or other data entered through a form to match your preferred format.

Solution

Use PHP functions and/or JavaScript methods to change capitalization on words and clean up and reformat phone numbers before they are recorded for future use.

Here are the relevant PHP methods:

ucfirst( )
> Capitalize the first letter in a string.

ucwords( )
> Capitalize the first letter in every word in a string.

strstr( )
> Get the first occurrence a string.

substr( )
> Get part of a string.

ereg( )
> Find a regular expression search pattern in a string.

ereg_replace( )
> Search and replace function using a regular expression.

Here are similar methods for JavaScript, where *string* is the string variable to operate on:

string.search( )
> Find a regular expression search pattern in a string.

string.replace( )
> Search and replace function using a regular expression.

string.toUpperCase( )
> Capitalize all letters in a string.

string.toLowerCase( )
> Make all letters in a string lowercase.

string.slice( )
> Get part of a string.

string.concat( )
> Join two strings together.

Discussion

Even with properly formatted sample data adjacent to your form fields (see Recipe 7.3), you can't always count on visitors to type in their information the way you want them to. There are the lazy (or aspiring poets) among your site visitors who disdain capitalization—even for their own names. Then there are the non-conformists who put slashes, periods, and who knows what else in their phone and fax numbers. If you want to generate mailing or call lists from information you collect online, you'll save yourself a lot of time later if you clean up the data and store it in a consistent format from the start.

You can combine some built-in JavaScript methods or PHP functions into custom functions that correct some common idiosyncrasies of user-entered information.

Capitalizing names

Use this simple PHP script to capitalize names:

```
<?
function formatName($name) {
 if (ereg("[A-Z]$",$name)) {
  $name = strtolower($name);
 }
 $name = ucwords($name);
return $name;
}
?>
```

This custom PHP function gets one parameter—$name—and first uses the built-in ereg( ) function to check if the user has typed his name in all caps. The search pattern [A-Z] followed by the dollar sign checks the last letter in the name to see if it's capitalized. If the name is all-caps, the built-in function strtolower( ) knocks every letter in the name down to its junior counterpart. Then the function uses the built-in function ucwords( ) to capitalize the first letter.

Writing your own functions gives you the advantage of modifying them as your needs change. For example, this function would convert the last name "o'reilly" into "O'reilly"—close, but no cigar. You can add another conditional to the function that handles these types of last names:

```
<?
function formatName($name) {
 if (ereg("[A-Z]$",$name)) {
  $name = strtolower($name);
 }
 $name = ucwords($name);
 if (strstr($name,"'")) {
   $name_split = split("'",$name);
   $name = $name_split[0]."'";
   $name .= ucfirst($name_split[1]);
  }
return $name;
}
?>
```

Here, the strstr( ) function looks for an apostrophe in the name. If so, it uses the split( ) function to divide the name into an array of two variables at the apostrophe—$name_split[0] and $name_split[1]. Then the last two new lines put $name back together: first, by appending the apostrophe back onto the front half of the name. Then by concatenating (using the .= operator) the existing $name variable with first-letter-capped version of the second half. This will cover the O'Reillys and D'Amicos, among others.

Then there are the McDonalds and McLaughlins. Without another addition to the function they will be recorded as "Mcdonald" and "Mclaughlin"—also not good.

```
<?
function formatName($name) {
 if (ereg("[A-Z]$",$name)) {
  $name = strtolower($name);
 }
 $name = ucwords($name);
if (strstr($name,"'")) {
   $name_split = split("'",$name);
   $name = $name_split[0]."'";
   $name .= ucfirst($name_split[1]);
  }
if (ereg("^Mc",$name)) {
   $name = "Mc".ucfirst(substr($name,2));
  }
return $name;
}
?>
```

An if statement that looks for "Mc" at the beginning of the name—the ^ character instructs ereg( ) to search from the beginning—allows the function to capitalize the rest of the name that follows when the condition is met. You can use this function as a base to expand its capabilities to other types of name spellings as the need arises.

You also can use JavaScript to perform similar name manipulation. JavaScript's string-handling capabilities are more limited than PHP's, but the changes get made before the user submits the form, saving a bit of processing resources on the web server:

```
<script type="text/JavaScript" language="JavaScript">
<!-- Begin
function formatName(field) {
if (name.search(/[A-Z]$/)) {
  name = name.toLowerCase();
 }
var name = field.value;
var firstltr = name.slice(0,1);
var remainder = name.slice(1);
firstltr = firstltr.toUpperCase();
var newvalue = firstltr.concat(remainder);
field.value = newvalue;
}
</script>
```

The formatName function takes one parameter called field, the name of the form field to be processed. The first three lines check for users who entered their names in all caps, and, if so, convert the string to all lowercase letters. Then three variables are defined: the value of the form field (var name), the first letter of the form field value (var firstltr), and the rest of the form field value (var remainder). JavaScript has two case-changing methods—toLowerCase and toUpperCase—that, as their names imply, are all-or-nothing actions. There are no methods for capping first letters in strings or first letters in words in strings as in PHP. That limitation complicates JavaScript's ability to handle two word last names and last names with more than one capital letter, as we were able to do with PHP. Adding those abilities to this function is left to the reader.

The function should be called from the input field to be processed using the onChange event handler:

```
<input name="fname" type="text" value="" size="10" maxlength="10"
       onChange="formatName(this.form.fname);">
```

Fixing phone numbers

This custom PHP function takes the oddly formatted phone number a visitor might throw at your server and turns it into a plain old telephone number:

```
<?
function formatPhone($phone) {
  $phone = ereg_replace("([[:punct:]])|([[:space:]])","",$phone);
  $phone = ereg_replace("^1","",$phone);
  $phone = substr($phone,0,3)."-".substr($phone,3,3)."-".substr($phone,6,4);
  return $phone;
}
?>
```

For this function and its JavaScript counterpart, I'm assuming a North American 3-3-4 phone number format. See Recipe 7.11 for more information.

The function formatPhone( ) gets one parameter, the phone number to be converted. On the first line. the ereg_replace( ) function gets two shorthand search patterns—[[:punct:]] and [[:space:]]—that remove all the punctuation and spaces in the number. The second line simply removes an extraneous "1" from the beginning of the number. Then the third line rebuilds the phone number to insert hyphens between the area code, exchange, and the rest of the number.

If you'd rather have straight 10-digit phone numbers, you can leave this line out.

JavaScript matches up better with PHP for phone number reformatting than it did for name reformatting. This function, like its name reformatting counterpart, can be called from the field to be processed using the onChange event handler:

```
<script type="text/JavaScript" language="JavaScript">
<!-- Begin
function formatPhone(field) {
var number = field.value;
```

```
number = number.replace(/(\s+)/g,"");
number = number.replace(/(\))/g,"");
number = number.replace(/(\()/g,"");
number = number.replace(/(\.)/g,"");
number = number.replace(/(\/)/g,"");
number = number.slice(0,3)+'-'+number.slice(3,6)+'-'+number.slice(6,10);
field.value = number;
}
// End -->
</script>
```

The formatPhone function gets the name of the field as a parameter and creates a variable (number) for the field value. Then, it uses the *string*.replace method several times to remove spaces and unwanted punctuation from the number. Finally, the *string*.slice method reformats the phone number the way you want it, with hyphens.

See Also

Recipe 7.3 shows how to add sample input to a form to help your users get formatting right on their own. Recipe 7.1 ensures that fields aren't left blank (making these forms pretty useless).

7.5   Generating Form Menu Choices from a Database

Problem

You want to create dynamic form menus from values stored in a database.

Solution

Create a PHP function that compiles all the values in a database table into a select menu that can be placed in a form. Then call the function as needed in various places on your web site:

```
<? echo makeSelectList(dbTable, dbFieldValue, dbFieldDisplay, menuField);  ?>
```

Discussion

The ability to grow painlessly is one of the most important qualities of a successful web site. If you have one or more forms on your site that require visitors to make choices from a large and ever-changing menu of options, then you may be able to save a lot of time by storing the menu choices in a database and using a PHP function to generate forms menus from records in that database.

This Recipe makes a couple of assumptions. Since it uses PHP scripting to manipulate the text, you'll need some familiarity with the use of variables and functions in that language. Also, you'll need to have access to an SQL database and some familiarity with creating queries for it.

For the function to work properly, you'll need to have an active connection to your web database. A basic connection to a MySQL database with PHP looks like this:

```
$dbName = "mydatabase";

$dbConnection = mysql_connect("dbhost","dbuser", "dbpassword")
  or die("Couldn't Connect.");

$db = mysql_select_db($dbName, $dbConnection)
  or die("Couldn't select database.");
```

 I recommend saving these three lines in an include file outside your web site's root directory, and then including it on any page where you'll need to use the makeSelectList function.

Now, on to the function itself. First, list the parameters that can be sent to the function; in this example, there are seven:

```
function makeSelectList(  $dbTable,
                          $dbFieldValue,
                          $dbFieldDisplay = "",
                          $menuField,
                          $idSelected = "--",
                          $size = 1,
                          $defaultText = "--")
   {
```

The first four define the table name, two fields, and the name of the HTML form element. The other three have default values in the function and are optional when the function is called from a web page. They will let you preset a selected value and default display text for the select menu that gets created, and convert the select menu to a select list by increasing size to something greater than 1.

Next, set up the variable that will become the HTML code product of the function ($menu) and the database query:

```
$menu = "";
    $query = "SELECT $dbFieldValue, $dbFieldDisplay " .
             "FROM $dbTable ORDER BY $dbFieldDisplay";
    $resultResource = mysql_query($query);
```

The bulk of the function is embedded in an if statement that tests for the existence of a result to the database query ($resultResource):

```
if ($resultResource)
   {
     $resultRows = mysql_num_rows($resultResource);
     $menu .= "<select name=\"$menuField\" size=\"$size\">\n";
```

Inside the conditional, the function gets a variable for the number of records found with the query ($resultRows) and begins to create the select menu stored in $menu.

```
if ($idSelected == "--")
   {
    $menu .= "<option value=\"--\" label=\"--\" " .
             "selected>$defaultText</option>\n";
   }
```

Then, if the function hasn't been given a new value for $idSelected, a first option is added to $menu with the default values. Next, the function adds options for each found record:

```
for ($rowIndex=0; $rowIndex<$resultRows; $rowIndex++)
 {
  $id = mysql_result($resultResource, $rowIndex, 0);
  $name = mysql_result($resultResource, $rowIndex, 1);
  if ($idSelected == $id)
     $menu .= "<option value=\"$id\" label=\"$name\" " .
              "selected>$name</option>\n";
  else
     $menu .= "<option value=\"$id\" label=\"$name\">" .
              "$name</option>\n";
 }
```

The for loop goes through each record in the found set and assigns values to two variables ($id and $name) for the two fields requested with the query. In the middle of the loop, the function checks the $id variable against the value of $idSelected. If they match, then that option in the menu will be selected.

Finally, the function closes the select menu, clears the query results from PHP's memory, and returns the HTML code stored in $menu:

```
$menu .= "</select>\n";
    mysql_free_result($resultResource);
   }
 return $menu;
}
```

Table 7-1 shows the rows, or records, in a hypothetical database table of favorite colors. I'll call this table *favcolors* in the examples that follow.

Table 7-1. This table lists the sample data to be displayed as a select menu

colorID	colorName
1	Red
2	Orange
3	Yellow
4	Green
5	Blue
6	Purple

Table 7-1. This table lists the sample data to be displayed as a select menu (continued)

colorID	colorName
7	Black
8	White
9	Pink
10	Brown

A typical function call might look like this:

```
<? echo makeSelectList(favcolors, colorID, colorName, favcolor, "--", 1, "Select your
favorite color") ?>
```

and the resulting code, like this:

```
<select name="favcolor" size="1">
 <option value="--" label="--" selected>Select your favorite color</option>
 <option value="1" label="Red">Red</option>
 <option value="2" label="Orange">Orange</option>
 <option value="3" label="Yellow">Yellow</option>
 <option value="4" label="Green">Green</option>
 <option value="5" label="Blue">Blue</option>
 <option value="6" label="Purple">Purple</option>
 <option value="7" label="Black">Black</option>
 <option value="8" label="White">White</option>
 <option value="9" label="Pink">Pink</option>
 <option value="10" label="Brown">Brown</option>
</select>
```

To create a list of values—rather than a menu—with one option already selected, use this function call, which leaves off the last argument for $defaultText:

```
<? echo makeSelectList(favcolors, colorID, colorName, favcolor, 7, 10) ?>
```

The results are shown in Figure 7-4.

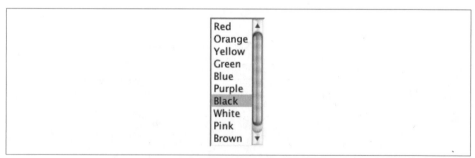

Figure 7-4. A select list generated from values in a database table

The complete PHP function looks like this:

```
function makeSelectList( $dbTable,
                         $dbFieldValue,
                         $dbFieldDisplay = "",
                         $menuField,
                         $idSelected = "--",
                         $size = 1,
                         $defaultText = "--")
{
$menu = "";
    $query = "SELECT $dbFieldValue, $dbFieldDisplay " .
            "FROM $dbTable ORDER BY $dbFieldDisplay";
    $resultResource = mysql_query($query);
if ($resultResource)
    {
      $resultRows = mysql_num_rows($resultResource);
      $menu .= "<select name=\"$menuField\" size=\"$size\">\n";
      if ($idSelected == "--")
          {
          $menu .= "<option value=\"--\" label=\"--\" " .
                  "selected>$defaultText</option>\n";
          }
      for ($rowIndex=0; $rowIndex<$resultRows; $rowIndex++)
      {
        $id = mysql_result($resultResource, $rowIndex, 0);
        $name = mysql_result($resultResource, $rowIndex, 1);
        if ($idSelected == $id)
          $menu .= "<option value=\"$id\" label=\"$name\" " .
                  "selected>$name</option>\n";
        else
          $menu .= "<option value=\"$id\" label=\"$name\">" .
                  "$name</option>\n";
      }
$menu .= "</select>\n";
      mysql_free_result($resultResource);
      }
  return $menu;
}
```

7.6   Storing Multiple Values in One Database Field

Problem

You need to store multiple answers from one form question in a single database field.

Solution

Set up your multi-input form fields to pass their values as an array by adding opening and closing bracket characters to the field name, like this:

```
<input type="checkbox" name="favcolors[]" value="Red">Red
```

Then use PHP's built-in implode( ) function to convert the array to a string separated by a unique character before storing the string in a single database field. In this Recipe, I'll use the pipe character (|) to separate unique values in the array-turned-string:

```
$favcolors_imp = implode("|",$favcolors);
```

Then you can insert the string $favcolors_imp into a text or varchar field in your SQL database.

If you need to convert the string back to an array, use the PHP explode function:

```
$favcolors_exp = explode("|",$favcolors_imp);
```

Discussion

HTML provides two form elements that allow users to select multiple choices: the checklist created with the input type="checkbox" tag shown above, and the multi-option select list created with this code:

```
<select name="favcolors[]" size="10" multiple>
 <option value="Green" label=" Green ">Green</option>
 <option value="Black" label=" Black ">Black</option>
 <option value="Brown" label="Brown">Brown</option>
</select>
```

The rendered versions of each type of list are shown in Figure 7-5.

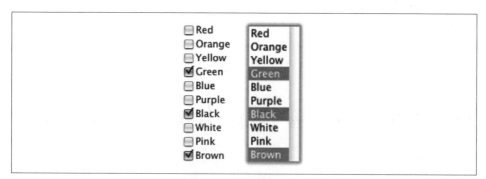

Figure 7-5. What's your favorite color? Checkboxes and multi-option select lists both let users choose more than one answer to a form question

The array-to-string-to-array process works with both types of form elements provided the value of the name attribute has [ ] at the end. Without the brackets, only the last value selected in the form ("Brown" in Figure 7-5) gets assigned to the

$favcolors variable that PHP creates from the POST or GET arguments sent to it from the form. When the array gets imploded into a pipe-delimited string, then all three values can be stored in the database, as Green|Black|Brown.

Wasted Space

You could take an alternative approach to this Recipe and create individual fields in your database for each possible answer, and then store a value of "1" (or "yes") in each one that the respondent selects on the form. In the example shown in Figure 7-5, the field-value pairs of the SQL insert query would look, in part, like this: green=1, black=1, brown=1.

This method has two downsides: first, it will only work with checklists, since each checkbox's <input> tag can have a unique field name, while the response options in a select list share a common field name defined in the <select> tag. Also, it can lead to an unnecessarily large database, as each new answer choice creates the need for a new field in the database. Storing multiple-choice form responses as a delimited string scales easily as your web site form questions and answers change and grow.

Finally, a note about searching for a single value in database fields containing multiple values—which at first glance might seem more complicated than individual values each stored in their own field. Fortunately, SQL provides some syntax for combining searches to find unique matches:

```
SELECT * FROM my_table
  WHERE (favcolor LIKE '%Brown|%' OR favcolor LIKE '%|Brown'
              OR favcolor='Brown')
```

In this query, the search conditions enclosed in parentheses starting after WHERE show three possible permutations of the favorite color "Brown" stored in a field with other favorite color choices or by itself. Combining the LIKE operator with the wildcard percent sign (%) matches "Brown" at the beginning, middle, or end of a string of multiple favorite color choices, while favcolor='Brown' matches records for form respondents who chose "Brown" as their only favorite color.

7.7   Using a Graphical Character String for Form Authentication

Problem

You need to make sure that bots or automated scripts are not able to abuse your web site's resources.

Solution

Distorted strings of random letters and numbers over an obscuring background of gradients, speckles, and lines (see Figure 7-6) have become an increasingly popular way to ensure that the user of a web form or other server resource is a human, rather than another computer. They even have their own acronym—*Captcha*—which stands for "completely automated public Turing test to tell computers and humans apart."

Figure 7-6. Hotmail uses a Captcha on its sign-up page to prevent spammers from signing up for throw-away email accounts

 In the early days of modern computing. Alan Turing proposed a method for testing a computer's skill at mimicking a human. You can add a human-readable graphical character string that must be retyped correctly for a form submission to be accepted using one of many Captcha generators and validators that are available for a variety of programming languages (refer to the "See Also" section in this Recipe for links to some of them).

You can sign up for a hosted Captcha service (free for non-commercial use) at *http://captchas.net* by emailing the developer to request a username. You'll receive a confirmation, a secret key, and a link to code samples for implementing the service with PHP (*http://captchas.net/sample/php/*). When I signed up, I waited only a day for my information.

Download *CaptchasDotNet.php* and you're ready to go. As an example, this solution creates two files—a form for posting a hypothetical blog comment and a script for processing the comment—based on the provided samples at Captchas.net. At the top of your form page, add these lines:

```
<?
include("CaptchasDotNet.php");
$captchas = new CaptchasDotNet('...my user name...', '...my secret key...');
$random = $captchas->random();
$url = $captchas->url();
?>
```

The first line loads all the custom functions for the Captchas.net service, and the next three lines define variables using some of those functions. The variable $captchas is based on the username and secret key I received from the developer.

The Captchas.net service creates the image and matching text value by concatenating my secret key with the value of $random, and then applying some of PHP's built-in cryptographic functions. The result is a six-character string of lowercase letters.

Your form can contain any fields you want, but it must pass the value that users type in to the text field ($typedpassword) and the value for $random as a hidden form input, like this:

```
<input type="text" name="typedpassword" size="6" maxlength="6" value="">
<input type="hidden" name="random" value="<?= $random; ?>">
```

The value of $url is the unique path to the Captcha image created and stored on the Captchas.net server. I displayed this on my form (see Figure 7-7) with the following code:

```
<img src="<?= $url; ?>" alt="Confirmation password is loading..." width="240"
height="80">
```

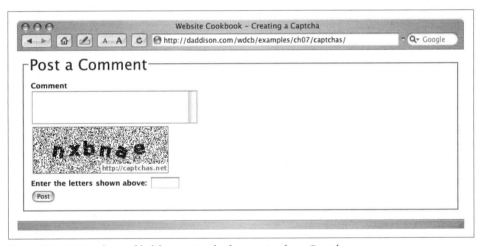

Figure 7-7. A Captcha-enabled form using the free service from Captchas.net

The script that receives the form submission also starts with a reference to the custom functions and defines the variable $captchas using your username and secret key:

```
include("CaptchasDotNet.php");
$captchas = new CaptchasDotNet('...my user name...', '...my secret key...');
```

Then the script uses a conditional to validate the $random variable and verify $typedpassword:

```
<?
if(!$captchas->validate($random))
{
```

```
   print"A Captcha can only be used once. The current Captcha has already been used.
   Try again.";
   }
   elseif (!$captchas->verify($typedpassword)) {
    print"<p><b>The password you entered is not correct. Blog posting is for humans
   only.</b><br>\n";
   } else {
    print"<h3>Thank you for submitting your comment</h3>\n";
    ...other comment-processing code...
   }
   ?>
```

The first condition—!$captchas->validate($random)—prevents the $random variable from being used more than once. The second condition tests the text the user entered into the form against the text value of the image stored on the Captchas.net server. If the text doesn't match the value from the server, the conditional prints an error message on the page. If the random variable is valid and the password the user typed matches the image value, then the user gets a confirmation that the comment has been accepted and the script processes the comment.

Discussion

Why would a computer want to use a web site? To sign up for a free email account to send spam, of course! Or to post advertisements for cheap Viagra and low mortgage rates in a blog comment. Or to influence the results of an online poll or sweepstakes.

The computers doing the dirty work aren't the evil spammers and prankish ballot box stuffers—their human creators are. But humans have to eat and sleep, and their wrists and eyes get tired after a long day of filling out the same Hotmail new account form over and over again. Automated programs can do the work a lot faster.

Enter Captchas, which first appeared on sign-up forms for free email accounts and have since been adopted by spam-blocking services and others (see Figures 7-8 and 7-9. As inline GIFs, JPGs, or PNGs, the characters in a Captcha can be read and typed into a verification field more easily by a human than by a computer.

 The common practice of describing an image in its alt attribute would defeat the purpose of the Captcha.

They also can't be read or used by blind and visually impaired visitors, or by the screen reading software they use to surf the web. For this reason, Captchas have been criticized by web site accessibility advocates. An *audio* Captcha provides a solution to the problem, but just a minority of the Captcha-protected sites (and software mentioned in the See Also section of this Recipe) offer this alternative.

Finally, Captchas are not impenetrable to computer-assisted "evil doers." As we saw in Recipe 5.5, devious web surfers intent on exploiting something on your site will

---

Figure 7-8. Spam Arrest challenges unknown email senders to enter the word shown in a Captcha before it will approve delivery of the message

Figure 7-9. A Captcha image from captcha.net

try to find a way to do so. Spammers can (and have) already found ways to circumvent Captchas, yet they remain a viable tool for preserving online resources for legitimate uses. Consider this and the known accessibility issues when implementing Captchas on your site.

See Also

The Captcha Project web site (*http://www.captcha.net*) describes the origins the nowubiquitous glyphs. Captcha generators and validators are available for a variety of programming languages, including Java (Jcaptcha, *http://jcaptcha.sourceforge.net/main.html*), PHP (Gotcha!, *http://phpbtree.com/captcha/index.php*), and Perl (Authen::Captcha, *http://search.cpan.org/dist/Authen-Captcha*). You also can sign up for a hosted Captcha service (free for non-commercial use) at *http://captchas.net*. The

Wikipedia entry about Captchas has links to other software and information about how some Captchas have been defeated— *http://en.wikipedia.org/wiki/Captcha*.

7.8 Putting Additional Information in mailto Links

Problem

You need to pre-format an email message generated from a link on your web site.

Solution

Extend the `mailto` link to include values for the message subject, body, and additional recipients.

A basic `mailto` link on a web page creates a new email message in the user's default email application. It's a good idea to make the actual address the link, because that helps reinforce for the user what happens when she selects the link:

```
<a href="mailto:address@domain.com">address@domain.com</a>
```

You can create more complex links that fill in parts of the message. With `Subject` and `Body`, you can ensure at least some meaningful content in the email messages you receive from your site:

```
<a href="mailto:address@domain.com?Subject=
    web site%20comment&Body=Type%20your%20message%20here:">
    address@domain.com</a>
```

 The characters %20 indicate a space in the encoded URL, though most browsers can handle an unencoded space.

You also can add additional recipients in the `To:`, `Cc:`, and `Bcc:` headers of the message by separating their addresses with commas:

```
<a href="mailto:address@domain.com,another@domain.com&
    Cc:afriend@domain.com&Bcc:someone@domain.com">address@domain.com</a>
```

Discussion

Unprotected email addresses in web page code are like blood in the water for spam sharks. If you must use linked email addresses on your site (rather than an email form that hides actual addresses), be sure to read Recipe 9.11 for more information. Most of the protection techniques described in that Recipe will still allow you to add the additional information to your email links described in this Recipe. On the positive side, however, pre-formatting prevents email messages from your web site from being rejected as spam before they get to you. A preset email subject line can help spam filters recognize a message sent from your web site as legitimate.

See Also

Recipe 9.11 will help you use these techniques and still keep a clean inbox.

7.9   Send Visitor Messages to Your Mobile Phone

Problem

You need to receive urgent messages from your web site on your mobile phone.

Solution

Create a simple email form that, combined with a JavaScript character counter, sends SMS messages from your web site to your mobile phone.

Discussion

Short Message Service (SMS) allows mobile phone users on nearly all major carriers to send and receive short alphanumeric messages. Also called *texting*, the practice is wildly popular in Europe and Asia and with younger cell phone users in the United States. Originally created for the GSM cell networks of Europe in the early 1990s, SMS traffic has grown from 250 billion messages sent in 2000 to more than 500 billion sent in 2004.

The SMS protocol can communicate with external systems, including email, which means that you can set up an emergency contact form on your web site that your customers, patients, or even boss can use to quickly send you important messages. Figure 7-10 shows a form I created to send SMS messages to my cell phone. Like other cell phone accounts, mine has an email address associated with it, which is my ten-digit mobile number @mobile.mycingular.com. My account also has a 160-character limit on SMS messages, so I've added some JavaScript to count characters as the visitor types his message, as well as a warning message that appears when the message is over the limit.

The JavaScript function smsLimiter takes three parameters: the name of the textarea field where the SMS message will be typed, the name of a read-only input field that counts down the number of characters remaining, and the maximum number of characters allowed in the message field:

```
function smsLimiter(message,counter,max)
{
    var strTemp = "";
    var strCharCounter = 0;
    for (var i = 0; i < message.value.length; i++)
    {
        var strChar = message.value.substring(i, i + 1);
        if (strChar == '\n')
        {
```

```
            strTemp += strChar;
            strCharCounter = 1;
        }
        else
        {
            strTemp += strChar;
            strCharCounter ++;
        }
    }
    counter.value = max - strTemp.length;
}
```

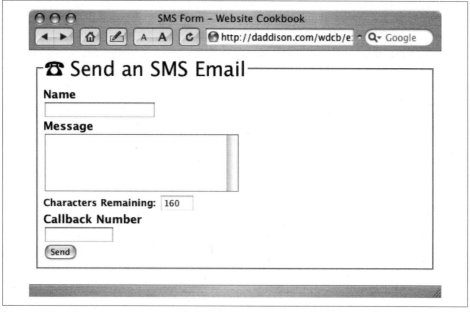

Figure 7-10. A form that generates an SMS message counts down the character limit as the sender types to prevent the message from exceeding the limits of the recipient's mobile phone plan

The code for the form looks like this:

```
<form action="sms.php" method="post">
<fieldset>
<legend>&#x260E; Send an SMS Email</legend>
  <h3>Name</h3>
    <input name="name" type="text" value="" size="20" maxlength="20">
  <h3>Message</h3>
    <textarea name="smsmsg" cols="35" rows="6"
onKeyUp="smsLimiter(this.form.smsmsg,this.form.remaining,160);"></textarea>
    <p><strong>Characters Remaining:</strong> <input name="remaining" type="text"
value="160" size="5" maxlength="5" readonly></p>
    <input name="remLines" type="hidden" value="10"/>
  <h3>Callback Number</h3>
    <input name="callback" type="text" value="" size="12" maxlength="12"><br/>
    <input name="Send" type="Submit" value="Send" onClick = "if
```

```
(this.form.remaining.value < '0'){alert('Your message is too long. Please make it
shorter.');return false;};"/><input name="f" type="hidden" value="send">
</fieldset>
</form>
```

 I used PHP's built-in email( ) function to send the message, but any
CGI capable of sending an email, such as formmail, will work.

The elements in the form have special attributes that work with the JavaScript function to keep messages under my carrier's SMS limit. The onKeyUp event handler calls
the smsLimiter function from the textarea element. The input element named
remaining counts down the characters remaining from an initial value of 160 (see
Figure 7-11). Because this form field is read-only, the user cannot change its value.

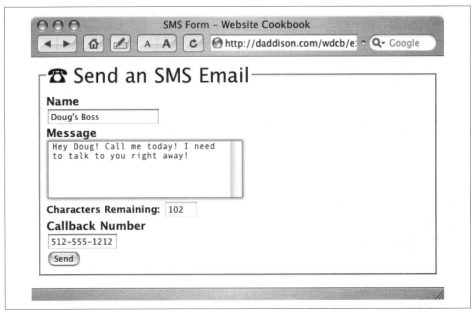

Figure 7-11. The Characters Remaining field counts down as the message is typed into the field
above it

If the message exceeds the limit, the onClick event handler in the code for the form's
submit button displays a warning message (see Figure 7-12). The message can't be
sent until the character limit is less than 160.

See Also

Wikipedia has an excellent entry about SMS at *http://en.wikipedia.org/wiki/Short_
message_service*. For a concise list of email address and message lengths for various
mobile phone plans in the United States and Canada, see *http://freesms.1888usa.com*.

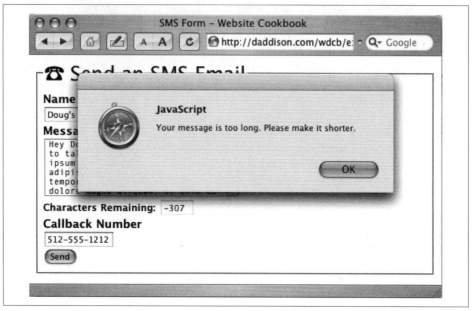

Figure 7-12. A message too long for my mobile service to handle prompts a warning message

7.10   Using Cookies to Remember Visitor Choices

Problem

You need to store small bits of information about your web site visitors' preferences and retrieve them on their subsequent visits to your site.

Solution

Record the settings as a cookie on a visitor's hard drive using the built-in PHP function setcookie( ), and then access it with PHP's built-in array of cookie variables associated with the current browser session, $_COOKIE.

Discussion

Browser cookies are an oft-debated *and* indispensable part of the Web. Privacy advocates rightfully point out that abuse can allow unscrupulous web sites to know much of the personal information and browsing habits of their visitors without their permission. But most of the world's most popular web sites—from Amazon.com to Yahoo!—would operate much differently without cookies. Whenever a site remembers your login information, or your name and address, it's using cookies to do so.

Cookies are small individual files, or indexed entries in one larger file, that store—on the visitor's own hard drive—a bit of information about a particular user for a particular web site. They typically have a name, the data to be stored, the host name of the site that controls the cookie, the file path on the host where the cookie is valid, and an expiration date. Cookies are exclusive to a specific browser on a specific computer. For example, if you have an account with the *New York Times* web site, you'll need a cookie on both your home and work computer to bypass the login screen and browse the site.

Your site might never have a need to record complex visitor preferences in a cookie. But even a simple use of a cookie can be a valuable way to tailor your visitors' experience with your site, such as choosing a language or plug-in preference. In this basic example, I'll explain how to set a cookie to remember a visitor preference using a choice screen. On our hypothetical home page (see Figure 7-13), a visitor must declare his relationship to the web site ("wholesaler" or "retailer") before proceeding to the site.

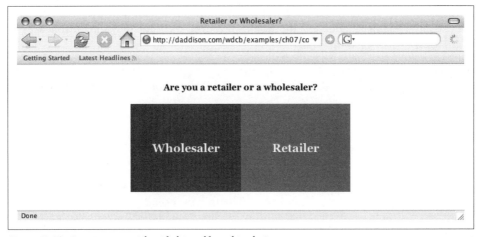

Figure 7-13. A visitor must identify himself on this choice page

The code for the page in Figure 7-13 uses a conditional statement to check for a cookie:

```
<?
 if (isset($_COOKIE["home"])) {
  header("Location: http://daddison.com/wscb/examples/ch07/cookies/php/".$_
COOKIE["home"]);
 } else {
?>
<!DOCTYPE HTML PUBLIC "-//W3C//DTD HTML 4.01 Transitional//EN"
"http://www.w3.org/TR/html4/loose.dtd">
<html>
<head>
```

```
    <meta http-equiv="Content-Type" content="text/html; charset=iso-8859-1">
    <title>Retailer or Wholesaler?</title>
    </head>
    <body>
    <table width="50%" height="300" align="center" cellpadding="0"  cellspacing="0">
      <tr align="center" valign="middle">
        <td colspan="2"><h3>Are you a retailer or a wholesaler?</h3></td>
      </tr>
      <tr align="center" valign="middle">
        <td width="50%" bgcolor="#0000FF"><a href="who.home.php">Wholesaler</a> </td>
        <td bgcolor="#FF0000"><p><a href="ret.home.php">Retailer</a></p>
        </td>
      </tr>
    </table>
    </body>
    </html>
    <? } ?>
```

At the top of the code, before any of the visible part of the page is sent to the browser, the condition isset($_COOKIE["home"]) checks for the presence of a cookie named *home*. If the variable has a value, which in this example will be the filename of a wholesaler- or retailer-specific home page, the built-in PHP function header( ) redirects the browser to that page.

On the retailer (*ret.home.php*) and wholesaler (*who.home.php*) home pages, two lines of PHP code define the expiration date and set the cookie when the chosen page loads:

```
<?
$expiry = time( )+60*60*24*365;
setcookie("home","ret.home.php",$expiry);
?>
```

The code defines the $expiry variable as one year from the current time and the setcookie( ) function records the cookie. The function sends three parameters to the browser: the cookie name (*home*), the value (*ret.home.php* or *who.home.php*), and the expiration date. The setcookie( ) function also can record optional information about the path, domain, and connection type for which the cookie applies. Since those values were left blank in this use of the function, Figure 7-14 shows them set to their default values.

See Also

For more about PHP's cookie-handling functions, see *http://us2.php.net/manual/en/ reserved.variables.php#reserved.variables.cookies and http://us2.php.net/manual/en/ function.setcookie.php.*

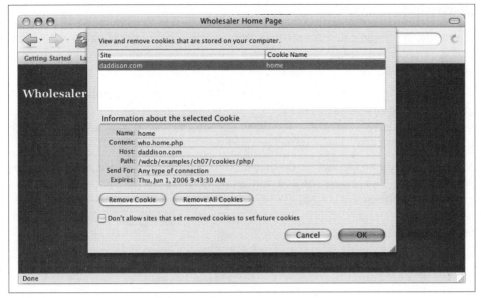

Figure 7-14. Information recorded as a cookie

7.11   Internationalizing Your Web Site

Problem

You need to make your site usable by a worldwide audience.

Solution

Internationalization is not the same as localization. Internationalized web sites strive to meet a wide range of users through a single version of the site. Localized sites offer a complete (or nearly complete) translation of every page on the site into all the languages spoken by frequent visitors to the site.

Here are some steps you can take to improve your web site's utility with a wide range of users through internationalization:

- Know your audience
- Use international time and date formats
- Design forms to accommodate non-U.S. addresses
- Avoid culturally specific icons and language
- Translate critical information
- Test or review

Discussion

Given that more than half the world's web surfers speak a non-English native language, international users likely make up a notable component of your web site's viewers.

A good web site statistics package should be able to give you some information about where your web site visitors live (see Recipe 9.9). After you've reviewed your site statistics, make a list of the top 10 or 15 countries from which you get hits to your site to guide your internationalization efforts.

Taking a global perspective is the key to successful internationalization. Perhaps you've seen the Australia-centric world maps with the South Pole at the top and most of the world in the bottom, northern half. A whimsical map is good for a laugh, but a web site operated with a narrow-minded view of who it's for will confuse visitors or turn them away.

For example, simple things like date notation mean different things to different people. In the United States, 6/1/2005 represents the first day of June, but much of the world would read it as January 6th. Whether it's a modification date on a web page or a timestamp in a list of articles or site postings, spell out the month in the date, either as "1 June 2005" or "June 1, 2005."

The same holds true with timezones; few of your non-U.S. site visitors will know what "noon ET" or "4 CDT" means. For live or real-time events such as online sales or webcasts, state the start time as two or three "local" times, such as "The webcast will begin at 9 p.m. on June 1st Austin time (3 a.m. the following day in London)."

On forms, inadequate character lengths, formatting requirements and blank field warnings can stymie non-U.S. respondents trying to join your mailing list or order one of your products. Although name, street address, and city are common to just about everyone's contact information, regional divisions, phone numbers, and postal code information varies widely.

 Use "postal code" rather than "Zip Code," since the latter is specific to U.S. addresses.

You should offer a select menu of state/province listings for your primary (North American) audience, as well as a fill-in-the-blank field for others to enter their county, prefecture, or territory, as the case may be. Make sure you specify enough space in a text field for names and addresses. Many names and addresses—particularly German, Arabic, and Latin American—are longer than their North American counterparts. A text input field can have attributes for both the amount of character space displayed in the form and the total number of characters that can be entered into the field, like this:

```
<input type=" text" name="address" size="30" maxlength="50" value="">
```

Also, be careful when using form validation schemes that expect 10-digit phone numbers and five-digit postal codes, as those bits of information may be longer or shorter in addresses outside North America. Use a select list for countries, too, that either defaults to the most frequently selected country or lists the most common choices at the top, rather than listing them alphabetically. If you do not ship to or do business with people in certain countries, make a note of it on the form.

Using icons can spell trouble for web sites geared toward a broad international audience. Because cultural interpretations can vary widely, avoid using icons that portray religious symbols, gestures, or sports analogies. Even the meaning of seemingly everyday objects such as mailboxes, shopping carts, stop lights, and telephones can get lost in translation. Best bet for icons: use them sparingly and with an adjacent text label when you do.

Translating your entire site into one or more languages can be costly and time-consuming to do and maintain. But offering multilingual versions of a few key pages—such as shipping policies or an About page—can be a hospitable addition. Be sure to see Recipe 4.2 for guidance on adding text to pages that's written in a language other than your site's main language.

Finally, take the time to check your work for the audiences you're trying to reach, either through site testing with a small group of users, or by enlisting the help of a usability consultant who can evaluate your site's effectiveness with a worldwide audience.

See Also

Recipe 4.2 will help you in displaying some of your pages in a foreign language.

7.12   Creating an Email Newsletter

Problem

You want to communicate with your web site visitors by email.

Solution

Email newsletters are a popular way to stay in touch with your most loyal web site visitors and give them reasons to come back to your site on a regular basis. In the already debate-prone world of web design, the subject of email newsletters—and especially HTML email newsletters—generates a tremendous amount of heated discussion about everything from coding techniques to the wisdom of creating and sending one in the first place.

Here's a checklist to consider before doing one of your own:

Choice

If your mailing list software allows you to do so, let your subscribers choose either plain-text format or HTML. Or send a combined "multipart/alternative" message that includes both the plain and fancy versions in one message. Personally, I prefer the latter method because it means one less thing for you and your subscribers to keep track of in the ongoing life of your email newsletter.

Design

Use a simple, table-based layout without any fancy CSS, JavaScript, or embedded Flash movies.

Content

Keep your messages short—four to six headlines and one or two other promo items or messages. Always give subscribers an easy way to unsubscribe and send you feedback.

Testing

Email clients and their particular rendering capabilities are much more varied than web browsers. Know your audience, their technology capabilities, and test your message format early and often.

Discussion

Sending an email newsletter is one web design task in which you cannot test and double-check your work enough. If you notice a stupid mistake on a web page, you can easily fix it before thousands of people see it. Not so with email newsletters. Not only are the mistakes easier to make, but many, many more people see them at the same time—including the boss. Proceed with caution.

That said, email newsletters—especially HTML emails—are a powerful marketing tool when done correctly. The combination of varied text sizes, colors, and images makes HTML email much easier to scan than plain text emails. The click-through rates for HTML email are higher—maybe twice as high as text email—and, all in all, they're a great way to extend and strengthen your web site's brand. Not all email clients can view HTML email, but depending on whom you ask, about three-quarters of Internet users have an email application that can.

Many people have compelling reasons to reject HTML email. They may connect to the Internet using America Online, whose software, until recently, did not handle HTML email very well. Or they use an old email client that can't—and never will—be able to view HTML email. Or they might read email offline, so they resent that embedded images in HTML email require them to reconnect to get the message's full effect. Some think all HTML email is spam, or that signing up for an email newsletter will result in more spam. Others resent being tracked by "spy GIFs" embedded in the message. A tracking image looks like a regular `img` tag, but its `src` attribute contains a URL to a script that records the user's receipt of the message. Most recent versions of popular email clients, however, let users open messages without viewing embedded graphics. But when the tracking image gets loaded, the sender will know.

 Feel free to use legitimate images and graphics to enhance your design, but don't rely on them to get your message across. Recipients who open your email and see nothing but unloaded images are likely to delete it without giving it a second thought.

There are some generally accepted coding and design tips, while others, which tend to contradict each other, will require you to make a choice based on personal preference and testing.

First, code your HTML email by hand, if you can.

Some email clients can trip over the slightest coding irregularity introduced into the message by a WYSIWYG editor or from code pasted from another web page, email, or word processing application.

Make sure you use absolute URLs for all your links and images.

This means the address of your links and images should begin with `http://`, followed by a domain name, path, and valid filename.

For the code structure, opt for a lowest common denominator—HTML 3.2.

You can include the `<html>`, `<head>`, and `<title>` tags or leave them out. Most web-based email services, such as Yahoo! and Hotmail, will only display the message content inside the `<body>` tags. They also will strip out `<meta>` tags, so you can leave those out, too. See Recipe 4.1 for more on HTML versions.

There are, however, at least two schools of thought on delineating text blocks: one favors the `<p>` tags that any conscientious web designer would already be using for paragraphs in her web pages:

```
<p style="font: normal 1em Verdana"> A message to our loyal web site visitors.</p>
```

The other viewpoint recommends `<font>` tags and `<br>` tags instead:

```
<font size="3" face="Verdana" class="normal" style="font: normal 1em Verdana">A
message to our loyal web site visitors.</font><br>
```

I've been using the latter method in the HTML emails that I produce. Of course you can try it the other way, but t-e-s-t.

Keep fancy designs and rich media to a minimum.

Avoid background images and image maps and don't include *any* JavaScript or Flash in your emails. Webmail services disable JavaScript and the scripts also can crash older email clients. Flash movies are generally just too big to force on email readers.

Use HTML-based tables (if you use tables at all).

Although tables are losing ground in web page design in favor of CSS-based layouts, table-based HTML emails ensure compatibility with older email clients. You can use fluid designs based on percentages so your message resizes with the email window, or assign a fixed width based on pixel values. I prefer fixed-width designs and see them more often in the HTML emails I receive. If you agree, then design your tables with a width no greater than 600 pixels. Some clients may have trouble with percentages, so be sure to check your design widely if you go that route.

Use CSS cautiously.

CSS should be used in conjunction with testing on target email clients if you do. CSS rules might be overridden, ignored, or improperly rendered, depending on the email platform used to view the message. Absolute positioning, as well as linked or imported style sheets, are a no-no, but embedded styles (listed in a group at the top of your code) and inline styles (listed within individual HTML elements) should work.

Test, test, and retest.

Before you send your first HTML email, call in your favors with family, friends, and colleagues. Build up a "focus group" of one or two dozen test recipients. Strive for a wide variety of platforms and versions; not just AOL, Outlook, and the web mail services, but as many lesser-known clients as possible: Eudora, Lotus Notes, Thunderbird, Apple Mail, Novell, Pegasus, or Squirrel Mail. Send your testers a screenshot of how the message is supposed to look, and then ask for feedback on how the version in their inbox compares. Tweak what you can and retest if necessary. Then build in time for mini-testing before you send additional messages, reviewing the message in as many email clients and services as possible before unleashing the message on your whole list.

See Also

For more on the often contradictory methods for building HTML email messages, see these two tutorials from veteran email marketers: *http://www.sitepoint.com/article/code-html-email-newsletters* and *http://css-discuss.incutio.com/?page=StyleInEmail*. America Online has a guide to creating HTML emails for its members at *http://webmaster.info.aol.com/htmlemail.html*.

CHAPTER 8

Promotion and E-Commerce

8.0 Introduction

Getting the word out and bringing the money in; those are the main preoccupations of many web site owners. Whether a web site sells a product, a service, a cause, or even its own visitors, the Internet provides a proven, cost-effective platform for reaching lots and lots of people and turning their visits into revenue. But before a web site visit can become a mutually beneficial exchange of dollars, information, and wares, both the site owner and its users have to be satisfied that their relationship with each other is fair and honest. Visitors have to able to trust the implicit promises of a web site; the online merchant has to distinguish between legitimate customers and those intent on perpetrating a scam at his expense. In this chapter, I'll explain the trust-building techniques and fraud-avoidance maneuvers that help secure both sides in an online transaction. I'll also explain some of the common methods of drawing an audience to your site, from search engine keywords and sponsored ads to email marketing, as well as some specific coding procedures that help ecommerce run smoothly.

8.1 Turning Site Traffic into Loyal Visitors and Customers

Problem

You need to form a relationship with your audience so that your site's traffic will grow and benefit your business.

Solution

Web sites succeed when they demonstrate their trustworthiness to their visitors. The process of establishing trust begins when you first start planning a site, and continues as an integral part of the ongoing job of running the site.

A web site that visitors can trust has the following:

- Information about the company
- An easy way to contact the owner of the site
- Grammatically correct, error-free text
- A consistent design
- A privacy policy
- SSL encryption for transmission of confidential information
- Fast-loading pages
- Well-written and useful error messages
- Fast responses to visitor messages
- A webmaster who tests the site to stay on top of new problems
- Frequently updated content

Discussion

The web-surfing population represents a spectrum of skepticism. Some will come to your site with preconceived notions and be wary of everything about it no matter what you do. Others will look past the inconsistencies and omissions that feed the skeptics and blithely conduct business with a site based on the recommendation of a friend or other trusted source. Your site should welcome both types of users—and everyone in between—but you'll have to work harder to satisfy the die-hard doubters.

When visiting your site, web surfers can't look you in the eye to gauge your integrity, or kick the proverbial "tires" of your products to determine their quality. Their assessment of you and your site's credibility will be derived from your ability to present a professional-looking site where people will feel comfortable doing business.

 Many of the Recipes in this book touch on techniques that affect a site's perceived trustworthiness. Individually, none of them is a silver bullet that will bury all doubts about your site. Together, though, they can help squelch skepticism about your site.

Trust-building should be part of your web site from day one, when you start to make decisions about design and navigation and compile content. Inconsistency can breed mistrust, so strive to make every page on your site share the same look and feel. The navigation should occupy a constant location on all pages, and the logo you use should match the one visitors see offline. Likewise, proofread your copy to get rid of all grammatical errors and misspellings. When you neglect these small details—like using proper punctuation—visitors are more likely to assume you can't handle the bigger details, like getting their order right.

Your web site should launch with some basic information about the enterprise that runs it, including an easy way to contact you. Don't procrastinate on these seemingly mundane details. When people can't satisfy their questions about who they're doing business with, they will take their business somewhere else. If you collect and use visitors' personal information, such as email addresses and phone numbers, you will need a privacy policy that spells out who, what, when, why, and how this information is handled (and protected). If the transactions include credit card numbers or other confidential information, you will need a secure server for encryption and a digital certificate for verifying the legitimacy of your web site to visitors.

In the day-to-day tasks that come along with running your site, you need to make a priority of eliminating problems that will challenge your visitors' ability to trust you. Surf your own site regularly to test links and forms, and uncover and correct any stumbling blocks before they start to drag on your online business. Optimize graphics and code to make sure that pages load quickly.

 The speed at which doubt forms in a visitor's mind is inversely related to the length of time a page from your site appears in her browser!

If necessary, contact your web hosting provider about upgrading your account to one that can handle more traffic. Make sure you have a well-written and useful general error page that can head off visitor confusion (doubt's cousin) when something goes wrong.

Finally, you should consider adding some of the following components to your site as they apply to the nature of your online business. Although leaving them out won't necessarily detract from your site's credibility, having them can help strengthen the trusting relationship you seek to form with your visitors.

Photographs
> Images of the company owner, the staff, or the business's physical location can help assure web surfers that they're giving their money and personal information to real people who work for a bona fide business.

Policies
> In addition to spelling out the privacy practices you use when handling visitors' personal information, create a page that answers questions about the ordering process itself: how soon are orders processed, what are the options for shipping methods and how much do they cost, how are customers notified when an order ships, and what is the store's return policy. Most of your visitors might never consult this information, but you should still make it easy to find for those who want it.

Credentials
> Display the logos of third parties, such as professional organizations, that can vouch for your site's legitimacy. Consider paying for a site audit from groups such as Truste or the Better Business Bureau—and address any problems they find—so you can display the auditor's stamp of approval logo on your site.

Testimonials
> It's human nature to want to identify with like-minded people. Use quotations from real, satisfied customers to sway the doubters' opinions.

Customer focus
> Sites that use affiliate links and pay-per-click ads (see Recipe 8.9) exist for the benefit of the site owner, not the visitor. You can't have it both ways. Curtail the income-generating site add-ons (or banish them altogether) and turn your efforts toward building a site that helps your visitors become *your* customers.

See Also

Security and privacy are further discussed in Recipes 6.1, 8.4, and 8.5. For more information on improving page load time and error messages, see Recipes 4.8, 5.1, and 9.1.

8.2   Creating an Effective Landing Page

Problem

You want to get sales or responses from visitors who arrive at your site from your sponsored search results ad, email campaign, or online banner ad.

Solution

Create a landing page for people who follow an external link to your site from an ad, email newsletter, or other promotional vehicle that you're using to drive traffic to your site. A landing page might be a web surfer's only look at your site, so it has to convey value and reliability to convert visitors into customers. The most successful landing pages do this by:

* Reiterating the search term to assure visitors they've come to the right place
* Encouraging one specific action—be it buying a product, registering for a demo, or requesting more information
* Displaying little, if any, navigation to other parts of the site
* Using easy-to-scan content, such as an enticing headline and bullet-list copy

Discussion

Landing pages are the infomercials of the web, and, like their broadcast world cousins, they begin and end with the goal of generating a response from their viewers. But the web is not TV (and don't let anyone tell you it is), a distinction that sets landing pages apart from infomercials, despite the similarity of their goals. Although infomercials employ a Chinese water torture approach to closing a sale, landing pages have to work fast—most of their visitors will back out within the first 10 seconds of arriving. But good landing pages have the advantage of addressing an audience predisposed to their message. (Does anyone ever consciously choose an infomercial from the program listings?)

To better understand how landing pages work, suppose that you're the purveyor of a complete line of upscale products for cat lovers and you want to send a free sample of your high-performance titanium kitty litter to new customers. To find people who will be interested in requesting a sample, you buy sponsored ads on search engine results pages tied to specific keyword searches, including "best kitty litter." Along comes a web surfer searching for "best kitty litter." Your ad appears next to the search results, with a link to your landing page. The searcher takes the bait and arrives at your landing page. The headline is "Tired of the rest? Try the best—Titanium Kitty Litter!"

The headline meets two goals that are key to making the landing page work: it reiterates the prospect's search query *and* it poses a problem that should resonate with the visitor. The copy that follows should introduce the product as the solution using the persuasive techniques of advertising and direct mail copywriting: emotional appeals or a story the prospect can identify with, a time limit on the offer (such as "Free samples for the first 250 respondents"), and incentives to sweeten the deal (such as "Act now to get a free catnip chew toy with your sample"). If your budget allows, you might want to consider hiring a professional writer to craft an effective message for your landing page.

The response device—i.e., the form that prospects will use to claim the offer—must be simple and straightforward. Make the "Submit" button big and eye-catching, and leave off the "Reset" button that you might include on other forms. Also, just ask for what you need, and nothing more. To get a free product sample, prospects must supply a name and mailing address. A request for a phone number, gender or birthday— as valuable as those can be to other marketing efforts—will turn off the more wary visitors and reduce the page's conversion rate.

Because they are so tightly focused, a landing page optimized for one product or keyword term shouldn't be used for other products, or for other sponsored search terms. But once you have a format that works, you can easily replicate it and tweak it for another offer.

You may want to have two (or more) landing pages for the same offer, to measure and compare their effectiveness.

See Also

Landing pages often are the destination for links found in sponsored search engine ads and email newsletters. For more information, see Recipes 7.12 and 8.9. Your visitors will respond to your landing page if they can trust your site. For more information, see Recipe 8.1.

8.3   Creating a Favicon

Problem

You want to create a graphical icon that appears in front of your web site's address, both in their browser's location bar and their bookmarks menu.

Solution

First, create a simplified, high-contrast version of your logo, or a new stripped-down glyph that will adequately represent your site. Because the end result will be 16 pixels square and use only 16 colors, there's not much room for creativity (see Figures 8-1 and 8-2).

Figure 8-1. Yahoo's favicon is a simple red "Y" that matches the typography of the site's logo

Figure 8-2. For a site I worked on recently, I cropped the glyph in the site's logo and used it as the favicon

Next, adjust the canvas size so the original image that will become your favicon is a square. Then, resize the original image to 16x16 pixels and save it as a 16-color PNG or GIF.

Open the PNG or GIF in a graphics application capable of creating Windows icon (*.ico*) files (Despite the name of the file type, there are several non-Windows graphics applications and browsers that can create and view favicons). I use GraphicConverter.

 Photoshop does not save files in *.ico* format, but there is a third-party plug-in that adds this functionality. Other options are listed in the "See Also" section of this Recipe.

Save the file as *favicon.ico* and upload it to the root directory of your web server.

Some browsers don't require you to alter your HTML code for the favicon to start showing up as long as it's in the root directory of your web server (and named *favicon.ico*). Also, browsers might cache the icon, so if you change it and don't see the change reflected, you might need to clear your browser cache. To ensure that your favicon displays in all browsers that support them, you should add a <link> tag to the <head> section of the pages on which you want to show the favicon. If you want to save the favicon somewhere other than your root directory or specify different favicons for different pages of sections of your site, you can do that with the <link> tag, too:

```
<link rel="shortcut icon" href="/path/to/favicon.ico" type="image/x-icon">
```

Discussion

Favicons were introduced with Version 4.0 of Internet Explorer for Windows. In fact, the Microsoft browser would request the favicon from the web server even if it didn't exist, and there was no link to it in the web page code. That clever little browser behavior led to a lot of webmaster consternation over the 404 errors noting a missing file (messages that filled their server logs). Several other newer browsers now support favicons, including Internet Explorer 5 and 6 (on Windows only), Netscape 7, Firefox and Mozilla (since Version 1.31), Opera (since Version 7), and Safari (for Macintosh).

See Also

Download the Photoshop Windows icon plug-in from Telegraphics at *http://www.telegraphics.com.au/sw*. IrfanView (*http://www.irfanview.com*), IconForge (*http://www.cursorarts.com/ca_if.html*), and GraphicConverter (*http://www.lemkesoft.com/en/graphcon.htm*) are three graphics applications that can save files in the Windows icon format.

8.4   Forcing a Secure Connection

Problem

You need to make sure that pages and forms that handle your visitors' confidential information are transmitted over a SSL connection between their browsers and your web server.

Solution

Use an Apache `mod_rewrite` rule in an *.htaccess* file to check the connection type, and switch to a secure connection before the page is returned to the visitor's browser:

```
RewriteEngine On
RewriteCond %{SERVER_PORT} !443$
RewriteRule ^(.*)$ https://yourwebsite.com/path/to/ssldir/$1 [R=301,L]
```

This rule will apply to every file in the same directory as the *.htaccess* file, and to all the files in its subdirectories as well.

Discussion

Many web surfers are familiar with the protocol acronym that signifies a secure web connection: the *https://* that precedes the location of the page they're requesting. That doesn't mean, though, that they'll always use it, even when it's in their best interest to do so. You can help matters by carefully coding your links with the *https://* prefix, especially when they target parts of your site where a secure connection is critical, such as your online store checkout or login form. But visitors who manually type in the address (or otherwise use *http://* rather than *https://*) might be unnecessarily exposing their confidential information without knowing what they're doing.

The rewrite rule I've presented in the Solution tests the connection type and switches to a secure connection if the browser has not requested one.

 As you've seen in other Recipes that use Apache's rewrite engine, the module must be enabled on your web server for this solution to work.

When Apache gets a request that begins with *https://*, it responds to the request over a different port than the one it uses for a standard request. Port 443 is Apache's default port number for secure connections, while port 80 is the standard port number for non-secure connections. When a visitor requests *https://yourwebsite.com*, Apache processes the request over port 443.

Ports are a rather esoteric concept, since they rarely appear in the actual URL of the browser request, and do not correspond to a physical component on the web server. Picture Apache as a old-fashioned telephone operator sitting behind a switchboard.

For most of the requests it receives, Apache plugs the line that completes the connection into a jack on the switchboard marked "80;" for secure connections, Apache connects the browser to a jack marked "443." The Apache module that encrypts data using SSL only works on port 443 connections (see Figure 8-3).

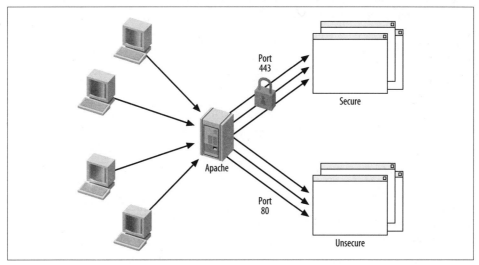

Figure 8-3. Much like an operator, a web server directs requests to where they need to go

The first line in the .htaccess file activates the rewrite engine. Then the conditional statement checks the port number of the connection.

 The port number need not be part of the URL the visitor requests for the rewrite rule to work.

Even though port 443 and the *https://* prefix go hand in hand, the conditional statement does not test the URL for the presence of *https://*; rather, it checks the port number, which is available to the rewrite engine through the Apache environment variable {SERVER_PORT}.

A connection over anything other than port 443—stated in the second line as !443$—activates the rule in the third line. The rule takes any URL not requested over port 443—^(.*)$—and redirects it to the same page over a secure connection, starting with *https://*.

See Also

Recipes 1.6 and 9.1 discuss other uses for Apache's rewrite engine.

8.5   Creating a Self-Signed SSL Certificate

Problem

You need to create a secure web site, but don't want—or need—to pay for an SSL certificate generated by a third party.

Solution

Generate your own self-signed certificate and install it on your web server:

1. Create a certificate authority key:

   ```
   openssl genrsa -des3 -out ca.key 1024
   ```

2. Create a self-signed certificate authority certificate:

   ```
   openssl req -new -x509 -days 365 -key ca.key -out ca.crt
   ```

3. Generate two private web server keys:

   ```
   openssl genrsa -des3 -out web server.key 1024
   openssl rsa -in web server.key -out web server.nopassword.key
   ```

4. Generate a certificate request:

   ```
   openssl req -new -key web server.key -out web server.csr
   ```

5. Sign the certificate request:

   ```
   openssl x509 -req -days 365 -in web server.csr
                -CA ca.crt -CAkey ca.key -signkey web server.key
                -set_serial 01 -out web server.crt
   ```

6. Create an SSL configuration file.

7. Enable SSL on the web server.

Discussion

A SSL certificate is a must-have for any online enterprise that asks its visitors to submit confidential information, such as credit card or Social Security numbers, through forms on its web site. When combined with an SSL-enabled web server, a certificate signed by a third-party certificate authority assures visitors that the personal information they are sharing will be sent to the company or organization operating the web site over an encrypted connection.

But SSL certificates are not cheap, and they must be renewed every year or two. The cost may seem high for what typically amounts to just two or three encrypted files on your web server, but the real value to the web site owner—and the justification for the money spent—comes from having the certificate authority's seal of approval. Web browsers know that an SSL certificate issued by VeriSign, Thawte, or GeoTrust is legitimate, and that means the visitor can trust the certified web site.

In certain scenarios, you can bypass the middleman, become your own certificate authority, generate your own certificate, and tell your web server to use it for encrypted connections. Most modern browsers will allow a user to view and accept an SSL certificate, even if it is signed by the web site owner him or herself. If your web site operates within a closed network, such as an intranet, or you have a small, focused audience of regular visitors with whom you have already established the trusting relationship that would otherwise come with using a third-party certificate, you may be able to create a self-signed certificate and save yourself a bit of money. If, however, you have a large, public audience of infrequent visitors who come to your web site to transact business with credit card numbers and other private information, then a third-party certificate is by far the better choice.

To create a self-signed SSL certificate, use the Unix-based `openssl` command-line tool on your own computer or through shell access to your web hosting account.

Create a certificate authority key

In the first step, you will bless yourself as a certificate authority (CA) by using openssl to create a public key with 1024-bit RSA encryption and Triple-DES. You will be prompted to enter a password for the key, which can be anything you choose, but don't forget what it is:

```
openssl genrsa -des3 -out ca.key 1024
```

This command generates output like this:

```
Generating RSA private key, 1024 bit long modulus
.....++++++
..............++++++
e is 65537 (0x10001)
Enter pass phrase for ca.key: password
Verifying - Enter pass phrase for ca.key: confirm_password
```

Create a self-signed certificate authority certificate

Next, you will create a self-signed CA certificate with the key and password you created in step one. Here, you must enter some information about your mock certificate authority, most of which is self-explanatory. One line is crucial: the Common Name must be the hostname or IP address of your web server.

```
openssl req -new -x509 -days 365 -key ca.key -out ca.crt
```

The output from this command looks like this:

```
Enter pass phrase for ca.key: password
You are about to be asked to enter information that will be incorporated
into your certificate request.
What you are about to enter is what is called a Distinguished Name or a DN.
There are quite a few fields but you can leave some blank
For some fields there will be a default value,
If you enter '.', the field will be left blank.
-----
Country Name (2 letter code) [AU]:US
State or Province Name (full name) [Some-State]:Texas
Locality Name (eg, city) []:Austin
```

```
Organization Name (eg, company :Doug Addison Web Productions
Organizational Unit Name (eg, section) []:Web Site Cookbook
Common Name (eg, YOUR name) []:localhost
Email Address []:doug@daddison.com
```

For a detailed explanation of the information you will be asked to provide for the self-signed certificate, see Table 8-1.

Table 8-1. Information required for creating self-signed certificates

openssl prompts for...	You enter
Country Name:	Your two-letter country code, such as US for the United States.
State or Province Name (full name):	Anything, but I put "Texas."
Locality Name (e.g., city) []:	The town where you live, such as "Austin."
Organization Name (e.g., company):	Doug Addison Web Productions.
Organizational Unit Name (e.g., section):	Web Site Cookbook.
Common Name (e.g., YOUR name):	*This one is important.* Don't enter your own name here. Enter the hostname or IP number of your web server here. I enter "localhost" because I created the certificate on my own machine, which hosts a test version of my own web site.
Email Address	Self-explanatory.
A challenge password []:	Optional, and not necessary for self-signed certificates.
An optional company name []:	Optional, and not necessary for self-signed certificates.

Generate two private web server keys: one with a password and one without

With your certificate authority established, now you must create two private keys for your web server:

```
openssl genrsa -des3 -out web server.key 1024
```

This command creates a key that you will use in the next two steps. You will be prompted to enter a password and confirm the password.

Now copy the first key, which is password protected, to another key, which doesn't require a password:

```
openssl rsa -in web server.key -out web server.nopassword.key
```

You will tell your Apache web server to use the second key when starting up, so you won't need to enter the key password every time you restart Apache.

Protect the no-password version of your private key by changing the permissions on the file with chmod so only you can read it:

```
chmod 400 web server.nopassword.key
```

 If you don't take this step to protect the no-password key, then anyone who gets access to it can use it decrypt data passed between browser and server.

Generate a certificate request

Now, use the first web server private key to create a certificate request. Enter the key password when prompted, and again, when prompted for a Common Name, enter the hostname or IP number for your web server:

```
openssl req -new -key web server.key -out web server.csr
```

This command will prompt you for the password for web server.key, as well as the same type of information you entered for the mock certificate authority certificate you've already created. Again, since this is a self-signed certificate, you can enter anything you want at the prompts. Be sure to enter your web server's hostname or IP address form Common Name. You can skip the last two prompts for challenge password and optional company name:

```
Enter pass phrase for web server.key:
You are about to be asked to enter information that will be incorporated
into your certificate request.
What you are about to enter is what is called a Distinguished Name or a DN.
There are quite a few fields but you can leave some blank
For some fields there will be a default value,
If you enter '.', the field will be left blank.
-----
Country Name (2 letter code) [AU]:US
State or Province Name (full name) [Some-State]:Texas
Locality Name (eg, city) []:Austin
Organization Name (eg, company) :Doug Addison Web Productions
Organizational Unit Name (eg, section) []:Web Site Cookbook
Common Name (eg, YOUR name) []:localhost
Email Address []:doug@daddison.com

Please enter the following 'extra' attributes
to be sent with your certificate request
A challenge password []:
An optional company name []:
```

Sign the certificate request

Finally, sign the certificate using the keys and request file that you just created. Enter the key passwords when prompted. The command below also includes a flag to serialize the certificate:

```
openssl x509 -req -days 365 -in web server.csr -CA ca.crt -CAkey ca.key -signkey
web server.key -set_serial 01 -out web server.crt
```

This command requires the passwords you entered earlier for the certificate authority key and the web server key. The output looks like this:

```
Signature ok
subject=/C=US/ST=Texas/L=Austin/O=Doug Addison Web Productions/
OU=Web Site Cookbook/CN=localhost/emailAddress=doug@daddison.com
Getting CA Private Key
Enter pass phrase for ca.key:CApassword
Getting Private key
Enter pass phrase for web server.key:WSpassword
```

Because the certificate you're creating expires after 365 days, you will have to generate a new one within a year. Serializing your certificates ensures that browsers with cached versions of an expired certificate will check for a newer certificate that is valid.

You should have six files when you're done:

- *ca.crt*
- *ca.key*
- *webserver.crt*
- *webserver.csr*
- *webserver.key*
- *webserver.nopassword.key*

Enable SSL on the web server

Your Apache web server may not be configured to respond to SSL connections by default, and you may need to upgrade your hosting account or pay extra for a web server that will. If you have access to the Apache configuration file, typically *httpd.conf*, you can enable the SSL functionality by uncommenting two lines that refer to apache's SSL module. Make sure the following two lines are not preceded by a #:

```
LoadModule ssl_module          libexec/httpd/libssl.so
AddModule mod_ssl.c
```

Add SSL directives to the Apache configuration file

Move the signed certificate file (*web server.crt*) and the no-password web server key (*web server.nopassword.key*) to a location on your web server where Apache can find them. Then modify the Apache configuration file to begin using the certificate.

> The location of Apache's configuration file—*httpd.conf*—is set at installation. The default location is */etc/httpd/conf/httpd.conf*. A commented, or inactive, line in the configuration file is preceded by a pound sign (#).

First, make sure the ServerName directive matches the Common Name entered for the mockup certificate:

```
ServerName: localhost
```

Then add this below the last line of the configuration file:

```
<IfModule mod_ssl.c>
Listen 80
Listen 443
SSLRandomSeed startup builtin
SSLRandomSeed connect builtin
<VirtualHost localhost:443>
SSLEngine on
ServerName localhost
ServerAdmin youremailaddress
ErrorLog /var/log/httpd/error_log
SSLCipherSuite ALL:!ADH:!EXPORT56:RC4+RSA:+HIGH:+MEDIUM:!LOW:!SSLv2:!EXP:!eNULL
SSLCertificateFile /absolute/path/to/web server.crt
SSLCertificateKeyFile /absolute/path/to/web server.nopassword.key
SSLCACertificateFile /absolute/path/to/ca.crt
</VirtualHost>
</IfModule>
```

After completing these steps, restart your web server (see Recipe 1.9 for details). To check your work, request a secure connection to your web site by preceding the web site URL with *https://*. Your browser should warn you not to trust the site because it can't verify the certificate. You can choose to accept the certificate permanently or, if you like repeat viewings of warning messages, just temporarily for this visit to your site (see Figure 8-4). Further examination of the certificate (see Figure 8-5) shows the detailed outcome of our little ruse.

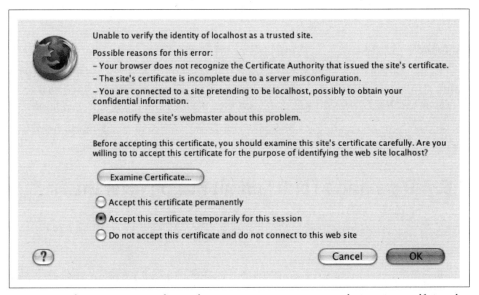

Figure 8-4. A browser warning when making a secure connection to a web site using a self-signed certificate is a likely outcome

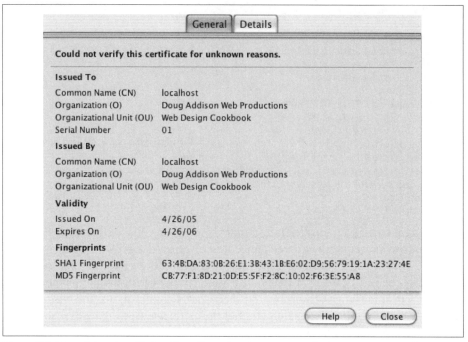

General | Details

Could not verify this certificate for unknown reasons.

Issued To

Common Name (CN)	localhost
Organization (O)	Doug Addison Web Productions
Organizational Unit (OU)	Web Design Cookbook
Serial Number	01

Issued By

Common Name (CN)	localhost
Organization (O)	Doug Addison Web Productions
Organizational Unit (OU)	Web Design Cookbook

Validity

Issued On	4/26/05
Expires On	4/26/06

Fingerprints

SHA1 Fingerprint	63:4B:DA:83:0B:26:E1:3B:43:1B:E6:02:D9:56:79:19:1A:23:27:4E
MD5 Fingerprint	CB:77:F1:8D:21:0D:E5:5F:F2:8C:10:02:F6:3E:55:A8

Help   Close

Figure 8-5. Examining the self-signed certificate in a browser reveals the imaginary certificate authority and web site owner to whom it was issued

See Also

For more information about using openssl see *http://www.openssl.org/*. RedHat Linux also has a guide to creating a self-signed certificate at *http://www.redhat.com/ docs/manuals/linux/RHL-7.3-Manual/custom-guide/s1-installation-selfsigned.html*.

For information on creating a self-signed certificate for Microsoft IIS see *http://www. xenocafe.com/tutorials/self_signed_cert_IIS/self_signed_cert_IIS-part1.php*.

8.6   Disabling a Form Submit Button After the First Click

Problem

You want to prevent visitors to your site from submitting a form more than once.

Solution

Add a JavaScript function to your form that submits the form, and then disables the submit button and changes its display value after the user clicks it.

This code goes in the <head> section of your web page code:

```
<script type="text/javascript" language="JavaScript">
var ordersent = false;
function placeOrder( ) {
if(ordersent == true) { return; }
document.orderform.submit( );
document.orderform.orderbtn.value = 'Please Wait...';
document.orderform.orderbtn.disabled = true;
ordersent = true;
}
</script>
```

Then, to ensure that the form works on browsers with JavaScript disabled, write the function-calling button on the page with the document.write( ) method and place the non-JavaScript button inside a <noscript> tag. The code for the form and buttons looks like this:

```
<form name="orderform" method="post" action="/cgi-bin/order.cgi">
<script type="text/javascript" language="JavaScript">
<!--
document.write('<input type="button" name="orderbtn" value="Place Order"
onclick="return placeOrder( );">');
//-->
</script>
<noscript>
<input type="submit" value="Place Order">
</noscript>
</form>
```

Discussion

Like elevator call buttons and watched pots on stovetops, web forms do not respond more quickly when given extra attention. When connecting to a credit card gateway (or to any other server over a slow Internet connection), web forms often take several seconds to return a result to the browser. Impatient web surfers (i.e., all of them) have the habit of clicking the submit button again and again in hopes of speeding up the process.

But unlike other everyday thumb-twiddlers, multiple clicks on a web site form can create big headaches for you and your visitors. Often, the extra clicks lead to additional unwanted orders, and you'll be the one left to sort out the details of refunding the money your visitors did not intend to spend.

First, the JavaScript defines a variable ordersent with a value of false. Then you create the function placeOrder( ), and on its first line use a conditional statement to check the value of ordersent. If it's true, the function will not be executed. The next three lines in the function submit the form, change its display value to "Please Wait..." (something web surfers will do grudgingly when explicitly told to do so), and disables the "Place Order" button, which prevents additional clicks from re-submitting the form. Finally, the function gives ordersent the value true, a second line of defense against additional clicks.

The JavaScript code presented in the Solution works only on a specific form (in this example, the one named orderform) and a specific "Place Order" button (named orderbtn). Also, note that because the placeOrder( ) function handles submitting the form with the submit( ) method, the input type of the "Place Order" button is button, rather than the more common submit. In the non-JavaScript section (within the <noscript> tags), the button type is submit, and its name and the form name do not matter. Also, note that the <noscript> version won't stop extra clicking, so you might need to include some text that warns users that extra clicks may lead to extra credit card charges.

See Also

Other JavaScript solutions for form-handling are covered in Recipes 7.1, 7.2, and 7.4.

8.7 Creating Complex Select Menus with optgroup

Problem

You want to group related choices logically on a form.

Solution

Use the <optgroup> element to create groups of similar options within one select menu.

```
<select name="name">
 <optgroup label="label">
  <option label=" label " value="value"> label </option>
  <option label=" label " value="value"> label </option>
 </optgroup>
</select>
```

Discussion

In a simple select menu, the options are listed together within the <select> element. Adding the <optgroup> element offers a way for you to group sub-lists of options hierarchically so the menu choices appear more clearly to the user. There's no limit to the number of <options> that can be listed within an <optgroup>, and no limit to the number of <optgroups> that can be included in one list.

You also can display one or many options on the page (using the size attribute) and allow the user to select more than one option by adding the multiple attribute to the <select> element (see Figures 8-6 and 8-7).

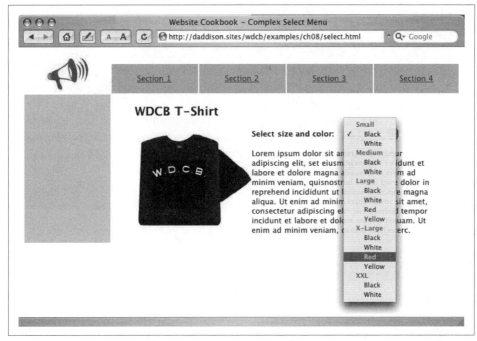

Figure 8-6. The <optgroup>values in this select menu (Small, Medium, etc.) are not selectable themselves, but serve to organize the <option> values indented and listed beneath them

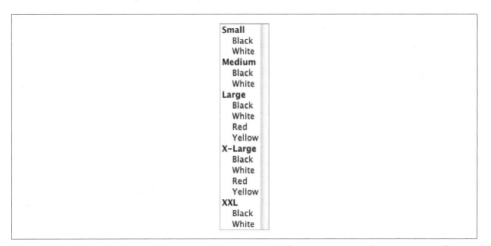

Figure 8-7. Adding the size attribute to a select menu with five <optgroup> elements causes the entire menu to be displayed in the browser, rather than requiring the user to click the menu so it pops up into view

Bear in mind that a select list of several dozen options can easily confuse users since they must scroll through the list to find the choice they want.

As the example in Figure 8-6 demonstrates, menus using the <optgroup> element are useful when the visitors must select two related options on a form, such as the size and color of an item they want to purchase from your online store. Other potential uses for you to consider include location information (grouped by state, then city), membership or subscription plans (grouped by level of service, then length of service), or ticket orders for performances (grouped by date, then time).

See Also

Recipe 7.5

8.8   Protecting Your Site from Fraud

Problem

You need to prevent fraudulent transactions from being accepted by your online store.

Solution

Take these steps, both preventative and proactive, to avoid the deceptive schemes that can inflict financial disaster on your web business:

- Validate and authorize the credit card numbers from your customers in real time.
- Enable the security features that your bank or authorizing authority provides, such as address (AVS) and card verification number (CVN or card verification value) checking.
- Report suspicious activity to your bank and/or authorizing authority as soon as possible.
- Refuse to do business with customers in countries known to be hotbeds of corruption and fraud (check the list referenced in the "See Also" section of this Recipe), and be careful of any overseas order.
- Ban visitors who appear to be attempting to make fraudulent transactions by blocking their IP address from connecting to your web server.
- Contact suspected fraudsters with a cease and desist letter or email, assuming they give you a valid address.
- *Don't ship* merchandise until payment is confirmed.

You might also consider these more extreme measures:

- Refuse orders where the billing and shipping address do not match.
- Refuse orders to be shipped to non-physical addresses, such as post office boxes.
- Refuse orders from customers using a free email account, such as Hotmail or Yahoo!.
- Confirm large orders by phone and/or request faxed copies of the credit card and customer signature.

Bear in mind that taking these extra steps will snub many honest customers along with the fraudsters. To address this problem, your might consider placing a pop-up window on your failed order page that allows customers to provide anonymous feedback about why their order failed. Or, since many people block automatic pop-up windows, send a follow-up email to shoppers whose orders were not accepted—if you can match up failed transactions with an email address.

Discussion

In these days of identity theft and phishing scams, web surfers have every right to be skeptical of the many web-based businesses seeking their money and personal information.

 Phishing is the slang term for the deceptive practice of attempting to collect account numbers or other confidential information through fake emails and web sites that impersonate the look and branding a reputable business. Many cases of so-called identity theft are perpetrated through phishing scams.

Although the risks are real and potentially large for consumers, online merchants face even higher stakes when hanging out their virtual shingle.

In general, a consumer whose credit card falls into the wrong hands is liable only for the first $50 worth of fraudulent charges. On the other hand, the merchant who ships goods to an imposter might be out every cent of an illegitimate transaction when the card holder contacts her bank to contest the charge. (Banks know they can get the money from the merchant more easily than from the legitimate card holder, and certainly, from the fraudster.)

Credit card companies do not publish statistics for online fraud, but experts estimate that it is far more prevalent than in face-to-face or even mail order and telephone transactions. Perhaps as many as one in 20 online transactions is fraudulent. That's because the credit and debit card payment systems were designed for in-person transactions in which the merchant has proof (a signature, card imprint, or card swipe on point-of-sale terminal) that the transaction is legitimate.

Web transactions offer much more anonymity than other types of credit card transactions, although the use of technical safeguards presented in the Solution (AVS and CVN) make it reasonably possible to link a real person (if not a face) and credit card (not just a number) to a transaction. With address verification enabled, the credit card authorizer will only approve the transaction if the provided billing address matches the billing address for the given credit card number. Requesting the CVN number—the little three-digit number that appears next to the account number in the signature box on Mastercard and Visa charge plates—confirms that the buyer has the card in hand (although not the means by which the card got in those hands).

Online fraud has become an appealing endeavor for a variety of criminal interests. Their favorite victims include sites that sell intangibles (such as subscriptions or downloads), items with good resale value, and those operated by inexperienced online merchants eager for their first "big" sale. Regardless of what you sell online, your best defense is to keep tabs on your e-commerce activity, trust your instincts, and listen to your inner pessimist—if it's too good to be true, it probably is.

Some other warning signs to look for include:

- Repeated failed orders from the same customer using one or more credit cards.
- A large order of seemingly random items, or a large quantity of the same item.
- Repeated inquiries about shipping status, or a customer offering to send his own "courier" for pick-up.
- A customer willing to pay any price for an item.
- An order amount far above the average transaction amount for your store.
- A request that the total transaction amount be charged on two or more cards for it to be approved.
- Extremely poor spelling and grammar in communications from a customer.
- Use of a free email address, when combined with several other warning signs.

See Also

For more on the flip-side of the relationship between online merchants and customers, see Recipe 8.1. Recipe 8.10 describes a way to turn away suspected fraudsters.

Transparency International list of the most corrupt countries is online at *http://www.transparency.org/pressreleases_archive/2004/2004.10.20.cpi.en.html*.

8.9   Generating Income from Traffic and Content

Problem

You want to use your site's content and traffic to produce revenue, even if you don't directly sell any products or services.

Solution

Build a site that can reliably send its visitors to e-commerce sites through pay-per-click ads and affiliate programs, where the money they spend will yield a small commission or finder's fee for you.

Discussion

Generating income from web site content is by no means a get-rich-quick scheme. Compared with the effort involved in running a true e-commerce site (such as the daily grind of order processing, inventory management, and fraud avoidance), web site builders might be tempted to think that selling their traffic through pay-per-click and affiliate programs offers a more efficient means of landing on dot-com Easy Street. In truth, the gains to be made by this method require a fair amount of hands-on tactics applied to the ongoing operation of the site.

To understand the steps involved, let's consider the hypothetical case of Walter Evans, the owner of a small construction company that specializes in ecologically friendly, energy-efficient new homes and remodels. Walter is an experienced contractor who has long been passionate about things like solar power, compact fluorescent light bulbs, and SEER ratings on air-conditioning systems. He has a web site that promotes his business and generates a few sales leads, but he'd like the site to do more to improve his bottom line.

Walter's extensive knowledge of his business is his greatest asset. Motivated by his interest in the subject matter (as well as his interest in making more money), Walter should start by adding content to the site that his visitors will find valuable. Short lists and product recommendations will be the easiest to create, since he can base them on his personal experiences—things like "Top 10 Inexpensive Ways to Reduce Your Electric Bill" or a review of the new *Renewal Resources for Dummies* book. Walter also will need devote some of his time to promoting his site by participating in the community it serves by, for example, posting comments on blogs related to his area of expertise.

 RSS feeds from other content providers offer another way to add valuable information to your site. See Recipe 6.7.

Content, of course, is only half the equation. Without an audience, Walter has nothing to sell to advertisers and affiliates. Call it what you want—selling your visitors, monetizing eyeballs—the revenue potential for a content-only web site is directly related to the volume of traffic it receives.

So Walter must find ways to lure web surfers to his site. A company that specializes in search engine optimization will perform this service, but at a cost that's likely to outweigh the revenue it generates. A do-it-yourself approach to increasing site traffic better fits Walter's budget, but getting results will require patience as well as compelling content. Here are some of the steps he should take:

1. Write a description for the site. Even a site that doesn't care a whit about its search engine ranking should have a <meta> tag description of 10 to 20 words in the <head> section of its web pages:

   ```
   <meta name="description" content="Walter Evans BuildDesign is an
   award-winning, residential construction company that specializes
   in green building, solar houses, and sustainable architecture in
   and around Austin, Texas.">
   ```

2. Register the site with web directories. Next, Walter should purchase commercial listings (using his site description) on the major search portals. A few hundred dollars (often payable annually) will buy listings on Yahoo!, MSN.com, LookSmart, and the other minor directories that get their listings from the big ones.

3. Choose keywords that people use in searches. Keywords augment the site description and help automated search engine spiders index a site. They are listed in a <meta> tag like this:

   ```
   <meta name="keywords" content="green building, solar house, sustainable
    architecture, home solar power, green design, green architecture,
    solar home, sustainable design, passive solar design, passive solar
    house, home solar energy, sustainable building, green building design,
    energy efficient building, solar design">
   ```

   Keywords should be listed in decreasing order of importance, ideally as two- or three-word phrases that align with the search queries of curious web surfers. For example, Walter might be considering three similar keyword phrases (among others) that he thinks his potential visitors would use to find his site: "green design," "sustainable design," and "sustainable building." When maximizing site traffic is the goal, the decision about which one to list first can't be made by guessing. Fortunately, there are several online keyword suggestion tools that can provide guidance on the search frequency of various keyword phrases. Google's AdSense program (*https://www.google.com/adsense*) will estimate keyword popularity when you sign up for the program. Digital Point Solutions' keyword suggestion tool combines Wordtracker's suggestion tool and Overture's keyword bidding tool into another powerful, free online resource for measuring the popularity of certain keywords (*http://www.digitalpoint.com/tools/suggestion/*).

4. Use microcontent to increase keyword density. HTML coding details such as page titles, alt attributes for images, and title attributes for links—not to mention the shrewd use of keyword phrases in the readable content and links of the pages themselves—can further enhance the relevance a search engine assigns to a page. For example, a picture of solar panels on Walter's site could include an alt attribute that reads:

   ```
   <img src="panels.jpg" alt="Residential solar panels are an
   increasingly popular option for homeowners seeking better energy efficiency.">
   ```

Keep in mind, however, that your site might suffer if you bend these page elements too far toward your own marketing goals, and away from the usability and accessibility benefits they were designed to provide. Refer to the "See Also" section for Recipes that discuss these specific techniques, as well as an online tool that will measure the keyword density of your site.

5. Keep tabs on search engine ranking. Tweaking his site to maintain a steady stream of new and repeat visitors will require Walter to monitor how his site measures up against others for the same keyword searches. By entering a keyword and his site's URL into RankWhere.com's web site ranking report tool (on the home page), Walter can track his site's ranking for that search term on Google, MSN, Lycos and other major search engines.

When Walter's efforts begin to bear fruit in the form of healthy and growing site traffic, he then must create ways to pass those visitors on to the sites who will pay him for his audience's attention and business. Many web site builders spend time trying to find new ways to *keep* visitors on their sites, but Walter's site will have a different agenda. The advertisements and affiliate links that Walter will place adjacent to his content should lead directly to the partner's site in the same browser window. Any navigational trickery, such as opening the link in a new window or in a frame below Walter's web site banner, could dilute the visitor's attention and jeopardize a potential sale.

 Refrain from clicking your own ads beyond an occasional test to make sure they're working; frequent "self-clicking" could be grounds for removal from the program.

In addition to the widely used pay-per-click systems (such as Google's AdSense) and affliate programs (such as the one offered at Amazon.com), Walter might consider some home-grown revenue generators. For example, he could refer visitors to the web sites of complementary businesses (such as architects, consultants, or realtors) in exchange for a finder's fee or a link back to his site.

 The number of sites that link to Walter's site can be another factor in determining its relevance in search engine rankings.

In the same vein, Walter could promote membership in related groups that represent his audience's interests, or encourage visitors to attend professional or consumer conferences in exchange for a referral fee from the organizers.

In addition to the effort involved, generating income from web site content is not without its pitfalls. In effect, doing so makes you a salesman working on commission. To succeed, you must become master of the soft sell. Web surfers are a jaded bunch, and you can easily alienate them by overselling. Work hard to match the products and services offered through your affiliate and ad links as closely as possible to your content. That way, your visitors will more naturally ease into buying mode, rather than feeling like they're being offered a great deal on a "Rolex" watch.

Also, beware of the imitators that success can bring. Since the barriers to entry for this type of business are low, when one site gets it right, others are sure to follow. Some might even be brazen enough to copy your content and keywords outright in a bid to replicate your results. Keeping ahead of the pack often becomes the last—and most important—tactic to master.

See Also

Use Search Engine World's keyword density analyzer (*http://www.searchengineworld. com/cgi-bin/kwda.cgi*) to measure your use of the search phrases web surfers are using to find your site. SEO Scanner (*http://seoscanner.com*) is a subscription-based set of online tools for monitoring the search engine optimization tactics you employ for the sites you manage.

Recipe 6.7 describes an increasingly popular method for adding third-party content to your site. Recipe 2.5 explains the importance of this often-overlooked code element. Recipe 6.3 describes how and why to use the title attribute in link tags.

8.10 Tracking and Blocking Visitors Based on Their IP Numbers

Problem

You need to determine the geographic location or Internet service provider of a visitor, possibly because you suspect he is attempting to abuse or defraud your site.

Solution

Make a note of the visitor's IP number, and then submit the IP number as a query to the American Registry for Internet Numbers (ARIN) *whois* search form at *http:// www.arin.net/whois*.

Discussion

IP numbers are unique identifiers for every machine connected to the Internet. They take the form of a *dotted quad*—four numbers between 0 and 255 separated by periods. For example, my PC's IP number is 70.113.31.107.

You should be able to get the IP number of a visitor from your web server access log or from your online store transaction records. If you receive an email from a visitor and can view the message header information with your email client, you might be able to get an IP number that way, too.

Search results from the ARIN database should supply you with the name, address, and phone number of the owner of the IP number (typically, the IP address belongs to an Internet service provider, not the end user). If the number is not in the ARIN registry, the results page might refer you to another regional registry where you can try another search. With this information, you can contact the ISP and report the suspicious activity.

You also might want to deny the visitor access to your site by blocking his IP number. Adding a few lines to an *.htaccess* file in your web site's root directory will prevent a specific IP number from accessing your web site:

```
<Limit GET POST>
order allow,deny
allow from all
deny from 70.113.31.107
</Limit>
```

To block a group of similar IP addresses—since dial–up accounts usually get a different IP for each online session—leave off the last dot and quad:

```
<Limit GET POST>
order allow,deny
allow from all
deny from 70.113.31
</Limit>
```

This rule will block all 256 possible IP numbers between 70.113.31.0 and 70.113.31. 255. Bear in mind when using this technique that when you deny large groups of IP addresses, you stand a good chance of blocking legitimate access to your site.

See Also

The Net World Map project web site provides some additional geographic information for IP numbers searched against their database (at *http://www.geobytes.com/IpLocator.htm*), but the results can be sketchy—and the site design is cheesy.

8.11   Soliciting Donations and Contributions

Problem

You want to collect money directly from visitors who support the cause advocated on your site, without setting up your own system for taking credit card payments online.

Solution

Use one of the many payment *pass-through systems* to allow visitors to donate or contribute to your organization through your web site after you first answer these questions:

- Will the contributions I collect be tax deductible?
- Does my organization need to be registered to collect donations?
- What information do I need to collect about contributors?
- How will I acknowledge contributions?

Discussion

Nonprofit organizations with tight budgets usually don't have the resources to set up their own custom donation collection engines, but that shouldn't stop you—or one of your clients—from using the web as a fundraising channel. What should stop you—or at least give you pause—are the little-known legal requirements of doing so. Online fundraising is a prime example of pre-Internet laws and regulations that take the ease out of transacting business over the Web, at least for the web site owner.

 This Recipe is intended to be an overview of the obstacles involved in collecting contributions online, not legal advice. For guidance regarding your specific situation, consult your tax adviser or attorney.

If your organization is a legal charity or nonprofit in the United States (and the donations you collect are tax deductible), then you must register with most of the 50 states in the union to solicit donations from residents of those states. These requirements apply not only to web-based solicitations, but to direct mail, telemarketing, and print advertisements as well. While there are some exemptions for religious groups, educational institutions, and organizations whose annual collections fall below a certain amount, you're better off knowing and fulfilling your legal obligations *before* the first donation hits your bank account. Failure to register can result in stiff penalties, including the loss of your nonprofit status and the ignominious end to your organization. The Multi-State Filer Project (see link in the "See Also" section of this Recipe) is a clearinghouse for information and resources regarding these regulations.

On the other hand, there also are federal requirements for web sites that are not run by a nonprofit, but who nonetheless seek contributions from visitors to help defray operating costs. In these situations, you must clearly state that the recipient of the contribution is *not* a registered nonprofit or charity and that the given funds are not tax deductible. Failure to do so might lead to big trouble with the IRS.

If you're still intent on adding a "Donate Now" button to your web site (and who wouldn't be), you have several options from which to choose. By enlisting the services of a third-party payment system, you can avoid having to set up your own credit card merchant account for online transactions and a full-fledged e-commerce system. PayPal is the most well-known of these services; others (see list referred to in the "See Also" section of this Recipe) are geared specifically toward nonprofits.

 If possible, make up names for your suggested donation levels—rather than asking for an open-ended contribution—and look for a donation-processing system that will let you customize pages to use those names on the payment pages.

Although terms and configuration options vary among services, generally they work by allowing an organization to use the service's merchant account and secure transaction processing systems in exchange for a percentage of each transaction, a monthly fee, or both (some also require a one-time setup fee). Many also provide customization tools that will let you create forms and receipt pages on the payment processor's server that bear a striking resemblance to the pages on your own site.

 Your receipt page should include the aforementioned legal language pertaining to the deductibility of the contribution.

There are a couple of notable, but not insurmountable, downsides to collecting donations this way—and together, they shouldn't be seen as outweighing the benefits of choosing this method of online fundraising for most organizations. I've already alluded to one of them: even if you make every effort to customize the payment pages hosted by your chosen service, they probably will not look exactly like the pages on your site. Some potential donors will not even notice, while others, when confronted with the visual discrepancy and a request for a credit card number, will balk. For those folks, you might want to offer a way to pledge online, and then pay offline.

You also might face limitations in the amount of donor information you can easily collect and archive using a third-party system. If you want to add donors to a mailing list or are legally required to collect certain information from donors (as is the case with some political contributions), look for a payment system that lets you add custom fields to your payment form and download payee information in a format that you can import into an offline database.

See Also

The Multi-State Filer Project (*http://www.multistatefiling.org*) consolidates the information and data requirements of all states that require registration of nonprofit organizations who solicit charitable donations within their jurisdictions.

You can find a comparative list of payment- and donation-collecting systems at *http://www.affinityresources.com/pgs/awz55Online.html*.

CHAPTER 9

Maintenance and Troubleshooting

9.0 Introduction

The fun part of web design begins when the designing is done and the live site starts to take on a life of its own. With frequent new content and ever-increasing functionality for a growing audience, a successful site bestows a well-deserved sense of satisfaction on the site builder—as well as an obligation to its visitors to maintain an acceptable level of quality, even while the site evolves and changes. In this phase of web design, your focus must shift from planning and creation to include the management skills you will need to anticipate, prevent, and respond to problems that can jeopardize your site. In this chapter, I'll discuss both the administrative tasks you should use to maintain your site, as well as the technical procedures you'll need to know to keep your site—and your job—trouble-free.

9.1 Handling Requests for Missing or Relocated Pages

Problem

You need to guide users through errors and keep them happily browsing your web site, even when things go wrong.

Solution

Missing pages accompanied by cryptic or meaningless error messages can turn visitors away from your site. Use a custom error page, HTML <meta> tag redirects, and web server Redirect directives and mod_rewrite rules to smoothly guide web surfers over rough patches on your site.

Also, make sure that the error messages your visitors encounter while browsing your site are helpful and user oriented. Here's a checklist to follow:

- State the specific problem and (if at all possible) a solution. If there is no solution for a typical user, it's probably an error the user shouldn't see in the first place.
- Keep the message brief, but include advice for avoiding the problem in the future.
- Use a basic, straightforward design. The error message should be the most prominent, if not the only, element on the page.
- Use friendly language and avoid strident language (including exclamation points) or "techy" words.

Discussion

An outdated bookmark, an old offsite link, or even a typo may lead web surfers to request a page that's not on your site. The HTTP error code for a missing page is 404, so in webmaster parlance a *404 page* is the page visitors see when the requested page is not found.

 A good web hosting provider will provide you with easy-to-read traffic statistics, where you can actively monitor bad links people are trying to load.

You can specify a custom 404 page in your Apache configuration file (*htppd.conf*) or with an *.htaccess* file in your web site's root directory. For more on creating and manipulating Apache configuration files, see Recipes 1.4–1.7.

Creating a custom error page

Your error page can be named anything you want, although typical choices are *error. php* or *missing.html*. The configuration line should look like this:

```
ErrorDocument 404 /error.php
```

If you don't specify an error page, users will see the web server's default error message (shown in Figures 9-1 and 9-2).

Not Found

The requested URL /foo.html was not found on this server.

Apache/1.3.33 Server at daddison.sites Port 80

Figure 9-1. Apache's default error page loads when the request page can't be found

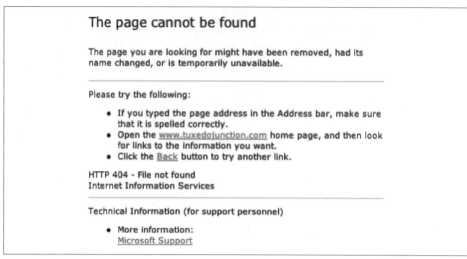

Figure 9-2. The default missing page for Windows IIS loads when the webmaster has not created a user-friendly error page

Your custom error page should be the last safety net for web site visitors who request a missing page. There are other, more sophisticated methods for handling old bookmarks and links when you rearrange or rename files on your site, but this should always be your first step.

Figure 9-3 shows a sample error page that loads when a user requests a file that does not exist (*foo.htm*); obviously much better than what you saw in Figure 9-2!

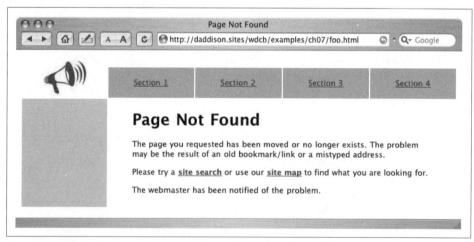

Figure 9-3. A custom error page explains the problem concisely and offers a way for web site visitors to get back on track

Note that the requested URL remains in the browser location field, even though the page that actually gets displayed is *error.php*.

The headline states the problem, the first paragraph explains why it happened, and the second paragraph offers solutions in the form of links to a site search and site map. Since the error page is a PHP script, it includes a bit of code that emails a "404 Report" containing the requested and referring page URLs to the webmaster:

```
mail("webmaster@daddison.com","404 Report",
    "request: $REQUEST_URI\n\nreferrer: $HTTP_REFERER",
    "From: webmaster@stardate.org\nX-Mailer: PHP/" . phpversion( ));
```

Redirecting users to a new page

When you move or rename pages on your web site, you should take steps to antici-pate users clicking on old bookmarks and links, and respond to them by forwarding their request to the new or moved page. Your custom 404 page *should not* be what visitors see, especially when you've made changes to your site layout—that's cer-tainly not the fault of the user!

Say you have a file on your site named *report.html* and decide to convert it to a PHP file named *report.php*. With a customized version of your old *report.html*, you can catch visitors still requesting the old page and automatically redirect them to the new page (see Figure 9-4).

Figure 9-4. A page that notifies visitors of a change and automatically redirects them to the new page

On this page, the headline and first paragraph state the problem and why it occurred. The solution: the user needs to update their bookmarks and links.

The <head> section of this page also has a <meta> tag that will make good on the stated promise that the visitor's browser will be automatically forwarded:

```
<meta HTTP-EQUIV="Refresh" content="10; URL=http://daddison.com/wscb/report.php">
```

After ten seconds, the HTTP-EQUIV="Refresh" attribute of this <meta> tag will load the new page in the visitor's browser.

Redirecting requests to a new directory

Now, let's imagine that you've done some wholesale remodeling on the site and you've moved all your reports from the *reports* directory to */analysis/reports*. In the old */reports* directory, create or modify an *.htaccess* file with this line:

```
Redirect /reports http://yoursite.com/analysis/reports
```

Note that the first, old directory name is relative to the web site root (*/reports*), while the destination of the redirect is a full URL (*http://yourdomain.com/analysis/reports*). Neither of these paths should have a trailing slash.

With the files relocated and the redirect in place, you can safely delete the files in the old directory.

Page-specific redirects

Apache redirects work from directory to directory, with the assumption that requests for files in the old directory can be fulfilled with same-named files in the new directory. For more complex redirects—for example, when files get moved *and* renamed—you need to use rewrite rules that get executed by the mod_rewrite module (Recipe 1.6 has more on determining if mod_rewrite is available on your web server, and how to enable it if it's not).

The rewrite rules go in an *.htaccess* file in the old directory—the one from which the files have been relocated. If you have simply moved and replaced the *.html* suffix with *.php* on all your files, then this rule will make sure visitors get the new page:

```
RewriteEngine On
RewriteRule (.*).html$ /analysis/reports/$1.php
```

The filename in front of the suffix has to be the same for both the old and new file for this rule to work successfully. In other words, the server will respond to a request for *http://yoursite.com/reports/PDAs.html* with the page *http://yoursite.com/analysis/reports/PDAs.php* using this rule. The dollar sign in the code indicates a match only at the end of the URL. The $1 placeholder indicates the replacement location for the wildcard search in parentheses: The regular expression pattern .* stands for one or more instances of any character before the *.html* suffix of the filename.

If, for example, the *PDAs.html* report page has been expanded, moved, *and* renamed to *mobiledevices.php*, then Apache needs a more specific rule.

```
RewriteRule PDAs.html$ /analysis/reports/mobiledevices.php
```

In this case, you might need to make a rewrite rule that maps each old filename to its successor.

See Also

Recipe 9.2 covers relaying the original requested file to your new page. The Apache web site has detailed information on using Redirects (*http://httpd.apache.org/docs/mod/ mod_alias.html*) and RewriteRules (*http://httpd.apache.org/docs/mod/mod_rewrite.html*). The 404 Research Lab (*http://www.plinko.net/404/*) provides guidance to webmasters on improving error pages.

9.2   Adding the Referring Page to a Form

Problem

You need to know the address of the last page a visitor was viewing before they contacted you through your web site.

Solution

Set the value of a hidden form field to the referring page address using the server-side include, or PHP tag for accessing this variable.

Using SSI:

```
<!--#echo var="HTTP_REFERER" -->
```

Using PHP:

```
<? echo $HTTP_REFERER; ?>
```

Discussion

When you solicit feedback from your web site through a contact form, one thing you'll get only once in a blue moon is the web page a visitor is writing to you about. Even if you explicitly ask people to include the URL of the problem page, you're much more likely to get cryptic messages like "There's a broken link on your site."

Fortunately, the pages on your site know the address of the page that contained the link that got them to your contact form. By embedding a simple environment variable in a hidden field, you'll stand a better chance of finding the problem a user has reported.

Using server-side includes, construct your hidden field like this:

```
<input type="text" size="100" maxlength="100" name="referrer"
       value="<!--#echo var="HTTP_REFERER" -->">
```

In the code of your form, the variable will appear as a complete URL: *http://domain.com/path/to/web page.html*.

 Both Apache and PHP spell "referrer" without the double "r" in the middle of the word.

If you're not using SSIs or PHP on your web site, you also can use the `referrer` property (note the double "r") of JavaScript's document object, but you have to wrap the whole form field tag in a `document.write` script, like this:

```
<script>document.write('<input type="hidden" name="referrer"
        value="'+document.referrer+'">');</script>
```

Another useful environment variable is the `HTTP_USER_AGENT`, which has the same name in both Apache and PHP. The user agent variable will tell you the browser and operating system of the respondent's computer, which can be critical information when hunting down site bugs and replicating user errors. The variable prints a long string of information that looks like this:

```
Mozilla/5.0 (Macintosh; U; PPC Mac OS X; en-us) AppleWebKit/312.1
    (KHTML, like Gecko) Safari/312
```

The code to embed the user agent in a hidden field using PHP looks like this:

```
<input type="hidden" name="agent" value="<? echo $HTTP_USER_AGENT; ?>">
```

See Also

Recipe 9.1 explains how to redirect users from missing or relocated pages; you may want to pair that with this Recipe to find out where they came from. Recipe 1.4 explains how to setup SSIs, and Recipe 4.4 explains how PHP and other scripts can be inserted into your pages.

Recipe 9.10 discusses ways to find and fix problems users encounter while visiting your web site.

9.3 Improving Site Performance

Problem

You want to decrease page load time and eliminate unnecessary hits on your web server.

Solution

Employ caching mechanisms to indicate to browsers in that web pages, images, and other site elements can be displayed from locally saved versions, and that must be refreshed from a newer version on the server. With Apache's `mod_expires` module, you can control caching by file type and directory. PHP's header( ) function and HTML <meta> tags provide caching control for individual pages.

Discussion

Cached files can speed the display of a web page. But lacking an expiration date for cached resources, a browser must still send a request to the server to check the validity of each file needed to render a page. Even when the server agrees that a file can be loaded from the cache, rather than downloading it again, the roundtrip between browser and server unnecessarily delays the page's load time and demands extra server processing cycles to complete. When the web server sends an explicit expiration time for each file, caching can eliminate the request-and-response routine the browser would otherwise need to validate its cache.

Apache's mod_expires module sets an expiration date for a resource and sends it to the browser in the Expires http response header for each request. The Expires header is a date and time after which a site file should not be cached. If you have access to your Apache configuration file (typically, *httpd.conf*) you can check to see if mod_expires has been installed for your web server, and enable the module if it was. Look for two lines similar to the following in adjacent sections of the configuration file, and uncomment them if necessary:

```
LoadModule expires_module      modules/mod_expires.so

AddModule mod_expires.c
```

 You need to restart Apache for any configuration change to take effect.

Then, in an *.htaccess* file, you can use mod_expires directives to set expiration dates for all files in a directory (and its subdirectories) or for specific types of files. For example, if you have a directory of images for your site navigation and logo, this code will enable caching for those files:

```
ExpiresActive On
ExpiresByType image/gif "access plus 1 month"
ExpiresByType image/jpg "access plus 1 month"
ExpiresByType image/png "access plus 1 month"
```

The first line activates the Expires header for files sent from the directory. Then for each possible web site image type (GIFs, JPGs, and PNGs), the directive command access plus 1 month ensures that images will remain in the client's cache for a month after they were requested. Cache durations can be specified either from the current time (access) or from the file's last modified time (as in modification plus 1 month) in multiples of years, months, weeks, days, hours, minutes, and seconds.

If you have carefully arranged your site files by type and function (see Recipe 2.3), then you can devise a sophisticated caching strategy for other files, such as JavaScript libraries and stylesheets, on a per-directory basis.

You also can send headers programmatically from your PHP scripts. Say, for example, that you have a dynamic page that displays a different FAQ from a database every day. To minimize load on the web server and the database on subsequent requests for the page by the same visitor on the same day, set an `Expires` header for midnight the following day:

```
<?
  header('Expires: ' . gmdate('D, d M Y', time()+24*60*60) . ' 00:00:00 -0500
GMT');
?>
```

Calls to the `header( )` function must be placed at the top of your PHP scripts, before any other PHP code or the `<html>` element that marks the beginning of the visible part of the page. As used above, the `header( )` function will output `Expires: Sat, 16 Jul 2005 00:00:00 -0500 GMT`. Only after midnight Central Time the following day will the page be refreshed from the browser and a new FAQ displayed.

HTML `<meta>` tags also can control page caching. To set an expiration date for a page this way, add a line like this to the `<head>` section of your web page code:

```
<meta http-equiv="Expires" content="Sat, 15 Jul 2006 00:00:00 -0500 GMT">
```

Setting the expiration date to some time in the future will cause the page to be saved in the user's browser cache until she requests the page again after that date or manually clears her browser cache. In contrast with dynamic PHP pages, there's no easy way to constantly update a `<meta>` tag expiration date in a static page, so using a future date works best on pages that you know will remain unchanged for a long time.

Often, `<meta>` tag expirations are set to a past date to force browsers to delete their cached version and request a fresh copy from the server:

```
<meta http-equiv="Expires" content="Mon, 15 Jul 1996 00:00:00 -0500 GMT">
```

Or, to ensure that both old and new browsers *never* cache a frequently updated page, there are two other `<meta>` tags to use. For HTTP 1.0-compliant browsers, use:

```
<meta HTTP-EQUIV="Pragma" content="no-cache">
```

And for HTTP 1.1. compliant browsers, use:

```
<meta HTTP-EQUIV="Cache-Control" content="no-cache" >
```

See Also

Recipe 2.3 provides more information on where certain files on your site should go. For an overview of mod_expires, see *http://httpd.apache.org/docs/mod/mod_expires.html*.

9.4   Tracking and Documenting Site Changes

Problem

You need to keep an ongoing record of modifications to pages on your web site.

Solution

Use one or more of the following methods to keep track of how your site evolves over time. If you need just a visual or documentary record of changes (rather than older versions of code that you can revert to):

- Add comments to your code when you make changes.
- Make notations about changes in an offline log book.
- Print pages before changing them and add them to the log book.
- Create an offline database (for example, in FileMaker Pro or Access) and record page changes in it.

If you need to keep a copy of the actual code from older version of your web pages:

- Save an offsite copy of each page before you change it.
- Keep multiple, regularly scheduled backups of your entire site.
- Use a site management tool (such as Macromedia's Dreamweaver/Contribute combination) to automate the creation of "roll back" versions of pages that get changed.
- Consider setting up a concurrent versions system (CVS) for your site.

Discussion

The web has a "here today, gone tomorrow" quality to it. A web site's page inventory can grow and change without regard for the print media tradition of keeping *back issues* or *older editions* of previously published material. Web surfers have adapted to this mindset: when a missing page elicits more than a shrug or furrowed brow, they have Google caching, the Internet Archive, or someone else's web site to fall back on. But a wise webmaster looks both forward to what's next for her site, while keeping an eye on (and a record, or better yet, a backup of) what's come before.

Backups are a key part of both choosing a provider to host your site (see Recipe 1.3) *and* running and maintaining your site on a daily basis. When last week's removed page becomes next week's update, a backup copy of old pages can be a big time-saver.

 If your hosting service does not back up your site, consult Recipe 2.7 for information on using the Unix `wget` to back up files.

For the sites I manage, I use Macromedia Dreamweaver to keep a local copy of the live site, which I then back up daily, weekly, and monthly to my PC's hard drive. For a couple of sites, I also use Macromedia's Contribute to automatically keep the three previous versions (called "roll back" versions) of every page on the site. Dreamweaver also offers webmasters the ability to enable file "check in/check out," which prevents pages from being changed by two people at the same time. A more thorough (although more complicated) solution to tracking and backing up web site changes requires the use of CVS to track and merge simultaneous changes to web page code, but it can be indispensable if site changes must be made simultaneously by multiple editors.

When your web site's design and development are done by a team, adding comments to the code is crucial to making the process go smoothly. It's also a good habit for the solo site builder, even if the comment amounts to just a name, date, and short description of a change made to a page.

Comments are sections of code that appear on the web page. HTML comments, which may span multiple lines, are enclosed by `<!--` and `-->` and look like this:

```
<!-- 7/15/2005: Added Joe's name and updated bio (DA) -->
```

In PHP and JavaScript, single-line comments must be preceded by two slashes:

```
// 7/15/2005: Added Joe's name and updated bio (DA)
```

PHP also allows single-line comments to be preceded by a pound sign (#), while multiline comment blocks in both languages must be enclosed with `/*` and `*/`:

```
/* This script contains functions
   for connecting  to the database
   and validating user logins
   7/15/2005 - Updated database hostname in connection function (DA)
*/
```

 HTML comments add to the file's weight and appear when viewing source; PHP comments do not appear in source or add to the file's weight.

In addition to providing a built-in way to track changes, comments also help explain a complex layout and delineate functions or nested loops in a script to someone else who must edit the code. They also can help *you* remember why you did something a certain way or—in PHP, JavaScript, and other languages—disable a subsection of code for debugging purposes. For that reason, you might find it useful to use the multiline style in PHP to record permanent information and changes to a script, and the single-line style to temporarily remove lines when trying to uncover and fix a problem.

See Also

Because HTML comments can add to your overall file size, you might want to keep them in your local copy of site files, but remove them from the version that gets published on the web. For more information, see Recipe 4.8. Recipe 2.7 describes how to use wget to back up files on a site.

9.5 Modifying an Auto-Indexed File List to Match Your Site's Design

Problem

You want to automate the creation of a menu page for a directory of files and make it look like any other page on your site.

Solution

Use the IndexOptions, HeaderName, ReadmeName, and IndexIgnore directives in an *.htaccess* file to instruct Apache's automatic index generation on how to customize the file list. The code below converts the file list on the left side of Figure 9-5 into the page shown on the right side of Figure 9-5:

```
Options Indexes
  IndexOptions FancyIndexing SuppressDescription SuppressHTMLPreamble
  HeaderName header.html
  ReadmeName footer.html
  IndexIgnore header.html footer.html .htaccess
```

Discussion

If the mod_autoindex module is enabled on your web server, Apache can generate an automatic list of files when a directory on your web server does not contain a default HTML page (typically named *index.html*).

If you have the ability to open and modify your Apache configuration file, check to make sure the following two lines are not commented out. The two lines you're looking for should be near the top of the file:

```
LoadModule autoindex_module
```

and:

```
AddModule mod_autoindex.c
```

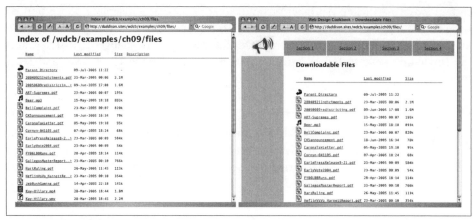

Figure 9-5. A few Apache commands make an auto-generated file list (left) more presentable

The location of Apache's configuration file—*httpd.conf*—is set at installation. The default location is */etc/httpd/conf/httpd.conf*. A commented, or inactive, line in the configuration file is preceded by a pound sign (#).

Any change you make to the file will require a web server restart to take effect (see Recipe 1.9).

Even with the module available for use, it's a good idea to turn off the indexing option at the web site root level, and then turn it on for specific sub-directories as needed with an *.htaccess* file in that directory. If you have the ability to edit your Apache configuration file, look for the lines that define options for your entire web site:

```
<Directory "/path/to/web site/root">
...other directives...
Options -Indexes ...other options...
...other directives...
</Directory>
```

If the indexing option is already enabled, you can either add a minus sign before the word Indexes or delete the word Indexes from the options list (you'll have to restart your web server for the change to take effect). Alternatively, you can use an *.htaccess* file in your web site's root directory: just the one line—Options -Indexes—will do the trick.

When you want an auto-generated file list, such as for a directory of frequently modified downloads, turn indexing on with the line Options Indexes in the *.htaccess* file for that directory. Then, you can specify additional options that mod_autoindex can use to create the page.

The IndexOptions directive can be followed by several display options, but the first one must be FancyIndexing to make the rest work. After that, the example shown in the Solution uses the `SuppressDescription` option to leave that column out of my reformatted page. Since the files shown in my example are mostly PDFs and images, there's no description to display. If the files had been HTML web pages, then I could leave out `SuppressDescription` and instead add the `ScanHTMLTitles` option, which would display the contents of each page's `title` element in the Description column. Suppress options are also available to hide the last modified and size columns and disable column sorting.

The second display option I use—`SuppressHTMLPreamble`—prevents the indexing module from adding its own `<html>`, `<head>`, and `<body>` tags to the page. I'll add those myself, along with other code for my site design, with the *header.html* and *footer.html* files listed in the third and fourth lines of the *.htaccess* code.

 Despite its name, the `ReadmeName` directive specifies the file that contains the code to end the page.

Finally, I use the `IndexIgnore` directive to prevent certain files from appearing on the list. For my example, that's just the header and footer files, as well as the *.htaccess* file itself. You can add any other files to the list that follows `IndexIgnore`, or use wildcard matches, such as **.pdf*, to cloak specific types of files with the same extension, like this:

```
IndexIgnore header.html footer.html .htaccess *.pdf
```

See Also

Other display options not described in this Recipe provide additional ways to customize the auto-index page, such as specifications for column widths and custom icons based on file type. See Apache's `mod_autoindex` documentation page at *http://httpd.apache.org/docs/mod/mod_autoindex.html* for more information.

9.6   Converting Source Documents to Web Pages

Problem

You need to produce clean, validly coded web pages out of documents created in a word processing or page layout program (without spending hours doing it).

Solution

Address the problem at both the starting point when documents are created, as well as at the point where you make the conversion.

- Get involved in the creation of documents destined for your web site.
- Explain what you need to the content creators.

- Set up templates that generate consistent, web-friendly documents.
- Use HTML processing utilities such as Dreamweaver, HTML Tidy, and/or Word Cleaner to develop methods for converting documents to web pages.
- Automate the routines wherever possible.
- Take a long lunch and go home early.

Discussion

The "Save as HTML" functions of many desktop applications—particularly the widely used Microsoft Office programs—are infamous for the bloated, non-standard code they generate. As a web site builder, you will almost certainly find yourself on the receiving end of these files as part of your site building or regular maintenance duties. These two strategies, especially when used together, can help make your job easier:

1. Optimize the creation of the source documents to make conversion as smooth as possible. Then employ one or more conversion utilities to generate web page code that meets the same standards as pages you create yourself. Although it's certainly easier said (and written) than done, your best strategy for improving the quality of the source documents you receive for your web site is to contribute to their creation by defining your requirements for the creators. This may simply be a matter of taking a list of your most aggravating conversion problems to the document creator(s) to find common ground in attempt to mitigate, if not solve, them.

2. Take matters more firmly into your own hands and create create (or modify) source document templates that are web-friendly and train the creators of the source documents on how to use them. (For example, Microsoft Word's default heading styles—Heading 1, Heading 2, etc.—map to standard HTML heading elements (<h1>, <h2>, etc.), so encourage their use over custom heading styles.) Trying to change habits and enforce discipline may not make you many new friends, but you may find that you prefer some mild animosity from co-workers at times to the hours of mind-numbing tedium required to fix the offending code all by yourself.

Some of the tedium also can be handed off to document conversion utilities or filters (see the list referenced in the See Also section of this Recipe). Dreamweaver offers a built-in "Clean Up Word HTML" function that removes most (but not all) of Word's wonky web page code. Other widely used applications, such as HTML Tidy and Word Cleaner, offer the same capabilities—as well as more configuration options—and the ability (unlike Dreamweaver) to batch-process multiple files. I took all three for a test drive on a Word-generated web page and found that none did exactly what I wanted with the file out-of-the-box. With a little trial and error, though, I was able to improve the output to my satisfaction—you should be able to do the same with minimal work.

These specific steps are not laid out here, since Word will often turn even two similar documents into wildly different HTML pages. You'll have to perform slightly different steps for each converted document.

Given a set of documents that follow the web-friendly formatting rules you've established, these utilities can automate an otherwise arduous task.

See Also

Recipe 4.8 discusses other code manipulation utilities and a way to use Perl to remove unwanted code fragments from one file or a batch.

Two popular and customizable HTML clean-up utilities are HTML Tidy (*http://tidy. sourceforge.net*) and Word Cleaner (*http://www.zapadoo.com/wordcleaner*). Although HTML Tidy is a command-line utility, it also is built in to the Windows HTML editor HomeSite (*http://www.macromedia.com/software/homesite*), and is available as a plug-in for BBEdit for Mac (*http://www.barebones.com*). The W3C maintains a comprehensive list of filters that will convert files from a variety of applications to HTML (*http://www.w3.org/Tools/Word_proc_filters.html*). Microsoft's HTML Filter (*http:// office.microsoft.com/downloads/2000/msohtmf2.aspx*) extends the capabilities of Word's built-in "Save as web page" function.

9.7   Coordinating Site Updates and Testing

Problem

You need to manage the testing and publishing of site updates created by multiple people.

Solution

Set up a basic development-staging-live web server configuration that allows contributors and developers to continuously work on the site, while testers and clients preview changes set to go live on a separate, password-protected copy of the site.

Discussion

A three-web server system provides an extra layer of protection against inadvertent site updates and data loss, while improving the efficiency of your development and testing efforts. In a typical setup, site contributors make all their file changes to copies on the development server. When a site update is ready for testing, proofreading, and/or client review, the lead site builder (or webmaster) moves the changed files to the staging server (see Figure 9-6).

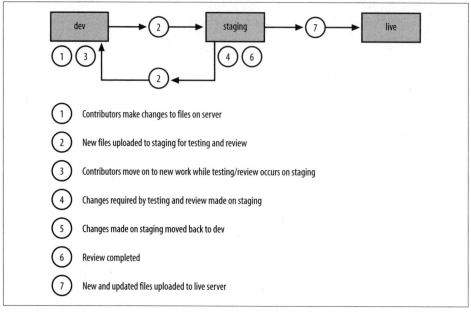

Figure 9-6. Site update process with a dev-staging-live server setup

Contributors and developers can move on to other work on the development server without having to wait for the testing and review process on the previous update. Any changes needed at this point are made to files on the staging server, and then those changed files are copied back down to the development server.

> Staging files also can be used to roll back unwanted changes on the development side, or provide backup for the live site.

After everyone reviews and approves the update, the new files from staging are copied over to the live, or production, server.

> The production site also can be the server on which you employ code optimization strategies discussed in Recipe 4.8.

Ideally, all three sites—and at least the staging and production sites—should be hosted on machines with identical configurations. You might even be able to keep both on the same physical server if your web hosting provider allows you to add *subdomains* to your account with their own root directories. Use that feature to create development and staging sites with host names like this:

- *http://dev.yoursite.com*
- *http://staging.yoursite.com*

Then copy all the files from your live site to the development and staging sites.

Next, be sure to restrict FTP access to the new sites so that only a few people on your site-building team have access to the staging site files, and fewer still to the live site (keeping the hands of novice coders, marketing interns, and the like off the live site will help you sleep better at night). Also, make sure curious web surfers and search engines can't view the pre-live sites.

 Failure to prevent duplicate content from being indexed can lead to ranking penalties from Google and other search engines.

Use password protection, IP-based access rules, or (if you're running your own web server on your network) firewall rules that allow only certain visitors access to the development and staging sites.

The process of managing three sites instead of just one adds a significant amount of complexity to a webmaster's job. And, to be sure, the Solution discussed in this Recipe simplifies what can end up being a very complicated arrangement for sites with elaborate web applications, e-commerce functionality, or dynamic, database content that must be synchronized along with static files and scripts. And without a CVS (see Recipe 9.4 for more on CVS), you can't reconcile and merge changes made by two or more site contributors to the same file at the same time. I'll leave the exploration of those matters to the reader.

Copying files with Perl

On the other hand, copying just the files that need to be copied between development and staging or staging and production can be handled with a Perl script that you can run manually from the command line, on a regular schedule with a cron job, or as needed through a web-based form. (See Recipe 1.8 for more information about using cron.) The following script copies newer files and directories from one site to another, provided both sites are on the same machine and the user running the script has read and write access to both sites' root directories:

```
#! /usr/local/bin/perl
use strict;
use File::Find;
use File::Copy;
```

First, the script needs to know the location of Perl on your server, which can vary depending on the operating system its running. The lines use strict, use File::Find, and use File::Copy identify Perl modules that must be loaded for use by the script.

Next, variables are defined for the source directory ($src_dir) to scan for new files and directories and the destination directory ($dest_dir) in which to mirror them.

With the umask command, it's easy to ensure that new files and directories will have the proper permissions:

```
my $src_dir = "/full/path/to/dev/site/";
my $dest_dir = "/full/path/to/staging/site/";
my $file_umask = 0133;
my $dir_umask = 0022;
umask $file_umask;
```

 This script could be modified so that it can be executed through a secure web-based form on which a site builder could specify values for `$src_dir` and `$dest_dir`.

Next, the script runs the subroutine update_web site, which traverses each directory, subdirectory, and file in the $src_dir tree:

```
MAIN:  {
find(\&update_web site, $src_dir);
exit;
}
```

If the file in the $src_dir tree is actually a directory and it does not exist in the $dest_dir tree, the script will create the directory in the appropriate place in the $dest_dir tree. If the file in the $src_dir tree was modified more recently than the version in the $dest_dir tree or it does not exist in the $dest_dir tree, the script will copy the file from the $src_dir tree into the corresponding place in the $dest_dir tree. If neither condition is true for a file, then the script will do nothing because that part of the $dest_dir tree is up to date.

The update_web site function

The script gets variables to hold the source filename and path, as well as the destination file path. The code s/$src_dir/$dest_dir/ swaps the source directory value with the destination directory value in the destination file path variable:

```
sub update_web site {
  my $src_file = $_;
  my $src_qual_file = $File::Find::name;
  my $dest_qual_file = $src_qual_file;
  $dest_qual_file =~ s/$src_dir/$dest_dir/;
```

First, the subroutine checks if the source file is actually a directory. If it doesn't exist in the same location in the destination tree, the script will create it:

```
unless ($src_file =~  /^\.\.?$/) {
  unless (-e $dest_qual_file) {
    if (-d $src_file) {
      umask $dir_umask;
      mkdir $dest_qual_file, 0755;
      die "Can't create directory $dest_qual_file: $!" unless -e $dest_qual_file;
      umask $file_umask;
    }
```

If the source file doesn't exist in the destination tree, the script will copy it to the analogous location there:

```
else {
  copy($src_file, $dest_qual_file)
    ||
  die "Can't copy file $src_qual_file to $dest_qual_file: $!\n";
  }
}
```

Finally, if the same files exist in both locations, the script defines variables for each file's last modification dates and compares the two dates. If the file in the source directory tree is newer than the same file in the destination directory tree, it gets copied to the destination site:

```
else {
  unless (-d $src_file) {
    my $src_file_age = -M $src_file;
    my $dest_file_age = -M $dest_qual_file;
    if ($src_file_age < $dest_file_age) {
     copy($src_file, $dest_qual_file)
       ||
     die "Can't copy file $src_qual_file to $dest_qual_file: $!\n";
    }
   }
  }
 }
}
```

See Also

Recipe 1.8 provides more information on using cron, while Recipe 2.7 explains how to use wget. For an explanation of methods to streamline the code on your production site, see Recipe 4.8.

9.8   Taking Care of Your Database

Problem

You want to keep your MySQL database running smoothly.

Solution

Use the mysqlcheck utility from the command-line prompt on your web server periodically, or set up a cron job to run the utility on a regular schedule.

The command to run is:

```
mysqlcheck -u MySQL username -ppassword -Avor
```

The four option flags at the end of the command (-Avor) instruct mysqlcheck to run on *A*ll your databases, echo the results *v*erbosely to your screen, *o*ptimize tables, and *r*epair any problems it finds.

Discussion

A damaged database can leave your site dead in the water, especially if you rely on it for your e-commerce sales, forum posts, or blog comments. Corruption can occur for many reasons, although problems are most common when the connection to a high-traffic database is not closed properly by the script that opens it.

The utility mysqlcheck, which should be available with your MySQL installation, can head off problems with your database. One of the advantages of mysqlcheck is that it can perform maintenance on databases while the MySQL server continues to run. However, during its optimization and repair routines, mysqlcheck locks the table it's working on, typically for just a few seconds (depending on the size of the table). For that reason, it's best to run the utility during off-hours or when you know traffic is light.

Database maintenance with mysqlcheck shouldn't be necessary more than once a week. To schedule a weekly tune-up using cron, enter something like the following in your *crontab* file on the web server:

```
0 3 * * 0 mysqlcheck -u MySQL username -ppassword -Avor
```

This command will run mysqlcheck every Sunday at 3:00 a.m.

When using PHP to connect to a MySQL database, you should use the mysql_close( ) function at the end of the script to make sure it closes the connection it has been using.

See Also

For more information on using cron, see Recipe 1.8. For more information on using mysqlcheck, see *http://dev.mysql.com/doc/mysql/en/using-mysqlcheck.html*. For more information on using PHP's mysql_close( ) function, see *http://www.php.net/manual/en/function.mysql-close.php*.

9.9   Evaluating Your Site with Metrics

Problem

You need to determine the effectiveness of your site by tracking the pages visitors look at, the number of pages they view each visit, and the last pages they look at before leaving your site.

Solution

Enable any tools your web host provides for distilling your server's raw logfiles into meaningful reports or set up your own offline log analysis tool to generate detailed reports about how visitors use your site.

The key metrics to track are:

Page views
> How many pages does the average visitor look at on my site?

Referrers
> Who is sending traffic to my site?

Entry pages
> What pages are most people seeing first?

Exit pages
> What are the last pages visitors see before leaving your site?

Discussion

In the early days of the Web, anyone with even a passing interest in a web site would boast gleefully about the number of "hits" it got. Phrases like "10,000 hits a day" or "a million hits a month" became the lingua franca of dot-com pioneers.

Web site hits, as you may already know, are a highly suspect measure of a web site's popularity, not to mention its effectiveness. Consider two of the most popular web sites: craigslist and Amazon.com. Since each downloaded element of the two sites' home pages is counted as a hit, Amazon's graphics-rich design wallops the Spartan craigslist on the hit parade 55 to 2. Does Amazon.com have more than 27 times the traffic of craigslist? Probably not, but looking only at hits would lead one to believe that it does.

Page views and unique visitors provide a more realistic gauge of a web site's popularity. By filtering out all the other files—images, stylesheets, JavaScripts, and the like—that each constitute a hit on the server, log analysis tools that tally page views give a webmaster a standard by which to compare his own site to others. Compiled over time, page view totals also paint a real, quantitative picture of a web site's growing popularity that everyone involved with the site can quote with confidence. Likewise, a count of unique visitors distills your logfiles' impersonal statistical entries into a more familiar framework—these people are your audience—and gives you a metric by which you can start to determine your site's effectiveness.

To be sure, the traffic trends shown in page view and unique visitor stats go a long way toward satisfying clients, marketing VPs, and advertisers. But growing traffic does not necessarily translate into more revenue, sales leads, or satisfied visitors. Whatever the goal for your site, its effectiveness in getting visitors to achieve that goal can't be determined without taking a deeper look at your web site statistics.

Measuring your site's effectiveness starts with knowing how well your efforts to drive traffic to it are working. When a new visitor arrives at your site, your web server should log the referring site, which is generally either a search engine or other web site. (No referrer is recorded for visitors who get to your site from a browser bookmark or by typing the site's URL directly into their browser.) Are your link-sharing and search engine optimization strategies bearing fruit? The answers are in the referrers list.

Next, take a measure of page views per visitor (simply page views divided by unique visitors over a given span of time) to get additional meaningful information about your site's effectiveness. For example, the designer of a site of more than 100 pages whose visitors average only 1.5 pages per visit might want to reevaluate what parts of the site—the navigation, the layout, the color scheme, the content, or the frequency of updates—prevent visitors from digging deeper into the site. (Probably all of them.)

A list of common entry and exit pages (which not all analysis tools create) puts an even finer point on understanding how visitors to your site behave and where design changes might be necessary. Of course, your home page likely will be the most common entry page; it's the pages that follow it in an entry-page list that provide more enlightenment. An entry-page list can provide both reassurance that your ad-linked landing pages are getting adequate traffic and revelations about the deep pages on your site that are surprisingly popular and perhaps deserving of more of your attention as a designer.

Knowing where visitors leave your site provides additional illumination. Consider a three-step checkout process where each step is contained on a separate file and tracked by the server log, as shown in Table 9-1.

Table 9-1. Flow rate for a three-step checkout process

Step	Visits per day	Progress	From previous	Percent of all visits
form.php	100	100%	-	25%
step2.php	75	75%	75.0%	18.75%
finish.php	5	5%	6.7%	1.25%

A webmaster might be satisfied in knowing that 25 percent of the visitors to her site view the order form every day (line one of Table 9-1) or that she's getting five orders a day (line two) when each pages' statistics are viewed individually. Seen together, a different story emerges: her ordering process is leaking visitors (and sales). Only 1 in 20 visitors who start the ordering process finish it. Although such metrics can't give a definitive "why," they provide a starting point for finding and correcting otherwise unseen traits about how your site and its visitors interact.

See Also

For generating site traffic reports, many hosting providers offer one or more of these common tools: Analog (*http://www.analog.cx*), Urchin (*http://www.urchin.com*), and The Webalizer (*http://www.mrunix.com/webalizer*). You also can download logs to your PC and analyze them with software such as WebTrends (*http://www.webtrends.com*), ClickTracks (*http://www.clicktracks.com*), AWStats (*http://awstats.sourceforge.net*), or FastStats (*http://www.mach5.com/products/analyzer*). The article "Measuring users' web activity to evaluate and enhance advertising effectiveness" (*http://www.findarticles.com/p/articles/mi_qa3694/is_200210/ai_n9108352*) offers a thorough, albeit academic, discussion of the terminology used in the area of web site analytics.

9.10   Developing Test Procedures for Your Site

Problem

You need to test your site to make sure it meets the goals you set for it, serves its visitors, and performs optimally.

Solution

Understand the types of testing that need to be done and incorporate them into your site building and maintenance process. The four main types of web site testing are:

- Usability testing
- Browser testing
- Quality assurance
- Load testing

Discussion

A former coworker and veteran web site tester once summed up her job to me: "Don't let anything get on the site that makes us look stupid." Of course, the reasons to test go beyond this simple mantra, but it also encapsulates (in its own blunt, self-serving way) why testing your site early and often matters. After the many hours you and others put into a site from concept to launch, failure to verify your plans and assumptions along the way can reduce your efforts to nothing more than a fool's errand.

Usability testing

Testing begins with your prospective visitors. Although you (like my old colleague) may worry about how an untested or unproven site will reflect poorly on your company or organization, the ones left looking (and feeling) stupid often are the site's naive users. When web surfers encounter a problem or confusing page on a site, they tend to blame themselves for what's gone wrong. The stubborn ones may try again, but many will give up and leave the site. If you haven't done the work to flush out and fix problems users may encounter on your site, you won't have to worry about the site continually making you look stupid—after a while, no one will be looking anymore.

The sooner in the site-development process you start collecting and acting on feedback from typical site visitors, the better your site will be. Fortunately, you don't have to interview hundreds of potential visitors or spend a fortune to accomplish meaningful usability testing. As Jakob Nielsen and other well-known usability experts have pointed out, *any* amount of usability testing is better than none, and a significant number of potential problems can be discovered by doing testing with just a handful of people.

Usability testing is not a means by which to justify a site design or reject a controversial color scheme. Rather, it is a means of soliciting feedback from potential users who are far enough removed from the creation process to provide a different and meaningful perspective on how it will "play" in real life. Likewise, usability tests are not focus groups, and from the subject's point of view should not even be considered a "test"—lest they fear getting something wrong. Usability testing should be done one-on-one in a comfortable and non-threatening setting for the subject.

If you have the foresight to do some testing before coding begins, you can use low-tech paper *prototypes* to represent your site. These can be nothing more than rough, hand-drawn representations of how you intend the site to look and how users will interact with it. Simple prototypes often are the best way to gauge how well users understand your site's concept and organization. When testing with an actual working copy of the site, interview your test users in their own homes or offices, using their own PCs. Here, you want to find out if people can actually use the site, how long it takes them, and if they understand your navigation, forms, buttons, and icons. Give them enough guidance to get the feedback you want, but refrain from leading them to the answers.

Browser testing

With methods in place to incorporate the results of user testing into your web site operations, you should turn your attention to your code and how it gets rendered by various browsers. Here again, early testing is crucial. The time to discover display inconsistencies among various browsers is not *after* every page on your site has been coded, but when the first mockups or templates have been translated to HTML. If you're coding to web standards, then the first step in browser testing is code validation against the document type, or DOCTYPE, you're using for your pages. (For more information, see Recipe 4.1). Nothing beats visual confirmation, though, so you also should take the time to install and view your sample pages in the browsers you expect your visitors to be using. (For more information, see Recipe 2.1 and the See Also section of this Recipe for an excellent online archive of old browsers).

Quality assurance

Quality assurance (QA) is an integral part of site maintenance and updating, as it combines the ability to think like a typical user with the site builder's acumen for understanding why something has gone wrong. The QA process incorporates the copyediting functions that every publisher needs—checking pages for spelling, grammar errors, and style inconsistencies—with the technical proofreading skills unique to the web: checking pages for broken links and unloaded images, verifying error messages, and provoking a web site into revealing its Achilles' heel. Ideally, every page on your site should go through QA before it is published. But your own role as producer, designer, or contributor to a site hinders your ability to QA your own work. Where possible, recruit or employ others to do this testing phase for you or consider one of the many online tools and utilities that will perform this service for you. Many of your visitors also will let you know when they find a problem. For more information on getting the most out of this dialog, see Recipe 9.3

Load testing

Performance benchmarking based on load testing can help you gauge how well your web server hardware and configuration can meet the needs of your site's traffic as it grows. It also can provide you with a useful metric on the effects of site enhancements you undertake, such as code and image optimization or caching.

But like any statistic, a measure of web site performance is most useful when you have previous statistics for comparison. That's why you should begin doing load tests on your site early in its lifetime—not when you begin to suspect a problem with performance—and continue the tests on a regular and consistent basis. In other words, a load test performed at the same time every week or month will have better validity in exposing performance trends than load tests done irregularly.

In addition to the many online load-testing tools (such as *http://www.netmechanic. com*) and paid monitoring services, Apache installs its own command-line benchmarking tool called *ab*. In order to ensure that the use of *ab* does not affect the results of your test, you should run the utility on a separate machine from the one being tested. From a shell prompt on a separate machine from your web site, run this command:

```
ab -n 100 -c 5 http://yoursite.com/index.php
```

The -n and -c flags are used to instruct *ab* to request the site's home page (*http://yoursite.com/index.php*) 100 times in batches of five concurrent requests. Although the output from *ab* (sample below) may not mean much on its own, a series of analogous reports collected over time can help you stay on top of your site's performance and anticipate the need to perform tune-ups or upgrade hardware before slow server responsiveness drives visitors away.

```
Benchmarking yoursite.com (be patient).....done
Server Software:        Apache/1.3.33
Server Hostname:        yoursite.com
Server Port:            80

Document Path:          /index.php
Document Length:        13642 bytes

Concurrency Level:      5
Time taken for tests:   17.089 seconds
Complete requests:      100
Failed requests:        0
Broken pipe errors:     0
Total transferred:      1406795 bytes
HTML transferred:       1389965 bytes
Requests per second:    5.85 [#/sec] (mean)
Time per request:       854.45 [ms] (mean)
Time per request:       170.89 [ms] (mean, across all concurrent requests)
Transfer rate:          82.32 [Kbytes/sec] received

Connnection Times (ms)
              min  mean[+/-sd] median    max
Connect:       48    53    3.2     53     65
Processing:   399   784  172.8    753   1296
Waiting:      347   783  172.8    752   1295
Total:        399   837  173.5    806   1349

Percentage of the requests served within a certain time (ms)
  50%    806
  66%    891
  75%    927
  80%    965
  90%   1049
  95%   1200
  98%   1327
  99%   1349
 100%   1349 (last request)
```

See Also

Your typical users and their browser requirements should be part of the functional specification for your web site, as described in Recipe 2.1. The site *http://browsers. evolt.org* provides an archive of just about every browser that's been used on the Web, while *http://www.anybrowser.com* will mimic how a variety of browsers will render your site through a web-based tool. Installing multiple versions of Internet Explorer on one Windows PC can be a challenge, but there's an excellent online tutorial for doing so at *http://www.quirksmode.org/browsers/multipleie.html*. For more information on web site load test and benchmarking, see *http://www. netmechanic.com* and the manual page for ab at *http://httpd.apache.org/docs/1.3/ programs/ab.html*.

9.11   Preventing Email Address Harvesting

Problem

You need to protect the email addresses listed on your site so they don't fall prey to spammers.

Solution

Employ one or more of these techniques:

- Don't list any unprotected email addresses on your site.
- Disguise addresses you must list on your site, without sacrificing your visitors' ability to click or copy them for legitimate use.
- Create a script that sends web site messages to your mail server using logic that hides the actual addresses.
- Block known harvesting agents—or *spambots*—from accessing your site.
- Set up a spambot trap.

Discussion

Taken all together, these methods are not guaranteed to stop spammers from getting addresses from your site. The only way to do that is to keep all email addresses—disguised or otherwise—off your site. But that's not practical for most web sites. And let's face it, the day when that becomes the only viable option will be the day the spammers have won.

One of the many ways that spammers get new addresses is with spambots, which crawl the web day and night to scrape web pages for email addresses. Spambots also scour Usenet and online forum postings, domain registrant information in whois databases, and poorly protected web-based mailing lists for new recipients their masters can barrage with junk. If you're not getting spam on at least one of your email accounts, you might want to check your pulse.

If you have unprotected email addresses in your web page code, remove them and consider ditching them altogether. New addresses that you must list on your site should be cloaked using encoding or JavaScript (the See Also section of this Recipe has a link to a well-known online tool for encoding email addresses).

Take the address *wscb@daddison.com*. Encoding it with the online tool produces a string of code in which every character has been converted to its HTML entity equivalent:

```
&#119;&#100;&#099;&#098;&#064;&#100;&#097;&#100;&#100;&#105;&#115;&#111;&#110;&#046
;&#099;&#111;&#109;
```

The character string can be pasted into your web page code, either in mailto links or not. Browsers will render the coded characters as *wscb@daddison.com*, allowing visitors to read, copy, or click the address as expected, while less sophisticated spambots will fail to recognize them as an email address.

This method has been around a while, so it's reasonable to assume that some spambots have gotten wise to this trick. I continue to use it as a first line of defense, although lately I've begun to mix other stumbling blocks into my concealed addresses. My hope is that combining encoded characters with unencoded characters and commented spaces will keep me one step ahead of the harvesters. For example:

```
<a href="mailto:
w&#100;&#099;b&#064;&#100;a&#100;&#100;&#105;s&#111;&#110;&#046;&#099;
&#111;&#109;">wdcb<!-- -->@<!-- -->daddison.com</a>
```

You also can use JavaScript's document.write( ) method to disguise email addresses. Break up the linked address into random segments, and then reassemble them on the page, like this:

```
<script language=javascript>
h='daddison.com';
n='wdcb';
document.write('<a href="mai');
document.write('lto:'+n+'@');
document.write(h+'">');
document.write(n+'@');
document.write(h);
document.write('</a>')
</script>
<noscript>wdcb(at)daddison.com</noscript>
```

Here the variables h (for host) and n (for name) are sprinkled into the code sections that together will create a standard email link. Since JavaScripts are run by the browser, the spambot's source view of the page shows the script itself (rather than its output). The rendered version that visitors see displays a linked address that's clickable and copyable. As with all client-side scripting solutions, the visitor must have JavaScript enabled for this method to work. The <noscript> section of the code provides a less functional alternative for those who do not.

A contact form is a better way to allow your site visitors to communicate with you via email. The widely used Perl script *formmail.pl* requires the recipient's address to be passed as an argument from the form. So, if you're using this basic method (or a similar one), the recipient field values in your form code must be disguised just like linked addresses. A less vulnerable script—which you can write yourself or find online—conceals the actual email address with logic. For example, you could define an array variable of names:

```
$names = ("doug","amy","bob","jane","eleanor","phoebe")
```

Then send the element number to the script in a form field, where the script concatenates it with the @*hostname*, and send the full recipient address and message to the mail server:

```
<select name="recipient">
<option label="Doug" value="0">Doug</option>
<option label="Amy" value="1">Amy</option>
<option label="Bob" value="2">Bob</option>
<option label="Jane" value="3">Jane</option>
<option label="Eleanor" value="4">Eleanor</option>
<option label="Phoebe" value="5">Phoebe</option>
</select>
```

After you've done your best to protect the email addresses on your site, it's time to take the fight to the spammers. First, set up a rewrite rule in your Apache configuration or an *.htaccess* file to use Apache's mod_rewrite module (if it's installed for your web server) to redirect known spambots—based on their self-identified user agent name—to their own special page on your site:

```
RewriteEngine on
RewriteCond $1 !^spam/index.html
RewriteCond %{HTTP_USER_AGENT} ^EmailSiphon [OR]
RewriteCond %{HTTP_USER_AGENT} ^EmailWolf [OR]
...conditions for other spambot agents...
RewriteRule (.*) /spam/index.html [L,R]
```

The first line of code enables the rewrite engine and the first condition checks to make sure the redirect has not already occurred to prevent the rewrite rule from looping endlessly. Then each subsequent condition identifies a spambot agent for which the rule will apply. If the client software accessing your site identifies itself as one of many known spambot agents, the server will redirect the request to */spam/ index.html*. (Check the See Also section of this Recipe for a link to a long-lived online discussion about using this method, as well as the names of many known spambot agents.)

Two notes of caution about using this method: first, believe it or not, many spambot agents do not identify themselves honestly. They might instead claim to be one of the many more common browser agents (Internet Explorer, Netscape, or Mozilla), and you can't redirect those requests without also turning away legitimate visitors to your site. Also, giving Apache a long list of user agents to check before responding to a request can significantly hinder performance if the server must do so for every directory on your site. For that reason, I recommend that you isolate this method for a specific file or in a specific directory where you must display email addresses, such as *http://yoursite.com/contact/*. In other words, let spambots roam the address-free pages of your site, but deflect them from the pages they really want to find.

On my special spambot page, I set a trap using the well-known Perl script *wpoison. pl*, which I embedded in the file */spam/index.html* using the server-side include tag

`<!--#include virtual="/cgi-bin/wpoison.pl"-->`. The Wpoison script (the download link is in the See Also section of this Recipe) generates a page of bogus email addresses and links to itself (see Figure 9-7). Confined to a self-referencing page, spambots will devour the garbage data, making it harder for their masters to dump their junk on you.

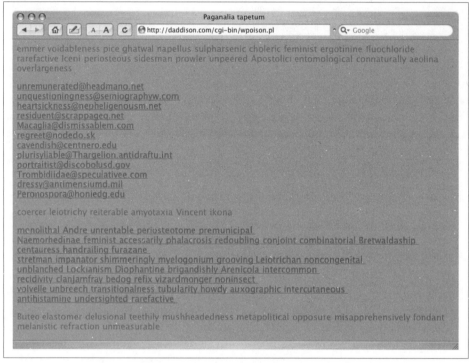

Figure 9-7. The spambot trap Wpoison generates pages of nonsense addresses and links

See Also

Encode your email addresses with this online tool: *http://www.wbwip.com/wbw/emailencoder.html*. For more information on redirecting spambots and setting a trap, check out this online discussion *http://www.webmasterworld.com/forum13/687-1-10.htm* and the Wpoison developer's site at *http://www.monkeys.com/wpoison*.

Index

A

advertising, design and, 65–67

ARIN (American Registry for Internet numbers), 222

authentication of forms, graphical character strings, 179–183

auto-indexed files, modifications, 237–239

automation, 19–22

B

background
  color
    color scheme and, 60–63
    text legibility and, 61
  images, 70–71

backups, 49

blank form fields, preventing, 161–163

blocking visitors, IP number and, 222–223

blocks of code in include files, 68

blocks of text in multiple pages, 94–100

blogs, RSS feeds and, 146

body copy, 87

body text, 86–90

breadcrumb links, 72–74

C

CA (certificate authority)
  private key creation, 208
  public key creation, 207
  self-signed, 207

capitalization in input formatting, 170

Captchas, 180

cell phones
  messages from web site, 185–187
  site available on, 158–160

certificate requests, 209

character strings, graphical in form authentication and, 179–183

characters
  foreign, 83–86
  special, 83–86

clip art, 116–118

code
  optimization, 103–107
  shared block in include files, 68

color
  background, text legibility and, 61
  color scheme creation, 60–63
  links, 61
  text, 61

command-line tools
  grep, 23, 25
  ps, 23, 26
  tail, 23

complex sites, flowcharts, 53–55

contact information, 126–128
  domain names, 6

content
  adding, 68–70
  income generation, 218–222
  isolating using CSS stylesheets, 69

conventions in book, xi

cookies, 188–190

copyright issues with images, 117

G

GD Graphics library, dynamic file generation
    and, 156
GIF (Graphics Interchange Format), 109
graphics
    clip art, 116–118
    GIF, 109
    JPEG, 110
    logo creation, 111–113
    optimization, 108–111
    PNG, 111
    stock photos, 116–118
    (see also images)
grep tool, 23
grep utility, 25

H

harvesting email addresses,
    prevention, 253–256
highlighting search results, 137–140
hosting, plan selection, 9–12
HTML (Hypertext Markup Language), 80
    converting text to, 100–103
    requisites for book, x
HTTP (Hypertext Transfer Protocol)
    daemon
        restarting, 22–23
hyphens
    discretionary, 92–94
    soft, 94

I

ICANN, domain registry and, 5
icons (see Favicons)
images
    background, 70–71
    clip art, 116–118
    copyright issues, 117
    downloading, disabling, 118–123
    logo creation, 111–113
    multiple appearing as one, 114–116
    naming conventions, 44
    pixilated, 110
    QuickTime movie preview, 147–149
    randomizing, 136–137
    recombining sliced, 114–116
    slicing, 114–116
    stock photos, 116–118
    watermarks, 123–125
    (see also graphics)
include files, shared code blocks, 68

income
    content and, 218–222
    traffic and, 218–222
index pages, naming conventions and, 43
input
    formatting, 168–??
        capitalization, 170
        phone numbers, 172
    sample, error reduction and, 165–168
internationalization, 191–??
inventory, site planning and, 39
IP number, visitor
        blocking/tracking, 222–223

J

JPEG (Joint Photographic Experts
    Group), 110

L

landing page, traffic and, 200–202
layout
    fixed, 56–60
    flexible, 56–60
links
    breadcrumb links, 72–74
    color, 60–63
    link to self, 76–77
    mailto, messages generated from, 184
    menus
        other pages, 74–76
        preview information, 131–132
        well-written, 128–131
logo creation, 111–113

M

mailto links, messages generated from, 184
maintenance
    databases, 245–246
    documenting changes, 235–237
    metrics and, 246–249
    performance, 232–235
    testing, procedure development, 249–252
    tracking changes, 235–237
materials for site, 38–40
menus
    forms, 173–177
    links to other pages, 74–76
    select menus, optgroup and, 214–216
messages, web site to cell phone, 185–187
metrics, 246–249
mirror sites, 49

About the Author

Doug Addison has more than 10 years of web development and content management experience and has worked professionally with numerous web technologies, including HTML, JavaScript/DHTML, CSS, Apache, PHP, MySQL, and Dreamweaver. Doug worked on Hoover's Online site and the *StarDate* and *Weatherwise* magazine web sites before starting his own web consultancy. He lives in Austin, Texas.

Colophon

The animal on the cover of *Web Site Cookbook* is the common or golden jackal (*Canis aureus*). Golden jackals have long been associated with superstitions about death and evil spirits, which were most likely inspired by their nocturnal habits, eerie howling, and affinity for lurking on the edges of deserts, especially near cemeteries. In fact, Anubis, the first Egyptian god of the dead, was depicted with a jackal's head and a human body.

Golden jackals are widespread throughout north and east Africa, southeastern Europe, and south Asia. They live in dry, open country, favoring savannas, deserts, and arid grasslands. Jackals are often described as having a strong physical resemblance to dogs, and if brought into the home as pups, they adopt similar temperaments to some dogs. Generally, they are between 70 and 85 centimeters long and have a tail of about 25 centimeters long. Not surprisingly, the golden jackal has sandy, golden-colored fur, which grows darker in the winter.

Jackals are among a small group of monogamous mammalian species. Most jackal families consist of a mated pair and their young. Sometimes, families have one or two extra adult members or "helpers" who assist parents in taking care of their pups. These units are vital to sustaining a family because it often takes a team effort to feed everyone. For example, both the parents and the helpers will scavenge and transport food in their stomachs to be regurgitated for pups or lactating mothers who can't hunt.

Jackals are omnivores. They are opportunistic eaters who feed on a wide range of prey, including young gazelles, rodents, snakes, insects, hares, ground birds, reptiles, frogs, fish, fruit, and grass. They'll also often follow lions and other big cats to pick over their kills. Of course, jackals have a few predators of their own to worry about, such as leopards, hyenas, eagles, and sometimes humans, who kill them for their fur.

The cover image is from *Lydekker's Royal History*. The cover font is Adobe ITC Garamond. The text font is Linotype Birka; the heading font is Adobe Myriad Condensed; and the code font is LucasFont's TheSans Mono Condensed.

Better than e-books

Buy *Web Site Cookbook* and access the
digital edition FREE on Safari for 45 days.

Go to www.oreilly.com/go/safarienabled
and type in coupon code WMMK-Y9YL-LA75-I3MY-EF9M

Search
thousands of
top tech books

Download
whole chapters

Cut and Paste
code examples

Find
answers fast

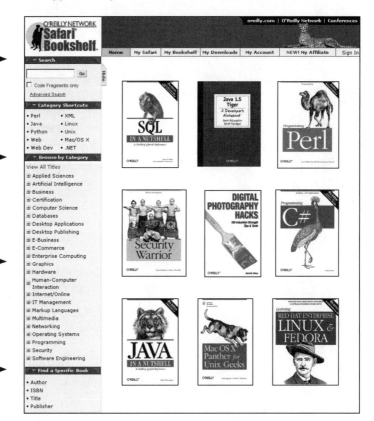

Search Safari! The premier electronic reference
library for programmers and IT professionals.

Related Titles from O'Reilly

Web Programming

ActionScript Cookbook

ActionScript for Flash MX: The Definitive Guide, *2nd Edition*

Dynamic HTML: The Definitive Reference, *2nd Edition*

Flash Hacks

Essential PHP Security

Google Hacks, *2nd Edition*

Google Pocket Guide

HTTP: The Definitive Guide

JavaScript & DHTML Cookbook

JavaScript Pocket Reference, *2nd Edition*

JavaScript: The Definitive Guide, *4th Edition*

Learning PHP 5

PayPal Hacks

PHP Cookbook

PHP in a Nutshell

PHP Pocket Reference, *2nd Edition*

PHPUnit Pocket Guide

Programming ColdFusion MX, *2nd Edition*

Programming PHP

Upgrading to PHP 5

Web Database Applications with PHP and MySQL, *2nd Edition*

Webmaster in a Nutshell, *3rd Edition*

Web Authoring and Design

Ambient Findability

Cascading Style Sheets: The Definitive Guide, *2nd Edition*

Creating Web Sites: The Missing Manual

CSS Cookbook

CSS Pocket Reference, *2nd Edition*

Dreamweaver 8: The Missing Manual

Essential ActionScript 2.0

Flash 8: The Missing Manual

Flash Hacks, *2nd Edition*

Flash Out of the Box

FrontPage 2003: The Missing Manual

Head First HTML with CSS & XHTML

HTML & XHTML: The Definitive Guide, *5th Edition*

HTML Pocket Reference, *2nd Edition*

Information Architecture for the World Wide Web, *2nd Edition*

Learning Web Design, *2nd Edition*

Programming Flash Communication Server

Web Design in a Nutshell, *3rd Edition*

Web Site Measurement Hacks

Web Administration

Apache Cookbook

Apache Pocket Reference

Apache: The Definitive Guide, *3rd Edition*

Perl for Web Site Management

Squid: The Definitive Guide

Web Performance Tuning, *2nd Edition*